Vällingby and Farsta—
from Idea to Reality

The MIT Press
Cambridge, Massachusetts, and
London, England

Vällingby and Farsta— from Idea to Reality

David Pass

The New Community Development
Process in Stockholm

Originally published in Stockholm, Sweden, as *Vällingby and
Farsta—from Idea to Reality: The suburban development
process in a large Swedish city*. Copyright © 1969 by David
Pass.

This book was designed by The MIT Press Design Department.
It was set in Lumitype Univers,
printed and bound
by Halliday Lithograph Corporation
in the United States of America.

ISBN 0 262 16 034 X (hardcover)

Library of Congress catalog card number: 73-118350

5

The Community Center
92

6

Selected Individuals and Organizations
110

7

Mass Transit
129

List of Figures

List of Tables

Preface

Vällingby and Farsta have been the subjects of numerous studies in urban problems and are usually offered as examples of an advanced, comprehensive development process. Little of the material, however, undertakes to illuminate the workings of the process itself; planners show a keen interest in Swedish new community building but largely ignore the political and administrative machinery of which it is so much a part. This study attempts to present the major patterns and characteristics of development as a routine, continuous process and, by doing so, to assist in making more accurate evaluations of the end results of that process.

One of the prime reasons for having selected Vällingby and Farsta for examination is that while they are quite similar in purpose and scope, they differ markedly in other respects. Vällingby, for example, was a public project planned under a Social Democratic administration; it was developed near a relatively prosperous suburb in an area of easy terrain but during a tight labor and money market. The more recently developed Farsta, on the other hand, was near a low-income area on a site of difficult terrain; its main period of development occurred during an easing labor and money market, it was planned under the more conservative Liberal-Conservative coalition, and its community center complex was planned and developed by private enterprise.

This report examines in detail the expressed goals for the two suburbs, the reasons for promoting them, the means of effecting them, the extent to which they were realized, and— perhaps just as important—the changes in the goals themselves as they underwent the various pressures of the development process. By way of perspective, the work offers a background to Stockholm's executive and legislative structure and a brief outline of the city's earlier planning efforts, but it concentrates on Vällingby and Farsta during the period from 1945 to 1960. The work also seeks to assess both the character and the extent of cooperation among the various public and private individuals and organizations that played pivotal roles in the development of the two suburbs. And it examines some of the quiet but often intense struggles that took place around the many plans, proposals, and counterproposals, as they aid in understanding the nature and limitations of the human elements in the development process.

In any organization there is only a rough correspondence between its formally defined structure and the internal principles that in fact govern behavior within it, between its public statements and documents and its internal motives and aims. Standard source material—official and semiofficial reports and records, memoranda and letters of public and private agencies, organizations, and individuals, and the like—have been supplemented, therefore, by a series of personal interviews, which the author conducted with a number of the principal actors engaged in the planning and development of Vällingby and Farsta. The interviews were conducted during the spring and summer of 1966. This seemed close enough to the chief period of planning and development for events to be still fresh in the minds of the interviewees; it also seemed far enough from it to have permitted realistic, experience-based assessments and to have softened any personal differences that might otherwise have impaired objectivity. For their candor and graciousness during these often lengthy sessions, I extend to these respondents my sincerest thanks.

For guidance, encouragement, and criticism I am indebted to Professors Erik Wirén, Hans Fog, and Kell Åström of the Royal Institute of Technology; Carl-Fredrik Ahlberg, Director of the Greater Stockholm Regional Planning Office; Dr. Lennart Holm, Director General of the National Swedish Board of Urban Planning; Professor Hans Meijer of the School of Political Science, University of Stockholm; former Stockholm Commissioners Yngve Larsson and Joakim Garpe; Professors Melvin M. Webber and I. M. Heyman of the Department of City and Regional Planning, University of California, Berkeley; Professor Thomas J. Anton of the School of Political Science, University of Michigan; Dr. Annmarie Walsh of the Institute of Public Administration, New York; and Martin Meyerson, formerly Dean of the College of Environmental Design, University of California, Berkeley, whose initial suggestions inspired this study. I am especially grateful to Miss Clare C. Cooper of the Institute of Planning and Development Research, University of California, Berkeley, for much of the material regarding the historical aspects of Stockholm city planning and to Mr. Bertil Gustavsson for his assistance in gathering material dealing with planning documents.

Research for this study was carried out with the support of the city of Stockholm, the Swedish National Building Research Council, the Tricentennial Fund of the Bank of Sweden, the Royal Institute of Technology, Stockholm, and the Swedish National Council for Applied Research. To these organizations I offer my deepest gratitude.

David Pass

Vällingby and Farsta—
from Idea to Reality

1
An Orientation to Vällingby and Farsta

Vällingby and Farsta, Stockholm's new suburban communities, have drawn praise from
both visitors and the international press. They
are attractive, efficient, complete, and
linked to the central city by a well-run rapid
transit system. Each has its own conveniently
located community center combining employment opportunities with commercial, cultural,
and social services. Parks and open space are
plentiful. There are playgrounds for children,
hospitals and other facilities for the elderly.
Separation of pedestrian and vehicular traffic
makes walking and driving safer. One sees no
slums, no pollution, no garish commercial
strips. Each community seems a well-modu-
lated urban entity, relieving and complementing Stockholm's central business district.

The physical planning seems to have been
almost a perfect textbook exercise. Certainly,
many of the planning principles incorporated
here were suggested years ago. Some were
developed in the garden city movement and
put into practice in Stockholm's own garden
suburbs, though these early examples were
simply residential dormitories, and not inte-
grated communities.

To fully appreciate what one sees at Vällingby
and Farsta, it is necessary to find out what
they underwent in process. Both the planning
solution and the housing design, while certainly interesting, played only small parts in
the larger process that structured them. Design and architecture, although in many ways
superior to results elsewhere, are incidental;
both are quite straightforward and traditional.
What is remarkable is the structure of the
development process: the formal and informal
rules and regulations, the way the game is
played.

The present approach to explaining this process begins with the problem Stockholm faced:
a precipitate housing shortage. The eventual
solution to this complex and much-discussed
problem was to develop vacant portions of
suburban Stockholm from the ground up.

By itself, however, a solution of this type

would have worsened the already overtaxed transportation system between the downtown area and the suburbs. Investigations led to proposals for incremental improvement: extension of the existing tramlines and construction of new lines, across intervening water where necessary, to suburbs as yet unserved; downtown the trams would run in tunnels. A public transportation system became a guiding principle. Through intense technical study and political discussion, tramline proposals gave way to an envisaged rapid transit system, one that would serve even the most distant suburbs. Construction began in earnest at the end of World War II.

The housing shortage, a municipal problem during the war, became a municipal responsibility shortly thereafter. Stockholm had to build new housing. The city owned large tracts of undeveloped suburban land (see Fig. 1.1). It could develop these new areas as self-sufficient satellite communities served by the transit system. People could live, shop, and work locally, needing to visit downtown Stockholm only occasionally. The proposed facilities mix for these new areas was the subject of some discussion among municipal politicians and planners, though what finally evolved was the result perhaps of factors beyond local control. There was general agreement, however, on the need for new housing.

Because of legal, institutionalized, local control of the development process—including planning, design, building, and timing—reinforced by city ownership of the developable land parcels, initiative, too, rested with the city. Experimental community developments on this scale were economically infeasible for individual private building contractors, so they accepted the city as developer-owner, and in return they carried out the actual construction. Private enterprise combined with the public sector, and together they achieved generally acceptable results with a minimum of conflict.

The city put up the front money and planned and improved the building sites. Municipal offices for real estate, city planning, streets,

transportation, water, electricity, and gas services worked together, formally and informally, coordinating activities. Municipal agencies for schools, medical services, and social welfare also participated. Housing, the general responsibility of the real estate department, was laid out and programmed in cooperation with the city planning department. Municipal companies and private contractors participated in construction.

Seldom did the public or the ordinary individual private citizen directly participate in the process.[1] (Indeed, no mechanism existed for such direct participation.) Those few individuals who can be identified as actors depended upon positions as politicians, civil servants, or spokesmen for recognized interest organizations. But the degree to which they contributed depended upon their individual abilities.

Law and the concentration of power in municipal hands structured the process that resulted in Vällingby and Farsta. However, through the exchange of information, interested outside organizations worked out numerous mutually beneficial accommodations. Moreover, while the general public remained outside this process, individuals with positions of legitimacy could exert pressure for certain publicly acceptable goals.

Vällingby and Farsta evolved in an atmosphere of uncertainty. To be sure, by most standards, they were planned and constructed efficiently, rapidly, and with a minimum of dislocation. Unselfconsciously, they satisfy a number of important objectives for new communities.[2] Yet their realization and success have close ties with socioeconomic conditions, political structures, and cultural attitudes specific to Sweden.

Five noteworthy physical planning ideas are often mentioned in reports on Vällingby and Farsta:

1 The communities are, like pearls on a string, linked to downtown by a rapid transit line (see Figs. 1.2, 1.3).

2 They are partly self-sufficient, with community centers and employment opportunities near housing areas.

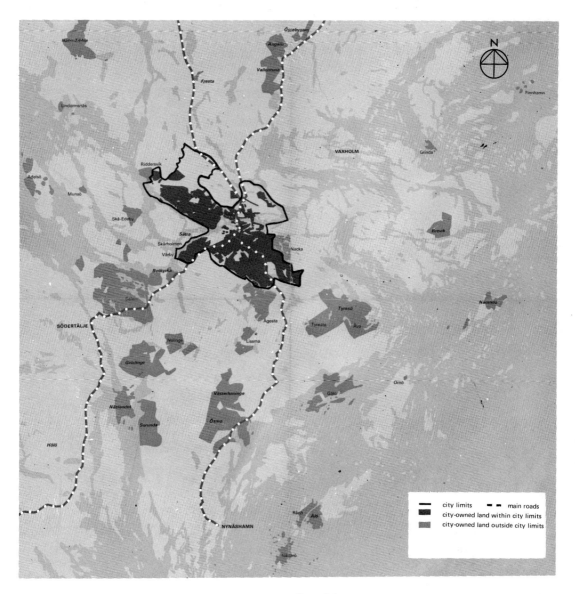

Figure 1.1
Land owned by the city of Stockholm, 1965.
 Source: Stadskollegiets Reklamkommitté, "Stockholms stads
markområden 1965" (Stockholm: Stadskollegiets Reklamkommitté, 1966).
 Names in roman type indicate purchase by the city before
1960; names in italics indicate purchase during 1960s.

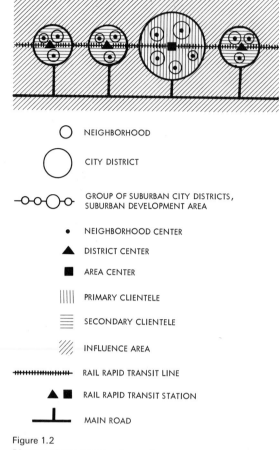

NEIGHBORHOOD

CITY DISTRICT

GROUP OF SUBURBAN CITY DISTRICTS, SUBURBAN DEVELOPMENT AREA

• NEIGHBORHOOD CENTER

▲ DISTRICT CENTER

■ AREA CENTER

||||| PRIMARY CLIENTELE

≡ SECONDARY CLIENTELE

//// INFLUENCE AREA

++++++++++++++ RAIL RAPID TRANSIT LINE

▲ ■ RAIL RAPID TRANSIT STATION

MAIN ROAD

Figure 1.2
Diagram of suburban development.

Figure 1.3
Schematic diagram of suburban community development.
   Source: Stockholms stads stadsplanekontor, *Generalplan
för Stockholm 1952* (Stockholm: Stockholms stads stadsplanekontor 1952), p. 180.
   Left: Two fully developed city districts with a common
industrial area and grouped around a radial suburban railway.
About 1,800 meters between the stations. About 33,000
inhabitants.
   Right: Two city districts developed solely with multistory
rental apartments and located partly around the radial suburban railway and partly close to the ring road with bus service.
About 1,100 meters between stations. About 24,000
inhabitants.

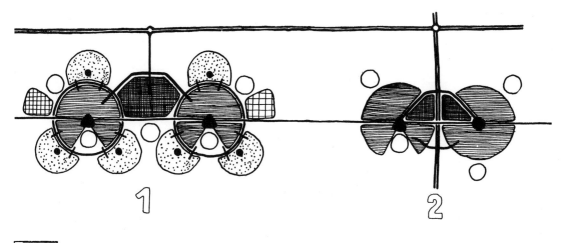

 multi-story rental apartments

 single-family detached homes

industry

 gardening area

 school

Figure 1.4
Schematic diagram of a suburban community served by rapid
transit.

Source: Stockholms stads stadsplanekontor, *Generalplan
för Stockholm 1952* (Stockholm: Stockholms stads stadsplanekontor, 1952), p. 123.

This model for Stockholm's post–World War II suburban
communities shows development taking place along the transit
line and the community center at the station. Multistory housing
is immediately adjacent to the center, with single-family housing
farther away. The center includes facilities for social activities
in the community hall and premises for cultural activities for the
community. However, in contrast to the English model, there
was no provision for local self-government.

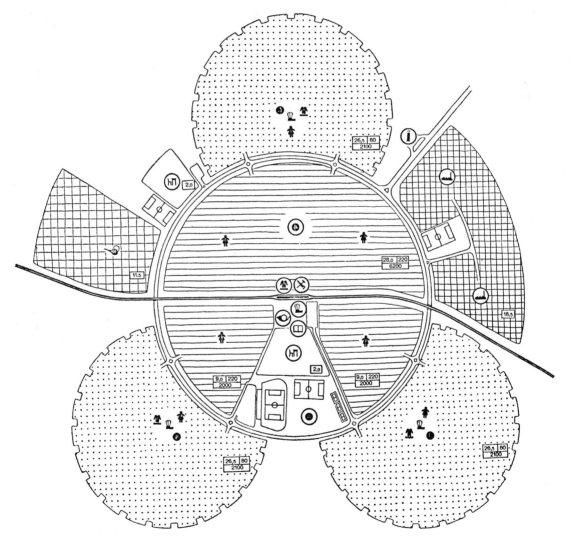

Type of dwelling	Number of inhabitants (approximate)	Percent
Multistory apartments	10,200	62
Row and detached single-family housing	6,300	38
Total	16,500	

Land use areas (approximate)	Hectares	Acres
Multistory apartments	46.0	113.66
Row and detached single-family housing	80.0	197.68
District center	1.0	2.47
Neighborhood center (three)	1.0	2.47
Schools (two)	5.0	12.35
Sports and festivals	7.0	17.29
Industry	16.5	40.77
Allotment gardens	11.0	27.18
Total	167.5	413.87

Population density	Inhabitants per hectare	Inhabitants per acre
Multistory apartments	220	89
Row and detached single-family housing	80	32

Distance from district center	Meters	Yards
To perimeter of multistory apartments	450	492
To perimeter of row and detached single-family housing	900	984
To perimeter of industrial area	600	656
To perimeter of allotment garden	600	656

Distance from neighborhood center	Meters	Yards
To perimeter of detached single-family housing	300	328
To district center	600	656

Symbols

- multistory apartments
- row and detached single-family housing
- larger shopping center
- smaller shopping center
- cultural center
- post office
- handicraft
- industry
- larger laundry
- smaller laundry
- auto service station
- nursery
- secondary school
- athletic field
- exercise field
- tennis court
- larger playground
- smaller playground
- allotment gardens

3   Each group of suburban communities has a large area center providing retail, commercial, social, and cultural services (see Figs. 1.2, 1.4).
4   Dwellings are arranged in small neighborhood units, often around a common green.
5   Different kinds of traffic are intentionally separated. People can walk to the neighborhood center and children to school without crossing roads.

Vällingby and Farsta are two among a number of areas of Stockholm planned along similar lines. During the 1930s and early 1940s, suburban development within corporate Stockholm was carried out at the neighborhood level. Development was concentrated primarily on residences and local shops. With the development of Blackeberg (and other areas) came a larger planning unit: a city district containing several neighborhoods. Planning viable district cultural and shopping centers became possible as a result of the increased population base.

An extension of these earlier developments is the Vällingby Development Area, which consists of six city districts, each with its own district center, and the Johannelund industrial area in the Vinsta city district. The city district of Vällingby is the site of the area center that provides the nearby city districts with services not available at their neighborhood centers (see Fig. 1.4). Large-scale suburban development has since been carried out elsewhere in Stockholm.[3] Farsta is a well-known example.

Boundaries

Stockholm is divided into a number of different historical, functional, and administrative districts, such as parishes, medical officers' districts, civil defense districts, and voting districts.[4] Often overlapping and occasionally congruent in area, they compose the city of Stockholm (see Fig. 1.5). While certain statistics are collected for these subdivisions, they enjoy no local autonomy or administration.

Though Vällingby and Farsta are specific city districts, their names have acquired a loose, popular connotation indicating an area center, a city district,[5] a development area (a group of city districts), or a retail service area. Area centers in Vällingby and Farsta, like the smaller district centers, serve a resident primary clientele. A secondary clientele, however, is necessary to support the area center's more extensive facilities, such as department stores; this clientele is drawn from neighboring city districts.

The suburban city districts of Blackeberg, Råcksta, Grimsta, Vällingby, Hässelby Gård, and Hässelby Strand, and the Johannelund industrial area constitute the Vällingby Development Area. Minus Blackeberg, this group of city districts has officially been known as Södra Spånga (see Figs. 1.6, 1.7, 1.8). Chronologically, these districts developed from east to west along the rapid transit line; development was continuous and during a very short time, mainly between 1950 and 1960.

The Farsta Development Area consists of the Fagersjö, Farsta, Farsta Strand, Gubbängen, Hökarängen, Larsboda, and Sköndal city districts (see Figs. 1.5, 1.9). Development was not continuous, as at Vällingby, and took considerably longer.

While Vällingby and Farsta Centers serve primarily the commercial, social, and cultural needs of the people of the nearby city districts, each attracts a clientele from a much larger influence area.

Figure 1.5
Stockholm parishes and city districts as of January 1, 1966.
  Source: Stockholms stadskansli, *Stockholms kommunal-
kalender 1966* (Stockholm: Stockholms kommunalförvaltning,
1966), p. 781.

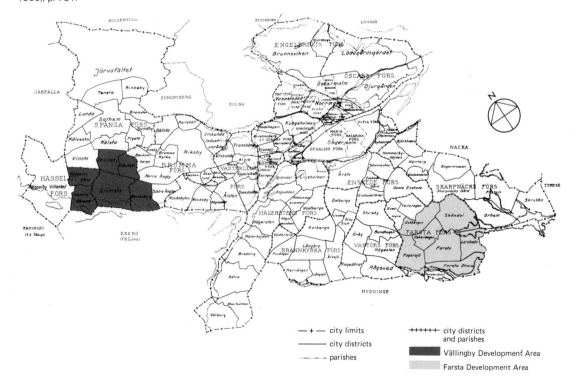

— + — city limits   ┼┼┼┼┼ city districts
                                             and parishes
——— city districts   ▓▓▓▓ Vällingby Development Area
-·—·—· parishes   ░░░░ Farsta Development Area

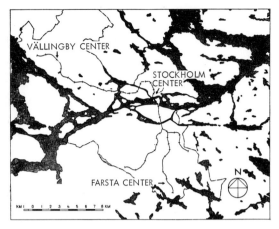

├──────┤ rapid transit ────·──·──· city limits

Figure 1.6
Vällingby and Farsta location map.
 Source: Lars Persson, *Kunderna i Vällingby* (Stockholm:
Stockholms kommunalförvaltning, 1960), p. 31.

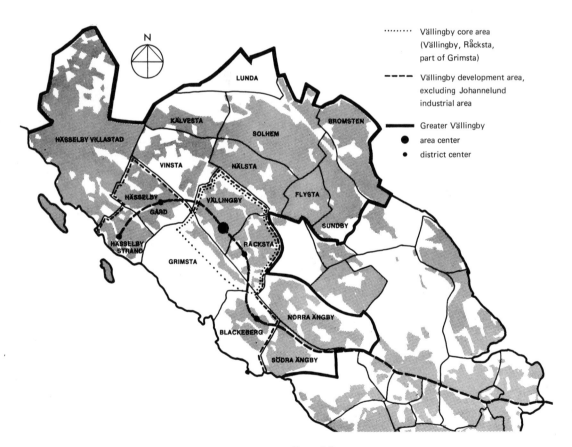

········· Vällingby core area
 (Vällingby, Råcksta,
 part of Grimsta)

──── Vällingby development area,
 excluding Johannelund
 industrial area

──── Greater Vällingby
● area center
• district center

Figure 1.7
Stockholm's western suburbs.
 Source: AB Svenska Bostäder, *Vällingby* (Stockholm: AB
Svenska Bostäder, 1966), p. 5.

Figure 1.8
Vällingby Development Area city districts.
  Source: Stockholm Office of Statistics, *Statistical Yearbook of Stockholm 1967* (Stockholm: Stockholm Office of Statistics, 1967), p. III.

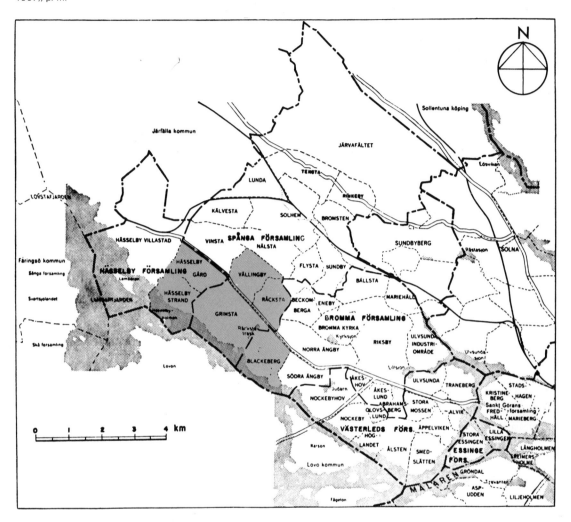

——·——·——·— city limits

-------------- city districts

  Vällingby Development Area

Figure 1.9
Farsta Development Area city districts.
  Source: Stockholm Office of Statistics, *Statistical Yearbook
of Stockholm 1967* (Stockholm: Stockholm Office of Statistics,
1967), p. II.

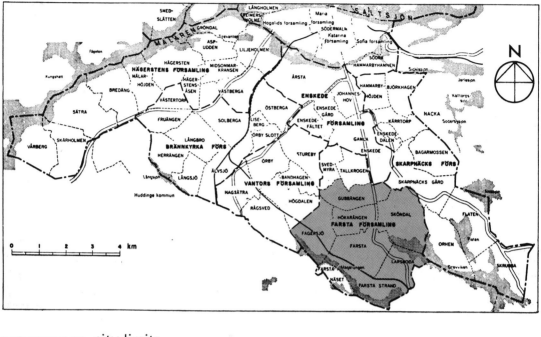

—·—·—·— city limits

------------ city districts

Farsta Development Area

The Vällingby Development Area[6]

All of the six city districts of the Vällingby Development Area, west of downtown Stockholm, are within a 3-kilometer radius of Vällingby Center. The population of the area in 1966 was 55,028, with a 1965 housing stock of 18,801 dwelling units (see Tables 1.1, 1.2; Figs. 1.10–1.13). Almost all land is municipally owned.

City Districts

Blackeberg   Southeast of Vällingby Center is the Blackeberg city district, consisting mainly of multistory rental apartments. Population increased from 1,500 in November 1951 to 8,500 in November 1952. Its 1966 population was 9,410, and it had a 1965 housing stock of 3,364 dwelling units. The straight-line distance to Vällingby Center ranges from 1.5 to 3 kilometers; to downtown Stockholm it is about 10 kilometers. Driving time to Vällingby Center is five to ten minutes, to downtown about twenty minutes. Blackeberg, lying on the rapid transit line, has good connections with Vällingby Center (five minutes) and central Stockholm (about twenty minutes). Local shopping is done primarily at Blackeberg Center, where there are some twenty shops, and at other, smaller concentrations of shops in the district.[7]

Råcksta   Råcksta, north of Blackeberg and east of Vällingby, had a 1966 population of 6,570 and a 1965 housing stock of 2,128 dwelling units, most of them constructed between 1951 and 1955.

The transit station in Råcksta serves not only the local inhabitants but also the almost 2,000 people employed in the new National Power Board administrative office complex in Råcksta.[8] The city district has a small shopping center that in 1957 consisted of thirteen stores. Because of its proximity to Vällingby Center, the complex has lost considerable business to it.

Vällingby   Vällingby is the nucleus of the development area, offering the neighboring city districts a wide range of facilities at Vällingby Center (see Fig. 1.14). The most intensive period of residential development in the Vällingby city district occurred between 1951 and 1955. By 1965, housing stock totaled 3,623 dwelling units, and the 1966 population was 10,531. Multistory rental apartments occupy an inner ring surrounding the center. Farther out are single-family detached homes and row houses. Throughout the area there are neighborhood shops for daily purchases. The distance to downtown Stockholm is 12 kilometers. Driving time is about twenty-five minutes; the rapid transit takes about the same time. Service is every twelve minutes during the day and evening and becomes infrequent during late night and early morning hours, when a double fare is charged.

Grimsta   The Grimsta city district, south of Vällingby, had a 1966 population of 4,924 and a 1965 housing stock of 1,654 dwelling units, constructed for the most part between 1951 and 1955. Residential development in Grimsta is concentrated in the northern portion of the area within easy walking distance of Vällingby, Vällingby Center, and the Vällingby transit station. The rest of Grimsta consists of woods and fields for recreational use. In 1957 there were some ten grocery and other stores in the Grimsta neighborhood.

Johannelund   Johannelund, an industrial park northwest of Vällingby Center in the city district of Vinsta, is considered part of the Vällingby Development Area. Development of Johannelund began at the same time as construction in the neighboring city districts (the first industry moved into Johannelund on June 1, 1954). There are good connections to and from Johannelund, both by highway and by rapid transit.

Hässelby Gård and Hässelby Strand   The two city districts southwest of Vällingby Center, Hässelby Gård and Hässelby Strand, form a densely developed modern suburban area consisting almost entirely of multistory rental apartment houses. From Vällingby Center to Hässelby Gård, the closer district, is about 1 kilometer. The most convenient road leading to downtown Stockholm passes within 200 meters of Vällingby Center. Driving time to

Vällingby Center is from five to fifteen minutes, to downtown about thirty minutes.

From the inauguration of Vällingby Center in the fall of 1954 until the fall of 1956, there was frequent bus service from Hässelby Gård and Hässelby Strand to the center. To continue downtown required a change to the rapid transit at Vällingby Center. By November 1956 the transit line extended to Hässelby Gård. Bus service continued between Hässelby Gård and Hässelby Strand until the rapid transit reached Hässelby Strand in the fall of 1958.

Hässelby Gård and Hässelby Strand developed later than Vällingby. When Vällingby Center opened, less than 1,000 persons were living in the two districts. By 1956 the population had increased to 13,200, and the number of dwellings had reached 4,800. In the spring of 1957 the population was 12,000 in Hässelby Gård and 5,000 in Hässelby Strand, a large proportion being children. As in the Vällingby area, in 1956 some 35 percent of the population was under sixteen years of age. On November 1, 1965, the number of dwelling units stood at 8,032, and on November 1, 1967, the population was 23,593.

A rather complete selection of shops was planned for Hässelby Gård and Hässelby Strand, and by 1966 the retail sales area at the Hässelby Gard Center had reached 1,200 square meters.

Residential Development Density

While column 5 in Table 1.1, entitled average gross density (population/acre), is only a rough measure, the figures reflect other information about the development area and each of the city districts.

All of the city districts have large areas of land reserved for greenbelts or other open space and for such purposes as transportation, commerce, shopping, and light industry. Residential use tends to be clustered; the density at primarily residential Blackeberg (24.25 people per acre) is typical of the early planning norm for the development of the entire area. Råcksta (23.11) and Vällingby (30.88) show similar densities.

The population density at Grimsta (7.24), though, is considerably lower because of decisions to preserve Grimsta Wood, which covers a large portion of the city district, and to confine development to the northern edge of Grimsta. Partly as a result of these decisions, the population density at Hässelby Gård (40.85) and Hässelby Strand (44.31) is significantly greater than in earlier developed city districts in the area. While the density of these two city districts is high, concentration in multistory residences leaves considerable open space.

Although the land area of Hässelby Gård and Hässelby Strand is less than half that of Grimsta, it houses almost five times as many people, and the total average gross density for the entire Vällingby Development Area (24.44) is much closer to the density for the three earliest city districts in the development, Blackeberg, Råcksta, and Vällingby.

The figures in Table 1.1 (col. 8) for average gross density of residential construction (dwelling units/acre), also a rough measure, induce conclusions closely parallel to those made concerning average gross population density (population/acre).

Employment

In the 1940s one of the explicit principles of the planning and development of suburban communities was the Walk-to-Work idea, which was to have precluded dormitory communities. To carry out the plan, it was necessary to create a balance between the housing supply and local employment opportunities. New housing would attract local services, but if the Walk-to-Work idea was to succeed, light industry and other nonlocal enterprises would have to locate in the developing areas. Some observers, however, have said that the aim of the Walk-to-Work idea was to create local jobs for only about 50 percent of the employable residents.

Before such a program at the Vällingby Development Area could be effected, several problems had to be solved. In the beginning especially, it was difficult to convince industry to locate at Johannelund, the industrial area

Table 1.1

Amount, Rate, and Intensity of Residential Development in the Vällingby Development Area

1. City district	2. Population Nov. 1, 1966[a]	3. Land area (hectares) Dec. 31, 1966[b]	4. Land area (acres)	5. Average gross population density (pop./acre)	Number of dwellings 6. 1960[c]	7. 1965[d]	8. Average gross density of residential construction, 1965 (dwelling units/acre)
Blackeberg	9,410	157	387.95	24.25	3,293	3,364	8.48
Råcksta	6,570	115	284.17	23.11	2,090	2,128	7.48
Vällingby	10,531	138	341.00	30.88	3,565	3,623	10.62
Grimsta	4,924	275	679.53	7.24	1,639	1,654	2.43
Hässelby Gård	13,629	135	333.59	40.85	4,601	4,667	13.99
Hässelby Strand	9,964	91	224.86	44.31	3,310	3,365	14.96
Totals	55,028	911	2,251.12	24.44	18,498	18,801	8.35

1. City district	Number of dwellings constructed[e] 9. 1946–1950	10. 1951–1955	11. 1955–1960	12. 1961–1965	13. Period of most intensive residential development	14. Number of dwelling units constructed before 1946 (16)–(15)	15. Number of dwelling units constructed 1946–1965	16. Number of dwelling units as of 1965	17. Percentage of dwelling units constructed 1946–1965 (15):(16)%
Blackeberg	—	2,759	370	149	1951–1955	86	3,278	3,364	97.44
Råcksta	1	1,840	271	—	1951–1955	16	2,112	2,128	99.24
Vällingby	—	2,829	655	74	1951–1955	65	3,558	3,623	98.20
Grimsta	—	1,109	542	—	1951–1955	3	1,651	1,654	99.81
Hässelby Gård	1	2,462	2,178	1	1951–1960	25	4,642	4,667	99.46
Hässelby Strand	—	42	3,322	1	1956–1960	0	3,365	3,365	100.00
Totals	2	11,041	7,338	225		195	18,606	18,801	99.00

[a] Stockholm Office of Statistics, *Statistical Yearbook of Stockholm 1967* (Stockholm: Stockholm Office of Statistics, 1967), Table 23, p. 32.
[b] *Ibid.*, Table 3, pp. 2–3.
[c] *Ibid.*, Table 129, pp. 137–139.
[d] Stockholms stads statistiska kontor, *Folk- och bostadsräkningen den 1 november 1965. Del IV Bostäder i Stor- Stockholm*, Mimeo. (Stockholm: Stockholms stads statistiska kontor, July 1968), Table 3, pp. 29–30.
[e] *Ibid.*, Table 2, pp. 17–18.

Table 1.2

Housing Developed in Vällingby by Municipally Owned Companies, January 1, 1966[a]

Company	Parish Bromma	Spånga	Hässelby	Totals
AB Familjebostäder	1,411	—	840	2,251
AB Stockholmshem	1,774	218	1,535	3,527
AB Svenska Bostäder	963	3,983	1,300	6,246
AB Stockholmsbyggen	—	—	—	—
Hyreshus i Stockholm AB	322	108	1,437	1,867
AB Råckstahus	—	1,390	—	1,390
Total number of units	4,470	5,699	5,112	15,281

[a] Source: Allmännyttiga Bostadsföretagen i Stockholm, *Kommunal bostadsbyggande i Stockholm* (Stockholm: Allmännyttiga bostadsföretagen i Stockholm, 1966), p. 45.

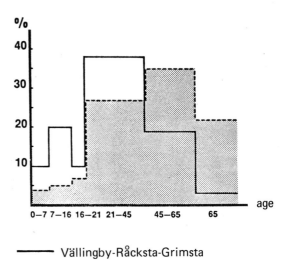

——— Vällingby-Råcksta-Grimsta

— — — central Stockholm

Figure 1.11
Comparative population structures of Vällingby-Råcksta-
Grimsta core area and central Stockholm, November 1964.
  Source: AB Svenska Bostäder, *Vällingby* (Stockholm: AB
Svenska Bostäder, 1966), p. 26.
  The difference between central Stockholm and the suburb
with regard to the age distribution of the population is shown
in the diagram. The comparison refers only to the core area
of Vällingby and central Stockholm, but the figures of Greater
Vällingby agree with those of the core area, even though
Greater Vällingby also includes a few older city districts.

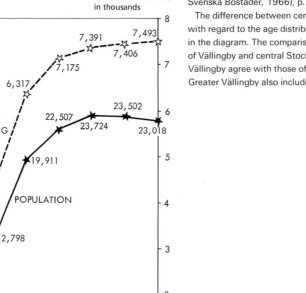

Figure 1.10
Population and number of dwelling units in Vällingby-Råcksta-
Grimsta, 1950–1964.
  Source: AB Svenska Bostäder, *Vällingby* (Stockholm: AB
Svenska Bostäder, 1966), p. 27.

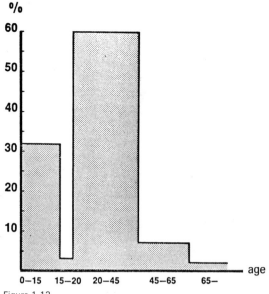

%

Figure 1.12
Population distribution at Vällingby city district by age, 1954.
    Source: AB Svenska Bostäder, *Vällingby* (Stockholm: AB
Svenska Bostäder, 1966), p. 26.
    The diagram shows the still greater proportion of younger
people at the time of moving in. This information refers only
to the city district of Vällingby, November 1, 1954, when about
5,000 people had moved in.

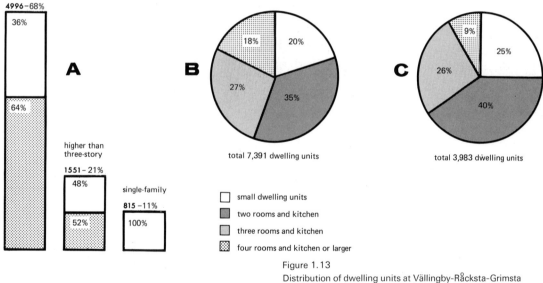

Figure 1.13
Distribution of dwelling units at Vällingby-Råcksta-Grimsta
by size of unit and type of building.
    Source: AB Svenska Bostäder, *Vällingby* (Stockholm: AB
Svenska Bostäder, 1966), p. 28.
    Distribution of dwelling units within Vällingby-Råcksta-
Grimsta:
A According to type of building (AB Svenska Bostäder, city-
     owned building company, in dotted area)
B According to size, all dwelling units
C According to size, AB Svenska Bostäder dwelling units

17   The Vällingby Development Area

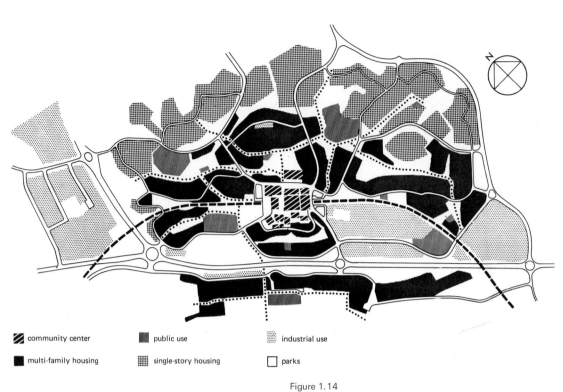

N

community center   public use   industrial use

multi-family housing   single-story housing   parks

Figure 1.14
Vällingby land use map.
   Source: AB Svenska Bostäder, *Vällingby* (Stockholm: AB
Svenska Bostäder, 1966), p. 7.

adjacent to Vällingby. The arguments against relocation were that Johannelund was a clay field 15 kilometers from the central business district, that nearby housing areas were either still in the planning stage or under construction, and that there was no railroad spur to the industrial area. (The area does however, have its own rapid transit station between Vällingby and Hässelby Gård.) Because of these factors, most of the enterprises that eventually located there did not do so until the residential areas were completed. This made it difficult for their employees to find housing near their jobs (see Table 1.3).

Except for heavy industry, most types of employers are represented at Vällingby, including production, assembly, and service. They employ both skilled and unskilled workers, male and female.[9] The community centers, too, play a role in employment. Companies at Vällingby Center alone employ some 2,200 persons in offices, shops, and service and social institutions. The National Power Board at Råcksta is one of the largest single employers, with 1,900 people in its administrative offices in 1966.

As Table 1.3 indicates, the number of jobs available within the Vällingby Development Area (including Johannelund) was 9,018 in 1960 and increased to 14,090 by 1965. In 1965, 3,158 jobs were available in the Johannelund industrial area, 7,379 in the Vällingby-Råcksta-Grimsta area.

Table 1.3 further shows that in 1960 the Vällingby Development Area (including Johannelund) could have employed 35.82 percent of the employable local residents but in fact employed only 19.64 percent; the other 80.35 percent commuted elsewhere to work. Of those working within the development area 54.83 percent also lived there. In 1965, these figures were 54.23 percent, 24.13 percent, 75.86 percent, and 44.49 percent, respectively.

The Farsta Development Area

Some 10 kilometers south of downtown Stockholm is the Farsta Development Area, consisting of the seven city districts of Gubbängen, Hökarängen, Sköndal, Larsboda, Farsta, Farsta Strand, and Fagersjö. Total 1966 population was 56,420 people living in 17,058 dwelling units (1965). Development at Farsta followed the same general pattern established at Vällingby, with several significant distinctions. Vällingby was almost exclusively a public project; Farsta was the product of private enterprise, with the city acting as overseer. The reasons for this departure were a blend of economic and political elements that will be dealt with in detail later. (For location map, site plan, and development breakdown, see Figs. 1.15, 1.16, and Table 1.4).

City Districts
Gubbängen North of the Farsta Development Area is the Gubbängen city district. The 1966 population was 7,160 persons, and in 1965 there were 2,363 dwelling units. Gubbängen is served by major highways running both east-west and north-south and by rapid transit from the station at the Gubbängen district center, which is bisected by a north-south road. Almost all development occurred after 1945; 1946 to 1950 was the most intensive period of residential construction.
Hökarängen The Hökarängen city district is south of Gubbängen, separated from it by a greenbelt. Hökarängen's 1966 population was 14,557; the 1965 housing stock was 4,420 dwelling units. Hökarängen is served by major north-south and east-west highways and the rapid transit station at Hökarängen's district center. Practically no development occurred in Hökarängen before 1945; the most active period of residential construction was from 1946 to 1950.
Sköndal The Sköndal city district, east of Gubbängen and Hökarängen, had a 1966 population of 6,775 people and a 1965 housing stock of 2,019 dwelling units. The district is near major roads, but for rapid transit, resi-

Table 1.3
Commuting within, into, and out of the Vällingby Development Area

1. City district	2. Nighttime population (number of residents)[a]	3. Nighttime employed population (number of employed residents)[b]	4. Percentage of residents employed (3):(2)	5. Daytime employed population (number of jobs available locally)[b]	6. Percentage of locally available jobs to residents (5):(2)	7. Percentage of locally available jobs to employed residents (5):(3)	8. Internal commuting or Walk to Work (number of employed residents employed locally)[b]
Blackeberg							
1960	10,131	4,483	44.25	1,383	13.65	30.84	584
1965	9,576	4,676	48.83	1,337	13.96	28.59	579
Råcksta							
1960	7,026	3,081	43.85	1,240	17.64	40.24	233
1965	6,693	3,212	47.99	3,199	47.79	99.59	323
Vällingby							
1960	11,402	4,772	41.85	3,054	26.78	63.99	656
1965	10,746	4,993	46.46	3,661	34.06	73.32	611
Grimsta							
1960	5,299	2,282	43.06	520	9.81	22.78	102
1965	5,023	2,337	46.52	519	10.33	22.20	87
Hasselby Gård							
1960	14,568	6,049	41.52	1,052	7.22	17.39	433
1965	13,938	6,208	44.54	1,536	11.02	24.74	453
Hässelby Strand							
1960	10,281	4,363	42.43	655	6.37	15.01	226
1965	10,002	4,430	44.29	680	6.79	15.34	234
Vinsta (incl. Johannelund)							
1960	309	140	45.30	1,114	360.51	795.71	41
1965	299	125	41.80	3,158	105.61	2,526.40	40
Total							
1960	59,016	25,170	42.64	9,018	15.28	35.82	4,945
1965	56,277	25,981	46.16	14,090	25.03	54.23	6,270

1. City district	9. Percentage of employed residents employed locally (8):(3)	10. Percentage of jobs available locally occupied by employed residents (8):(5)	11. Number commuting out (3)−(8)	12. Percentage of employed residents commuting out (11):(3)	13. Number commuting in (5)−(8)	14. Percentage of jobs available locally occupied by nonresidents (13):(5)
Blackeberg						
1960	13.02	42.22	3,899	86.97	799	57.77
1965	12.38	43.30	4,097	87.61	758	56.69
Råcksta						
1960	7.56	18.79	2,848	92.43	1,007	81.20
1965	10.05	10.09	2,889	89.94	2,876	89.90
Vällingby						
1960	13.74	21.48	4,116	86.25	2,398	78.51
1965	12.23	16.68	4,382	87.76	3,050	83.31
Grimsta						
1960	44.69	19.61	2,180	95.53	418	80.38
1965	37.22	16.76	2,250	96.27	432	83.23
Hässelby Gård						
1960	7.15	41.15	5,616	92.84	619	58.84
1965	7.29	29.49	5,755	92.70	1,083	70.50
Hässelby Strand						
1960	51.79	34.50	4,137	94.82	429	65.49
1965	52.82	34.41	4,196	94.71	446	65.58
Vinsta (incl. Johannelund)						
1960	29.28	3.68	99	70.71	1,073	96.31
1965	32.00	1.26	85	68.00	3,118	98.73
Total						
1960	19.64	54.83	20,225	80.35	4,073	45.16
1965	24.13	44.49	19,711	75.86	7,820	55.50

[a] Population figures from Stockholm Office of Statistics, *Housing Census of Stockholm 1960* (Stockholm: Stockholm Office of Statistics, 1965), Table 40, pp. 201−202, and *Statistical Yearbook of Stockholm 1967* (Stockholm: Stockholm Office of Statistics, 1967), Table 23, p. 32. Registered residents approximately equal residents.
[b] Data provided by Jon H. Léons, Research Section, Stockholm City Planning Office, from raw material in the 1960 and 1965 *Folk- och Bostadsräkningen*. Excluded are registered residents with unknown or mobile places of employment, for example, cab drivers, seamen.

Table 1.4
Amount, Rate, and Intensity of Residential Development at the Farsta Development Area

1. City district	2. Population Nov. 1, 1966[a]	3. Land area (hectares) Dec. 31, 1966[b]	4. Land area (acres)	5. Average gross population density (pop./acre)	Number of dwellings		8. Average gross density of residential construction, 1965 (dwelling units/acre)
					6. 1960[c]	7. 1965[d]	
Gubbängen	7,160	178	439.84	16.27	2,326	2,363	5.37
Hökarängen	14,557	142	350.88	41.48	4,007	4,420	12.59
Sköndal	6,775	266	657.29	10.30	1,702	2,019	3.07
Larsboda	1,989	123	303.93	6.54	605	660	2.17
Farsta	16,441	237	585.63	28.07	4,003	4,847	8.27
Farsta Strand	6,330	156	385.48	16.42	719	1,884	4.88
Fagersjö	3,168	180	444.78	7.12	55	865	1.94
Total	56,420	1,282	3,167.88	17.81	13,417	17,058	5.38

1. City district	Number of dwellings constructed[e]				13. Period of most intensive residential development	14. Number of dwelling units before 1946 (16)–(15)	15. Number of dwelling units constructed 1946–1965	16. Number of dwelling units 1965	17. Percentage of dwelling units constructed 1946–1965 (15)–(16)%
	9. 1946–1950	10. 1951–1955	11. 1955–1960	12. 1961–1965					
Gubbängen	2,133	127	3	7	1946–1950	93	2,270	2,363	96.06
Hökarängen	3,353	278	219	561	1946–1950	9	4,411	4,420	99.79
Sköndal	273	703	733	276	1951–1960	34	1,985	2,019	98.31
Larsboda	—	3	617	5	1956–1960	35	625	660	94.69
Farsta	270	1	3,560	974	1956–1960	42	4,805	4,847	99.13
Farsta Strand	5	—	737	1,102	1961–1965	40	1,844	1,884	97.87
Fagersjö	—	—	—	820	1961–1965	45	820	865	94.97
Total	6,034	1,112	5,869	3,745		298	16,760	17,058	98.0

[a] Stockholm Office of Statistics, *Statistical Yearbook of Stockholm 1967* (Stockholm: Stockholm Office of Statistics, 1967), Table 23, p. 32.
[b] *Ibid.*, Table 3, pp. 2–3.
[c] *Ibid.*, Table 129, pp. 138–139.
[d] Stockholms statistiska kontor, *Folk- och bostadsräkningen den 1 november 1965. Del IV Bostäder i Stor-Stockholm*, Mimeo. (Stockholm: Stockholms statistiska kontor, July 1968), Table 3, pp. 29–30.
[e] *Ibid.*, Table 2, pp. 17–18.

dents must rely on connecting bus service to the Hökarängen or Farsta stations. Residential and commercial construction continues in Sköndal, which is the site of Stora Sköndal Diakonanstalt, a large private retirement community.[10] Almost all development has occurred since 1945; 1951 to 1960 was the most active period of residential construction.

Fagersjö   The Fagersjö city district, west of Gubbängen and Hökarängen, had a 1966 population of 3,168 persons and a 1965 housing stock of 865 dwelling units. Major roads connect the district with Hökarängen to the northeast, Farsta to the southeast, and Högdalen to the northwest. There is bus service to transit stations at Högdalen and Farsta, and there is a railroad station at Fagersjö. Practically no development occurred in the area before 1960, and the most active period of residential construction was 1961 to 1965, though it is still largely undeveloped.

Farsta   The Farsta city district, south of Fagersjö, Hökarängen, and Sköndal, and with a greenbelt on the north, had a 1966 population of 16,441 persons and a 1965 housing stock of 4,847 dwelling units. The district has good north-south and east-west roads, a network of bus lines, a railroad station, and a transit station at Farsta Center. Little development occurred before 1945, and the most active period of residential construction was from 1956 to 1960. Farsta Center, located in the Farsta city district, was planned to serve the entire development area.

Larsboda   The Larsboda city district, southeast of Farsta, had a 1966 population of 1,989 people and a 1965 housing stock of 660 dwelling units. The district is bisected by a major north-south highway and has bus service to the Farsta transit station and to the Södertörns Villastad railroad station. Little development occurred before 1955, and the most active period of residential construction was 1956 to 1960. Large areas of Larsboda have been set aside for industrial use.

Farsta Strand   The Farsta Strand city district, south of Farsta and Larsboda, had a 1966 population of 6,330 persons and a 1965

Figure 1.15
Farsta location map.
   Source: AB Farsta Centrum, *Farsta* (Stockholm: AB Farsta Centrum, 1959).

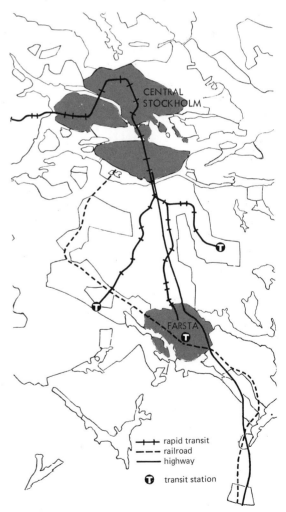

rapid transit
railroad
highway

T   transit station

1. Farsta Center
2. parking lot
3. rapid transit station
4. secondary school
5. secondary school
6. primary school
7. day nursery
8. gymnasium and outdoor
   swimming pool
9. athletic field
10. riding school
11. Farsta Gård (reserved for
    leisure time use)
12. atomic powered heating
    substation
13. central boiler
14. offices and laboratories for
    National Telecommunica-
    tions Board administration
15. industrial area
16. small boat harbor

====== railroad
------ rapid transit
············ pedestrian paths
—+—+— city district boundary

Figure 1.16
Site plan of the Farsta, Farsta Strand, and Larsboda city
districts.
 Source: ''Farsta Centrum,'' *Arkitektur*, 1961, No. 3.

housing stock of 1,884 dwelling units. The district is served by main north-south roads and bus service to the Södertörns Villastad railroad station and the Farsta transit station. The transit line that now terminates at Farsta will eventually extend to Farsta Strand. Practically no development occurred in the district before 1955, and the most intensive period of residential construction was 1961 to 1965.

Residential Development Density

Column 5 in Table 1.4—average gross population density (population/acre)—is only a rough measure, but the figures reflect other information about the development area and each of the city districts.

The city districts reserve land for greenbelts and other uses such as transportation, commerce, shopping, and light industry, so residential use tends to be clustered. Farsta city district is the best example of this; other city districts differ in detail.

Gubbängen's population density of 16.27 people per acre is about average for the development area (17.81). Land use in the city district is devoted chiefly to residences and services (shopping, transportation, schools), but southern Gubbängen is given over to a large greenbelt. Development accounts for a greater portion of Hökarängen than Gubbängen, but land use is otherwise similar. Hökarängen is primarily residential; its high population density (41.48) reflects its development (between 1946 and 1950) as an area of small, poorly equipped units of category housing for larger, less affluent families. Some physical improvements have been made since then.

At Sköndal there are detached single-family dwellings and multistory rental housing. Its only other major development is the private retirement community, Stora Sköndal Diakonanstalt. A large area of the city district remains in open space. Except for land given over to industrial use and some residential development, the city district is largely undeveloped.

Land use at Farsta is diverse, and its population is clustered at Farsta Center in apartment buildings of up to sixteen stories.

Development at Farsta Strand is almost entirely residential; population density is about that of Gubbängen. Like Larsboda, Fagersjö is largely undeveloped open space. Residential development is clustered, but the overall population density is low.

The disparate population densities of the city districts in the Farsta Development Area no doubt reflect local variations in terrain and other technical obstacles; when compared with the Vällingby Development Area, though, they suggest a less highly developed municipal housing commitment. [11]

The variations in the figures in Table 1.4 (col. 8) for average gross density of residential construction (dwelling units/acre), also a rough measure, closely parallel those for average gross population density.

Employment

As Table 1.5 indicates, fewer Farsta Development Area residents walk to work than do Vällingby Development Area residents. In 1960 the number of jobs available in the Farsta Development Area was 5,694; in the Farsta city district, 2,874. In 1965 the figures were 8,632 and 5,338, respectively.

Table 1.5 indicates that in 1960 the Farsta Development Area had employment opportunities for 28.20 percent of the employable resident population. However, only 12.34 percent of this population held local jobs; the rest (87.65 percent) were commuters who worked elsewhere. Of the total number of persons working within the development area, 43.74 percent lived there. In 1965 these figures were 33.37 percent, 14.95 percent, 85.04 percent, and 44.79 percent, respectively. This represents not so much a less successful attempt to effect local employment policy as it does a change in outlook toward the policy itself, a matter that will be examined closely in succeeding chapters.

Table 1.5
Commuting within, into, and out of the Farsta Development Area

1. City district	2. Nighttime population (number of residents)[a]	3. Nighttime employed population (number of employed residents)[b]	4. Percentage of residents employed (3:2)	5. Daytime employed population (number of jobs available locally)[b]	6. Percentage of locally available jobs to residents (5:2)	7. Percentage of locally available jobs to employed residents (5:3)	8 Internal commuting or Walk to Work (number of employed residents employed locally)[b]
Gubbängen
1960	7,855	3,596	45.77	799	10.17	22.21	276
1965	7,378	3,937	53.36	725	9.82	18.41	181
Hökarängen
1960	14,624	6,192	42.34	1,067	7.29	17.23	421
1965	14,808	7,143	48.23	1,028	6.94	14.39	372
Sköndal
1960	5,533	2,590	46.81	553	9.99	21.35	235
1965	6,299	3,015	47.86	877	13.72	29.08	298
Larsboda
1960	1,957	859	43.89	80	4.08	9.31	31
1965	2,064	955	46.26	158	7.65	16.54	38
Farsta
1960	13,421	5,818	43.34	2,874	21.41	49.39	581
1965	16,679	6,919	41.48	5,338	32.00	77.14	1,025
Farsta Strand
1960	2,235	1,055	47.20	197	8.81	18.67	25
1965	6,267	2,540	40.52	248	3.95	9.76	51
Fagersjö
1960	176	75	42.61	124	70.45	165.33	12
1965	3,143	1,354	43.07	258	8.20	19.05	54
Total
1960	45,801	20,185	44.07	5,694	12.43	28.20	2,491
1965	56,638	25,863	45.66	8,632	15.24	33.37	3,867

1. City district	9. Percentage of employed residents employed locally (8:3)	10. Percentage of jobs available locally occupied by employed residents (8.5)	11. Number commuting out (3–8)	12. Percentage of employed residents commuting out (11:3)	13. Number commuting in (5–8)	14. Percentage of jobs available locally occupied by nonresidents (13:5)
Gubbängen						
1960	7.67	34.54	3,320	92.32	523	65.45
1965	4.59	24.96	3,756	95.40	544	75.03
Hökarängen						
1960	6.79	39.45	5,771	93.20	646	60.54
1965	5.20	36.18	6,771	94.79	656	63.81
Sköndal						
1960	9.07	42.49	2,355	90.92	318	57.50
1965	9.88	33.97	2,717	90.11	579	66.02
Larsboda						
1960	3.60	38.75	828	96.39	49	61.25
1965	3.97	24.05	917	96.02	120	75.94
Farsta						
1960	9.98	20.21	5,237	90.01	2,293	79.78
1965	14.81	19.20	5,892	85.15	4,313	80.79
Farsta Strand						
1960	2.36	12.69	1,030	97.63	172	87.30
1965	2.00	20.56	2,489	97.99	197	79.43
Fagersjö						
1960	16.00	9.67	63	84.00	112	90.32
1965	3.98	14.18	1,300	96.01	204	79.06
Total						
1960	12.34	43.74	17,694	87.65	3,203	56.25
1965	14.95	44.79	21,996	85.04	4,765	55.20

[a] Population figures from Stockholm Office of Statistics, *Housing Census of Stockholm 1960* (Stockholm: Stockholm Office of Statistics, 1965), Table 40, pp. 201–202, and *Statistical Yearbook of Stockholm 1967* (Stockholm: Stockholm Office of Statistics, 1967), Table 23, p. 32. Registered residents approximately equal residents.

[b] Data provided by Jon H. Léons, Research Section, Stockholm City Planning Office, from law material in the 1960 and 1965 *Folk- och Bostadsräkningen*. Excluded are registered residents with unknown or mobile places of employment, for example, cab drivers, seamen.

2
The Background to Stockholm Suburban Planning and Development

Vällingby and Farsta, while representing sharp departures from the past, are products of a well-established tradition of municipally initiated housing development. It seems useful, therefore, to examine briefly the cornerstones of this tradition and the degree of success that each achieved.

Stockholm's attempts to accommodate orderly urban growth—prior to the development of large-scale suburban communities such as Vällingby and Farsta—is comprised of three elements: the city's extensive purchase of land beginning in the early twentieth century; the development of garden suburbs of single-family houses in the 1920s and early 1930s; and the construction of larger, planned suburban communities of mixed housing types and limited community facilities during and immediately after World War II.

Municipal Land Purchases

Throughout the century, Stockholm has been buying land, generally large private estates and, where possible, extending its city limits to incorporate the new land. The first important acquisition was the purchase of 600 hectares (1,482 acres) in Enskede Gård in the spring of 1904 and was followed later that year by the purchase of four plots of land in Bromma with a total area of 1,355 hectares (3,350 acres). In less than a year, the city had bought almost 2,000 hectares (5,000 acres), at a time when the total built-up area of the city was only 1,700 hectares (4,200 acres).[1] (See Fig. 2.1 for all city land purchases.) The cost, totaling 3.6 million kronor ($720,000), was sanctioned by an almost unanimous vote in the city council, which was then comprised almost exclusively of businessmen. Succeeding land purchases, however, were more difficult, as for instance in 1912 when the city council proposed the purchase of a 645-hectare (1,600-acre) farm at Farsta. Many council members considered it a waste of public funds to purchase land so far from the central city, an understandable viewpoint, perhaps, since the property was not to be developed for some forty years. An influential bank director of the time, K. A. Wallenberg, summed up the pro-expansion position: "Those who believe in the future of our municipality must vote for this proposition. Those who believe that our city is going to stagnate ought to vote against it."[2]

In 1927 there was public criticism over the purchase of two estates, Beckomberga and Råcksta, totaling 508 hectares (1,255 acres), and the newspapers accused the city of squandering public money.[3] The purchases continued, however, as in 1931 when the city purchased a site outside its western boundary consisting of four square miles of country estates formerly used for hunting and farming. Today this area is Vällingby.

By 1965 the city owned some 10,000 hectares (24,700 acres), or about two-thirds of the total corporate area surrounding the inner city. By this time critics of land policy were complaining that the city had not been active enough in the field of land acquisition. Such a complaint has come from former commissioner Joakim Garpe, who writes: "This doesn't mean that it hasn't bought a great deal of land. Stockholm has, on the contrary, invested unusually large sums in land purchase, but still not enough."[4]

No less important than land acquisition is the question of its disposition.[5] From the very beginning, Stockholm has, through a system of leasehold rights, parceled out the land to create housing areas for the less well-to-do. By the leasehold method the city controls both the ownership and the price of land, maintaining for itself maximum latitude in the economics and timing of future plans.

The city reserves the right to reclaim the land, after a certain period, should it be needed for another function. A national law of 1907 sets this period, in the case of Stockholm, at sixty years for residences and twenty-six to one hundred years for industrial property. In 1953 the leaseholder's contract was extended to cover an "unlimited period." However, the city may still reclaim the land after the first sixty years if it needs it for other purposes; otherwise, the contract is extended through another forty years. The city may reclaim nonresidential land after twenty years, but as a rule the first period is eighty years.

Although these new regulations strengthen the leaseholder's position, they also benefit the city. If the city reclaims a piece of property after the first period, it must compensate the lessee to the extent of the value of the improvements. On the other hand, the city may now make up for increases in land prices by raising the ground rent or leasehold fee. The leasehold fee is revised every twenty years for residences and every ten years for other types of buildings.[6]

The chief aim of the fee is to cover the cost of development of and interest on land; there is no attempt to recover original capital outlay. The land is valued at a very low price, only

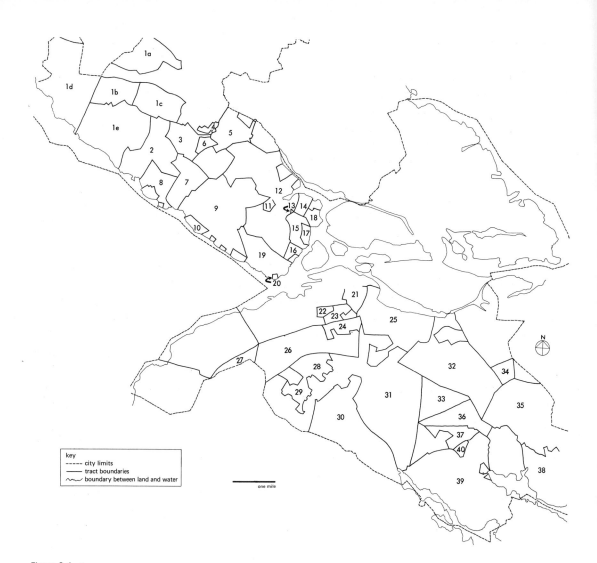

Figure 2.1
Land owned by city of Stockholm in western and southern
suburbs, by tract, date of purchase, area, price, and price per
unit area.
  Source: Prepared by Axel Wallenberg for Yngve Larsson.
Courtesy Yngve Larsson.

Index number	Tract name	Parish	Purchase year	Purchase price in thousands, kronor	Area in hectares	Price per hectare in kronor
1a.	Lunda		1931		206	
1b.	Vinsta		1931		97	
1c.	Nälsta		1931		58	
1d.	Hässelby villastad		1931		134	
1e.	Hässelby		1931		478	
1a–1e.	Hässelby	Spånga	1931	3,030.0	973	3,110
2.	Råcksta	Spånga	1927 ⎫	1,580.0	508	3,110
3.	Beckomberga	Bromma	1927 ⎭			
4.	Flysta	Spånga	1938 ⎫	2,500.0	157	15,950
5.	Bällsta	Bromma	1938 ⎭			
6.	Eneby gård	Bromma	1938	276.0	22	12,500
7.	St. Ängby	Bromma	1904	100.0	156	640
8.	Blackeberg	Bromma	1947	2,845.0	84	33,830
9.	Åkeshov och Stora Nockebyhov	Bromma	1904	400.0	584	680
10.	Åkeshov	Bromma	1935	400.0	24	16,970
11.	Lillsjönäs	Bromma	1908	150.0	9	15,970
12.	Ulvsunda	Bromma	1904	909.6	587	1,550
13.	Vidängen	Bromma	1932	100.0	2	52,080
14.	Johannelund	Bromma	1919	1,673.7	40	41,480
15.	Äppelviken och Alvik	Bromma	1908	1,270.0	75	16,920
16.	Smedslätten	Bromma	1922	621.0	21	30,000
17.	Alvik	Bromma	1931	450.0	16	27,780
18.	Traneberg	Bromma	1904	190.0	28	6,790
19.	Ålsten	Bromma	1905	295.0	181	1,630
20.	Skogsbo	Bromma	1920	134.6	2	68,350
21.	Nybohov	Brännkyrka	1939	2,500.0	67	37,260
22.	Stadsägeområdet No. 16 å Brännkyrka (del av)	Brännkyrka	1938	300.0	22	13,500
23.	Midsommarkransen	Brännkyrka	1937	1,000.0	29	34,720
24.	Norra Västberga	Brännkyrka	1937	1,750.0	74	23,680
25.	Årsta	Brännkyrka	1905	2,300.0	380	6,050
26.	Västberga	Brännkyrka	1935	1,645.0	426	3,860
27.	Sätra	Brännkyrka	1937	120.7	30	4,090
28.	Långbro	Brännkyrka	1937	600.0	160	3,750
29.	Herrängen	Enskede	1930	260.0	130	2,000
30.	Älvsjö	Brännkyrka	1930	700.0	496	1,410
31.	Örby	Brännkyrka	1950	8,336.8	394	21,140
32.	Enskede	Enskede	1904	2,000.0	607	3,300
33.	Svedmyra	Enskede	1905	155.0	131	1,190
34.	Kärrtorp	Enskede	1947	1,500.0	26	58,710
35.	Skarpnäck	Enskede	1922	2,400.0	670	3,580
36.	Mossen	Enskede	1905	175.0	137	1,280
37.	Gubbängen	Enskede	1908	200.0	76	2,630
38.	Orhem	Enskede	1913	225.0	193	1,170
39.	Södertörns villastad (Farsta och Lilla Sköndal m.m.)	Enskede	1912	1,000.0	645	1,550
40.	Starrmyran	Enskede	1939	100.0	8	12,890

Conversions

1 hectare ≃ 2.5 acres   1 hectare = 10,000 square meters

1 krona ≃ $U.S.0.20

3.5 kronor per square meter. Commercial leasehold fees are based on current values in the open market.

The importance of the leasehold system in accommodating Stockholm's growth, particularly in terms of housing, can be gauged from the fact that about 70 percent of the dwellings in the suburbs of the city (120,000 out of 170,000) are built on land leased from the city. Folke Lundin notes,

For the planning of a functional and systematic development of a big city it is essential that the municipality be able to decide in which order the different areas are to be built, where the traffic routes are to be situated, how the land is to be divided among industries, shopping centers, offices, flat blocks [apartment houses], one-family houses, and so on. To have to deal with a varying number of private landowners is a hindrance to timed construction and a rational distribution of the ground. . . . The real estate office can control the drawings, and the members of the real estate board can assert their opinions concerning the plans and the sizes of dwellings, etc. . . . The leasehold system is without doubt of great importance for the construction of the new suburbs.[7]

The Garden City Movement[8]

Ebenezer Howard's book *Garden Cities of Tomorrow* (1902) was a major influence on the development of new towns and garden cities around the world.[9] However, small developments foreshadowing some of his ideas had grown up before that time in a number of countries; Sweden was no exception.

Stockholm was among other large cities throughout the world that toward the end of the nineteenth century experienced an urban exodus as a reaction to overcrowding. Most of those who moved were affluent people who settled in communities like Djursholm.[10] Further accommodation was offered with the establishment of suburbs such as Sundbyberg (1876), about 11.5 kilometers from the central city, and the resortlike coastal towns of Saltsjöbaden and Nynäshamn just after 1900.

It was then that the city instituted its policy of assisting the less well-to-do to obtain low-cost housing. The first development of single-family houses on municipally owned land took place in Enskede Gård shortly after its purchase.

Most of those who acquired homes in the new garden suburbs were manual laborers and building trades workers, since buyers often reduced costs by contributing their own labor to the construction of their homes. As the city imposed stricter building standards, however, self-builders were replaced by regular building contractors. The result of this development was that builders began to demand down payments of 20 to 25 percent from prospective owners. This, together with the reputation that the new garden suburbs were gaining as agreeable residential districts, led to their attracting a more prosperous class of people than the city had intended.

To counter this, a small private society calling itself Homes by Your Own Labor was formed in 1920. Through this society it was possible for people to acquire homes with no down payment except the labor of their own hands. Other societies followed, but it was not until the city itself took action that building for the less affluent began on a large scale.

In 1926 the city council approved an estates department proposal for building 200 cottages during the following year. The city furnished all the materials (in factory-prepared standard dimensions), supplied building directions, and made arrangements for the more skilled work such as plumbing, electrical wiring, and sheet-metal work. This came to about 90 percent of the building costs. The owner provided the other 10 percent (about 1,000 kronor, or $200) by helping to prepare the foundations and erecting the frame. All he had to lay out in cash was 300 kronor ($60) to cover one year's ground rent and part of the expense of the ground plan.

The build-your-own-home movement in the 1920s and 1930s was a considerable success largely because of the moderate prices and the great desire of many people to own their own small home and garden. Axel Dahlberg, Stockholm's real estate director from 1935 to 1943, estimated in 1939 that standardization of building materials saved 10 percent, central purchasing 10 percent, and the builder's own labor another 10 percent. The fact that the home was mortgaged at up to 90 percent of its cost made this plan a very attractive one. [11]

The income limit for buyers was 5,000 kronor ($1,000) a year; a lower limit of 3,500 kronor ($700) also applied since the city felt that families with an income lower than that would have difficulty meeting the payments and maintenance costs.

The city succeeded in reversing the trend away from home buying by the less affluent, and at the end of the 1930s it was estimated that of all the cottage builders of the previous decade, about 60 percent were manual laborers and factory workers; about 20 percent were service workers such as policemen, transit workers, and firemen; and only about 20 percent were in such occupations as public service and the military.

By 1939 there were 3,500 cottages housing 12,500 people. Developed were a fairly extensive area northwest of central Stockholm, including Olovslund (1927) and Norra Ängby (1931–1938), and sections to the south, in Enskedefältet (1930–1931) and Tallkrogen (1933–1938). Today the narrow, curving streets and lush foliage of the garden suburbs lend them an almost rural charm, especially when contrasted with the stark lines of the multistory apartment buildings in the nearby new suburbs of Vällingby and Farsta. One of the leading figures in the garden city movement, Axel Dahlberg, sums up the spirit behind it:

It is possible to solve the housing question for the group . . . that . . . displays relatively small incomes and is lacking in capital. . . . But if it lacks capital, it must possess the will to work and a willingness to sacrifice leisure, Sundays and evenings, for a year and devote the time to hard work. . . . [Whoever has] that will and that willingness, can solve [his] housing problem. He can, in fact, obtain a dwelling that not only provides a roof over his head and a place where he and his family can eat and sleep, but he can have a spacious dwelling, where he can feel himself at home, entirely his own master, a *home* which gives him and his family something, both financially and in the satisfaction derived from doing something useful. . . . He may cultivate the soil, something which ought to be the right of every man, since there is no work which provides such satisfaction as that. [12]

During and after World War II

Cottage building in the 1920s and 1930s occurred partly as a reaction to the "city of stone," as the inner city of Stockholm came to be known. Paralleling it was the development of suburban apartment houses, most of them the long, three-story buildings that exist today in Abrahamsberg to the west, Solna and Sundbyberg to the north, and Hägersten, Västberga, Midsommarkransen, Aspudden, Årsta, and Hammarbyhöjden to the south. These dormitory suburbs were not, of course, without their critics. There were numerous complaints that such areas were culturally sterile and devoid of activity. Many of them lacked recreation areas, cinemas, and meeting places, which made socializing particularly difficult for young people. [13]

With the advent of the 1940s came the provision of more recreation facilities, especially in areas of multifamily housing. Still, there was little in the way of a systematic basis for planning or locating them. Toward the end of the 1940s, however, Sweden began to feel the influence of English thinking on community centers, which had evolved from the settlement-house movement of the late nineteenth century [14] and from the principles of neighborhood planning developed in the United States by Clarence Perry and put into practice in the "greenbelt cities." [15]

Professional planners and interested politicians—among them, Uno Åhrén, Carl-Fredrik Ahlberg, Sven Markelius, and Yngve Larsson—began to demand a greater role for neighborhood planning, particularly the planning for extensive community centers containing a wide variety of facilities. The first actual attempt at neighborhood planning within the Stockholm area began with a planning competition for Gubbängen. Other suburbs planned in the late 1940s and containing local centers after the community center idea were Björkhagen, Kärrtorp, Västertorp, Midsommarkransen, and Årsta.

Of these, the most carefully planned, certainly the one receiving the greatest attention, was Årsta, which is in the inner suburbs just south of the central city. The 1940 site development plan for Årsta comprises three adjoining housing groups, each with approximately 10,000 residents, separated from each other by narrow greenbelts. In 1943 Svenska Riksbyggen (headed by Professor Uno Åhrén), which had built much of the housing in Årsta, proposed the construction of a community center at Årsta Square (see site plan, Fig. 6.1). The chief purposes of such a center were to provide local cohesion and a strong sense of community, thereby making Årsta more culturally independent of central Stockholm.

By the time Årsta Center had been constructed, however, Sweden's leading planners were beginning to be somewhat more hesitant about the goals of neighborhood planning. Their enthusiasm in the early 1940s, when neighborhood planning seemed the obvious answer to the critics of the "sterile" garden suburbs, gave way to a healthy skepticism in the early 1950s. Uno Åhrén said in an interview in 1953,

In the beginning of the 1940s we were optimistic and had great plans. We read the English authors and believed in men's education in democracy through collective activity. Most of what we planned for neighborhood life was thwarted because many thought the country lacked the labor and materials to do it. We had time to think, and we found that our ideology was perhaps a little out of touch with reality. We had time to study our projects in more detail, and we discovered how little we·actually knew about the reality we were planning for. We are groping our way forward; we need more research, clearer lines to work toward. [16]

In 1954–1956, at the city's behest, Gunnar Åsvärn and Bertil Mathsson undertook a sociological study [17] to discover how the inhabitants of Årsta used the new recreation center and whether they felt the cohesion and sense of community that the planners had hoped for. The results were disappointing; with the exception of the movie theater and library in the center building, most residents used recreational facilities outside Årsta. Many of the young people did not even know of the center's existence. The study rooms at the center, however, were actively used for adult education, and two-thirds of the respondents said they approved of the central location. It was significant, though, that very few mentioned as a reason for this approval the opportunity for personal contacts with other Årsta residents, which was one of the major goals of the center. Though some of its findings were important for the future planning of such centers, [18] the study is more significant for the fact that it tested planning theories that up until then, in Sweden as in many other countries, had been put into effect without undergoing an empirical testing of their possible results.

Another example from the 1940s is Hägerstensåsen-Hökmossen, in the southwestern inner suburbs. In this area the city houses approximately 17,000 people, predominantly in narrow four-story apartment houses and tower apartment buildings; there is also an area of small cottages. The planners' knowledge of how such a development is used and viewed by its inhabitants was considerably enhanced with the publication in 1951 of a community social survey of the area, commissioned by the Stockholm city planning board and undertaken by sociologist Edmund Dahlström. The chief interest of the study was, as stated in the English summary, ". . . in the development of certain sociological conditions in a physical environment of this planned type, in order to furnish planners with points of departure for future residential construction."[19]

Because of the housing shortage, the majority of prospective residents had only the choice between moving to Hägerstensåsen-Hökmossen or staying where they were. It is not surprising that a good many were less than satisfied with their new homes. On the whole, residents were satisfied with the shopping facilities, the architectural appearance of the area, the open areas, and their neighbors. Among the things they considered insufficient were transportation to work and to the city center; recreational facilities; and facilities for the care of preschool children, including not

only preschool play areas but also day nurseries, the lack of which prevented many women from contributing to the family income.

An important finding of Dahlström's study was that it was the quality of the housing and its convenience to work—not the cultural and recreational facilities in the area—that were decisive in keeping residents there or causing them to move. Many had complaints about certain facilities, but the desire to move did not correspond to the degree of dissatisfaction with them. Most informants considered their dwellings in Hägerstensåsen-Hökmossen bright, well planned, modern, and with splendid views, but these qualities did not compensate for lack of space, the most frequent complaint. Of those who wanted to move from the area (including fully two-thirds of the married couples), more than half wanted larger quarters and would have moved to any part of Stockholm to get them.

These studies of Årsta and Hägerstensåsen-Hökmossen, together with others conducted elsewhere in the country, [20] had considerable influence on planners and architects trying to foresee the needs of new residential areas. As assessments were made of past planning efforts, the stage was set for a new series of developments in the accommodation of city growth.

Seeds of the New Concepts

The first of these new ideas on neighborhood planning came to Sweden from the English-speaking world. In 1942 the Swedish edition of Lewis Mumford's *The Culture of Cities* appeared; it was widely read and discussed. Shortly after this, a few copies of the Abercrombie-Forshaw plan for the London County Council became available in Sweden and received similar attention.

As the city planning director, Göran Sidenbladh, has pointed out, there were a number of other factors in the immediate postwar years that coincided with the new interest in neighborhood planning: the city now owned considerable tracts of land; national legislation dating from 1943 provided the financial machinery for city-directed suburban development; and new population forecasts indicated that the city's population would grow at a much faster rate than previously anticipated.[21]

It was soon obvious to the planners that such provisions as those made for Årsta, with its limited shopping and transportation facilities, could no longer be considered sufficient. The very size of the city's expected growth demanded a different sort of plan from the one the city originally envisaged—the idea of a central high-density area surrounded by a ring of low-density suburbs was causing serious second thoughts.

As early as 1945, a city planning office proposal had recommended the creation of a number of administratively and geographically separate satellite towns, each with a suitable ratio of industrial and commercial activities to residences.[22] But by the time the master plan was published in 1952, the earlier proposal had been discarded. Future growth would take the form of a ring of fairly high-density neighborhoods within corporate Stockholm, separated from each other by narrow greenbelts, each with a center offering commercial, social, and cultural services and each linked to the central city by rapid transit or a suburban railroad.

3

A Political-Administrative Framework

Stockholm Government[1]

Stockholm has no mayor or city manager. A popularly elected city council of one hundred members makes legislative decisions; executive power rests with the central board of administration and the board of commissioners.[2] The central board of administration is made up of twelve members and twelve alternates, whom the city council chooses from its own membership. The board of commissioners is composed of nine paid officials, appointed by the council to four-year terms. Each commissioner presides over one of the city's administrative divisions. (See Table 3.1 and Figs. 3.1–3.9 for the political and administrative makeup of the city from 1934 to 1967.)

City council members serve for a term of four years, and all are elected at the same time. The council meets publicly one evening a month except during the vacation months of July and August; passage of the budget each December usually requires several additional sessions. On important matters, the council almost always votes along party lines.

During the first meeting of the council each year on October 15, the members elect a chairman and two vice-chairmen. The chairman decides the council's agenda, presides over its sessions, and represents the city on official occasions, While the terms of the chairman and vice-chairman are one year, it is customary to reelect them throughout the four years the council sits. The chairman and vice-chairmen of the council may be appointed to the central board of administration too but may not serve as either chairman or vice-chairman of the board. Commissioners, whether or not they are also city councilmen, may not sit on the board of administration.

The central board of administration meets regularly once a week. Its chairman, who serves without salary, supervises and co-ordinates the activities of the fifty or so boards and committees of the city's nine administrative divisions and prepares matters to be submitted to the city council.

The board of commissioners is made up of the administrative chiefs of Stockholm's nine divisions: finance; staff administration; real estate; streets and traffic; harbors, gas, electricity, and water; social welfare; culture and education; public health; and greater Stockholm (planning and regional affairs). The commissioner serves a four-year appointment, is salaried, and is entitled to a full retirement pension after serving twelve years. He is appointed by the city council at its first meeting,[3] and he automatically becomes the chairman of the boards belonging to his division.[4] He reports to the central board of administration and the city council on the various matters being handled by the boards under him, each of which is, for budget purposes, treated as a separate entity.

Each of the boards in a division has its "office," a staff of professional administrators and technical experts who plan methods of carrying out policy decisions and make studies for future projects. The office is guided by the director, a nonpolitical expert in the field his board administers.

The Building Board

The powers and activities of Stockholm's city planning board and real estate board, together with their administrators, were determining forces in the development of Vällingby and Farsta. At one time Stockholm's building board functioned exclusively as a building control board. Today it combines this function with that of a city planning commission, and the chief administrator directs both city planning and building control.

By law every city must have a building board responsible for local application of the national building law.[5] The board makes studies and recommendations for planning, real estate development, and construction; it cooperates with other authorities whose activities concern its area of responsibility; it prepares advice and information for public consumption; and it sees to the application of rules and regulations in construction work.

To assist it, the building board has a city architect, a building inspector, a city engineer, and others concerned with surveying, map making, and deed recording. In larger cities the work of the city architect and the building inspector is carried out by a number of officials; one architect may issue building permits, and another may plan. In Stockholm, for example, the city planning office employs several hundred workers and is divided into several subunits with different responsibilities. The city architect heads the bureau for building permits, the chief engineer oversees building inspection, and the city engineer is in charge of the surveying office. Special bureaus take care of general plan work, detailed site planning, and traffic questions.

A building board can, to a limited degree, delegate its decision-making powers, but decisions must be approved by the national government's county administration, which in Stockholm was, until January, 1, 1968, the office of the governor of Stockholm. The city architect frequently makes decisions regarding changes in building orders and other less important activities.

Table 3.1
Composition of Stockholm City Council by Parties (1935–1962)[a]

1. Period	2. Conservatives	3. Liberals	4. Bourgeois Majority (2 + 3)	5. Social Democrats	6. Socialists	7. Communists	8. Total (2 + 3 + 5 + 6 + 7)
Apr. 1, 1935– Sep. 30, 1938	33	14	47	45	7	1	100
Oct. 1, 1938– Sep. 30, 1942	26	14	40	55	2	3	100
Oct. 15, 1942– Oct. 14, 1946	29	16	45	46	0	9	100
Oct. 15, 1946– Oct. 14, 1950	22	23	45	38	0	17	100
Oct. 15, 1950– Oct. 14, 1954	17	35	52	43	0	5	100
Oct. 15, 1954– Oct. 14, 1958	20	31	51	41	0	8	100
Oct. 15, 1958– Oct. 14, 1962	29	20	49	45	0	6	100

[a]Source: Stockholm Office of Statistics, *Statistisk Årsbok för Stockholms Stad 1964–1965* (Stockholm: Stockholm Office of Statistics, 1965), Table 85, p. 103.

Figure 3.1
Selected functions (1935–1960) by commissioner, party, and
division of city government.

Source: Compiled from Stockholms stadskansli, *Stockholms
kommunalkalender* 1936–1961 (Stockholm: Stockholms
kommunalförvaltning, 1936–1961).

[a]Municipal election years.

[b]The municipal election of 1942 did not affect incumbent
commissioners; those appointed in 1940 remained at their
posts until October 1946.

[c]Chairman of building board, but not commissioner of division.

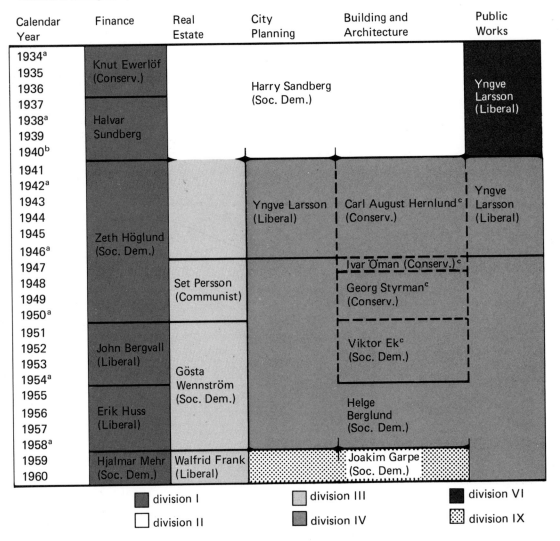

Figure 3.2
Selected municipal functions (1935–1960) by director.
  Source: Stockholms stadskansli, *Stockholms kommunal-kalender*, 1936–1961 (Stockholm: Stockholms kommunal-förvaltning, 1936–1961).

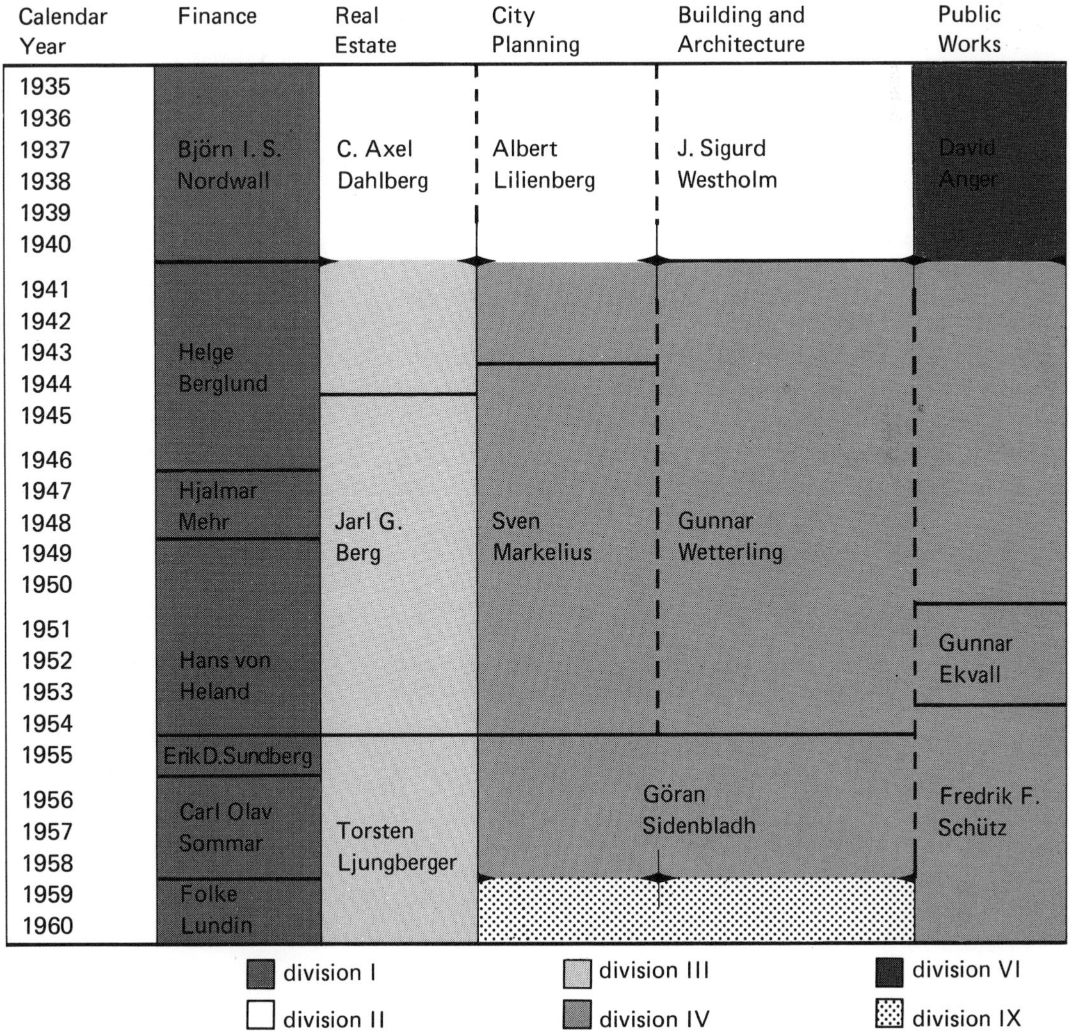

Calendar Year	Finance	Real Estate	City Planning	Building and Architecture	Public Works
1935					
1936					
1937	Björn I. S.	C. Axel	Albert	J. Sigurd	David
1938	Nordwall	Dahlberg	Lilienberg	Westholm	Anger
1939					
1940					
1941					
1942					
1943	Helge				
1944	Berglund				
1945					
1946					
1947	Hjalmar				
1948	Mehr	Jarl G.	Sven	Gunnar	
1949		Berg	Markelius	Wetterling	
1950					
1951					
1952	Hans von				Gunnar
1953	Heland				Ekvall
1954					
1955	Erik D.Sundberg				
1956	Carl Olav		Göran		Fredrik F.
1957	Sommar	Torsten	Sidenbladh		Schütz
1958		Ljungberger			
1959	Folke				
1960	Lundin				

■ division I   ▨ division III   ■ division VI
□ division II   ▨ division IV   ▨ division IX

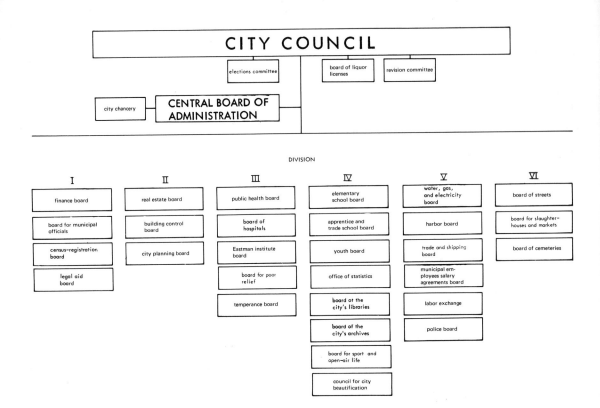

CITY COUNCIL

elections committee

board of liquor licenses

revision committee

city chancery

CENTRAL BOARD OF ADMINISTRATION

DIVISION

I	II	III	IV	V	VI
finance board	real estate board	public health board	elementary school board	water, gas, and electricity board	board of streets
board for municipal officials	building control board	board of hospitals	apprentice and trade school board	harbor board	board for slaughter-houses and markets
census-registration board	city planning board	Eastman institute board	youth board	trade and shipping board	board of cemeteries
legal aid board		board for poor relief	office of statistics	municipal employees salary agreements board	
		temperance board	board of the city's libraries	labor exchange	
			board of the city's archives	police board	
			board for sport and open-air life		
			council for city beautification		

Figure 3.3
Organization of Stockholm city administration at the end of 1935.

Source: Stockholms stadskansli, *Stockholms kommunal-kalender 1936* (Stockholm: Stockholms kommunalförvaltning, 1936).

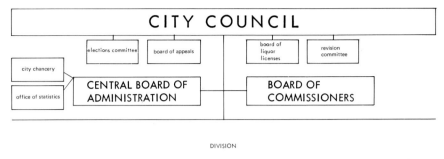

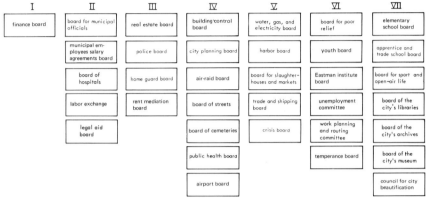

CITY COUNCIL

elections committee | board of appeals | board of liquor licenses | revision committee

city chancery | office of statistics

CENTRAL BOARD OF ADMINISTRATION | BOARD OF COMMISSIONERS

DIVISION

I	II	III	IV	V	VI	VII
finance board	board for municipal officials	real estate board	building control board	water, gas, and electricity board	board for poor relief	elementary school board
	municipal employees salary agreements board	police board	city planning board	harbor board	youth board	apprentice and trade school board
	board of hospitals	home guard board	air-raid board	board for slaughter-houses and markets	Eastman institute board	board for sport and open-air life
	labor exchange	rent mediation board	board of streets	trade and shipping board	unemployment committee	board of the city's libraries
	legal aid board		board of cemeteries	crisis board	work planning and routing committee	board of the city's archives
			public health board		temperance board	board of the city's museum
			airport board			council for city beautification

Figure 3.4
Organization of Stockholm city administration at the end of 1940.

Source: Stockholms stadskansli, *Stockholms kommunal-kalender 1941* (Stockholm: Stockholms kommunalförvaltning, 1941).

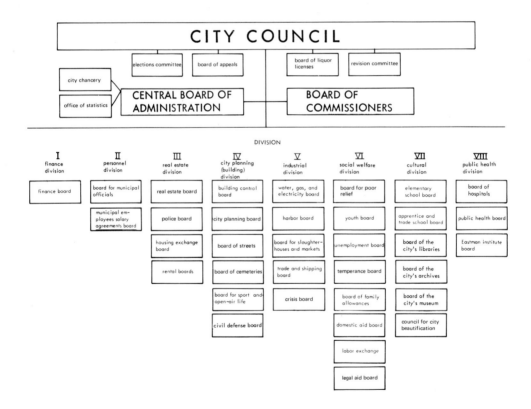

Figure 3.5
Organization of Stockholm city administration at the end of
1946.
  Source: Stockholms stadskansli, *Stockholms kommunal-
kalender 1947* (Stockholm: Stockholms kommunalförvaltning,
1947).

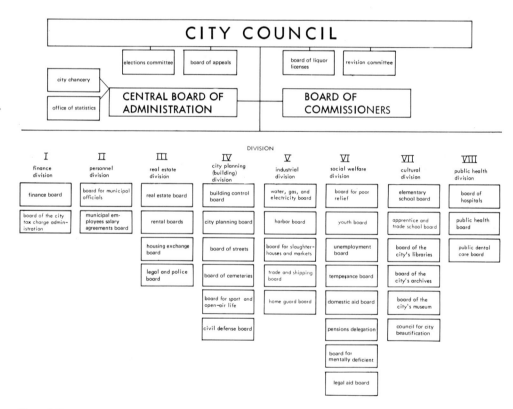

Figure 3.6
Organization of Stockholm city administration at the end of
1951
 Source: Stockholms stadskansli, *Stockholms kommunal-
kalender 1952* (Stockholm: Stockholms kommunalförvaltning,
1952).

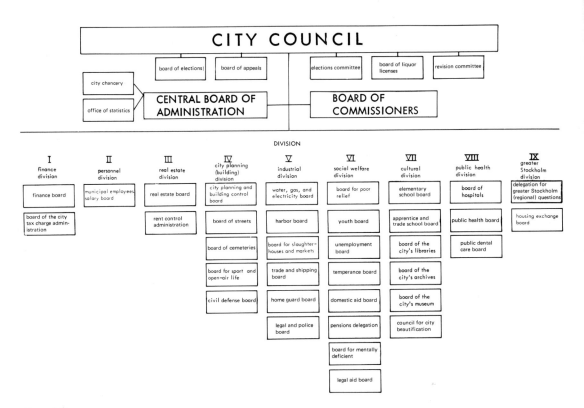

Figure 3.7
Organization of Stockholm city administration at the end of
1955.

Source: Stockholms stadskansli, *Stockholms kommunal-
kalender 1956* (Stockholm: Stockholms kommunalförvaltning,
1956).

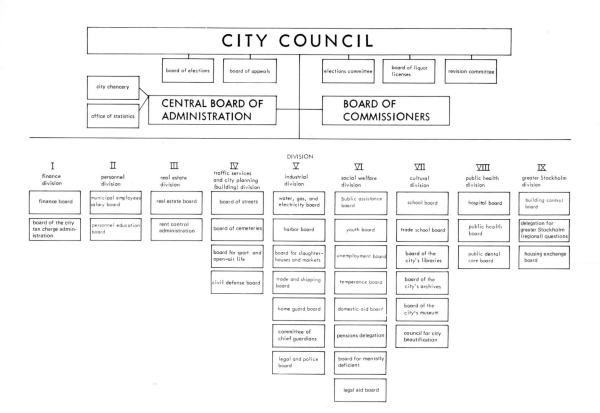

CITY COUNCIL

| board of elections | board of appeals | | elections committee | board of liquor licenses | revision committee |

city chancery

office of statistics

CENTRAL BOARD OF ADMINISTRATION

BOARD OF COMMISSIONERS

DIVISION

I	II	III	IV	V	VI	VII	VIII	IX
finance division	personnel division	real estate division	traffic services and city planning (building) division	industrial division	social welfare division	cultural division	public health division	greater Stockholm division
finance board	municipal employees salary board	real estate board	board of streets	water, gas, and electricity board	public assistance board	school board	hospital board	building control board
board of the city tax charge administration	personnel education board	rent control administration	board of cemeteries	harbor board	youth board	trade school board	public health board	delegation for greater Stockholm (regional) questions
			board for sport and open-air life	board for slaughter-houses and markets	unemployment board	board of the city's libraries	public dental care board	housing exchange board
			civil defense board	trade and shipping board	temperance board	board of the city's archives		
				home guard board	domestic aid board	board of the city's museum		
				committee of chief guardians	pensions delegation	council for city beautification		
				legal and police board	board for mentally deficient			
					legal aid board			

Figure 3.8
Organization of Stockholm city administration at the end of 1960.
  Source: Stockholms stadskansli, *Stockholms kommunal-kalender 1961* (Stockholm: Stockholms kommunalförvaltning, 1961).

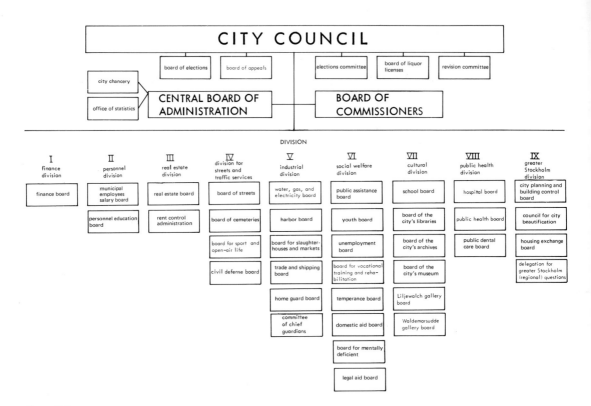

Figure 3.9
Organization of Stockholm city administration in 1967.
  Source: Chart, "Stockholms stads förvaltnings organisation,"
Stockholms stads personalutbildningsnämnd, 1967.

As Figures 3.10–3.15 show, during the 1940s and 1950s there were separate boards for building, public works, and city planning, each with its own supporting office and staff. Singly and together they worked with the real estate board and its servicing office, which administered real estate, property management, and housing.

Until 1955 the city planning board and the building board were separate and distinct, though their interests often overlapped. The planning board's chief duties were to make proposals for new and revised site development and traffic route plans. The building board was responsible for administering site apportionments, controlling building and repair, and passing judgment on planning board proposals.

In one respect the building board was unique. As already mentioned, when the central board of administration appoints a commissioner, he automatically becomes chairman of each of the boards within the division. This was not always the case with the building board. Since the 1920s, the board had chosen its chairman from within its own five-man membership. While the system worked well enough under the city architect Westholm,[6] it began showing strain with the advent of extensive downtown redevelopment planning.[7] Part of the problem lay in the fact that the planning board had no direct link to the city council; plans and proposals had to go through the building board, which could, if it chose, kill them simply by not passing them on to the council. This veto power, along with the almost inevitable personal differences that arose between members of the two boards because of their sometimes conflicting jurisdictions, compounded the irritation the planning board felt as a result of its division commissioner's being unable to assist in steering planning proposals through the building board. In fact, neither Yngve Larsson, public works and city planning commissioner from 1940 to 1946, nor Helge Berglund, his successor, was even allowed to attend building board meetings.

The city's director of organization is responsible for structural improvements in Stockholm's municipal government. In 1953 director Joakim Garpe recommended combining the building and planning boards into one body. Garpe, whose office seldom operated as high as the board level, was aware that he was somewhat beyond his province; he felt, though, that the gains of consolidation warranted the departure. It was his opinion that the friction that had existed between the two boards since the 1940s was a major source of waste and inefficiency and could only worsen. As a first corrective step, Garpe suggested that the building board invite division commissioner Berglund to its meetings as a nonvoting observer with the right to participate in discussions. Wary of any attempt to dilute its powers, the building board replied that while there might be some merit in the suggestion, it could not allow Berglund blanket permission to attend all its meetings; it would, however, discuss at each meeting whether to invite him to the next one. To this gambit Garpe replied, "I shall annihilate you the faster for it."[8]

On January 11, 1954, the city council made a decision in principle to combine the two boards. On December 7, 1954, after Garpe himself had become commissioner of the Greater Stockholm division, the council made its decision final, and on January 1, 1955, the building and planning boards were officially merged to form the planning and building control board, with Berglund as chairman.

In consolidating the old city planning and building boards into a new nine-man board, the city council made three new provisions. First, in appointing members to the board, the city council must always appoint the commissioner of the city planning division as a member. Second, the board must choose the commissioner as chairman. Finally, municipal officials, for example the city architect and the city engineer, and others when their interests require it, may attend board meetings, participate in the board discussions, and have their views entered in the report of the proceedings. The merger streamlined the treat-

Figure 3.10
Organization of Stockholm real estate, building, and city
planning boards at the end of 1936.

Source: Stockholms stadskansli. *Stockholms Kommunal-
kalender 1937* (Stockholm: Stockholms kommunalförvaltning,
1937).

[a]Only delegations concerned with suburban activities are
shown.

Figure 3.11
Organization of Stockholm real estate, building, and city
planning boards at the end of 1940.

Source: Stockholms stadskansli, *Stockholms kommunal-
kalender 1941* (Stockholm: Stockholms kommunalförvaltning,
1941).

[a]Only delegations concerned with suburban activities are
shown.

[b]The division commissioner did not at this time sit on this
board.

Figure 3.12
Organization of Stockholm real estate, building, and city
planning boards at the end of 1946.

Source: Stockholms stadskansli, *Stockholms kommunal-
kalender 1946* (Stockholm: Stockholms kommunalförvaltning,
1946).

[a]Only delegations concerned with suburban activities are
shown.

[b]The division commissioner did not at this time sit on this
board.

Figure 3.13
Organization of Stockholm real estate, building and city
planning boards at the end of 1951.
    Source: Stockholms stadskansli, *Stockholms kommunal-
kalender 1952* (Stockholm: Stockholms kommunalförvaltning,
1952).
    [a]Only delegations concerned with suburban activities are
shown.
    [b]The division commissioner did not at this time sit on this
board.

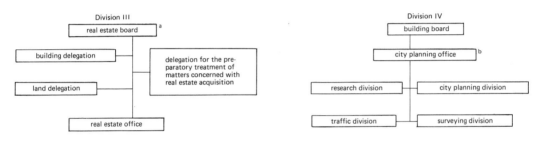

Figure 3.14
Organization of Stockholm real estate and building (merged
planning and building control) boards at the end of 1955.
    Source: Stockholms stadskansli, *Stockholms kommunal-
kalender 1956* (Stockholm: Stockholms kommunalförvaltning,
1956).
    [a]Only delegations concerned with suburban activities are
shown.
    [b]Only selected divisions are presented.

Figure 3.15
Organization of Stockholm real estate and building (merged
planning and building control) boards at the end of 1960.
    Source: Stockholms stadskansli, *Stockholms kommunal-
kalender 1961* (Stockholm: Stockholms kommunalförvaltning,
1961).
    [a]Only delegations concerned with suburban activities are
shown.
    [b]Only selected divisions are presented.

ment of planning proposals by doing away with one step in the passage of planning documents, a step that was usually difficult and always time-consuming.[9]

Formal Preparation and Approval of Planning Documents

To develop new suburban communities, national law requires that a city have formal planning documents. Since 1947 the national government has legally distinguished between comprehensive planning, which requires a master plan, and detailed planning, which requires a site development plan.

The main purpose of a master plan is to earmark land for specific uses. There are three types of master plans: (1) those that the Crown has to approve; (2) those that the city council adopts; and (3) those that the city council informally prepares but does not formally adopt even if the council discusses them. The third type need not even be passed by the building board. Stockholm's 1952 master plan is the third kind. It is quite informal, even though the city council discussed it, printed it, and used it as an aid in city development.

As areas become available for new uses, detailed development plans are prepared within the master plan. To prevent undertaking projects based on obsolete plans, the 1947 law states that a site development plan must not embrace an area larger than can be developed within a reasonably brief period of time.[10]

A site development plan is more simply categorized than a master plan: either it is or it isn't. The document can begin as a proposed site development plan or as a proposed change to an existing site development plan. The city planning office is continually making proposals; as soon as the city council adopts a proposal, it is formally referred to as a site development plan. As Kell Åström in *City Planning in Sweden* puts it: "Although the Crown must still put its seal of approval on . . . site plans, a decision once taken at the local level is seldom nullified by the central government."[11]

According to the current city planning director, Göran Sidenbladh, after the war it was a constant problem to find developable land near public transportation routes. Office directors held informal conferences three or four times a year to determine what land would be available for development and when. Conference members included the directors for streets, real estate, city planning, the city transit company, and social welfare, as well as the city architect and the city planning commissioner. Göran Sidenbladh notes that during this period, the city planning department was working under an informal commission from the real estate department: "This was all discussed at the directors' conferences. The informal decisions reached at these directors' conferences were confirmed either by letter from the director of real estate to us or by a kind of protocol."[12]

Theoretically, when land is marked for development, the real estate board or the real estate office sends a letter to the city planning office "commissioning" it to prepare a master plan and site development plans. In fact, however, by this time the planning office has already begun work. City planner Josef Stäck comments, "Usually this letter is just a piece of paper, because we already know where and how we have to plan. We will already have worked on the planning for some months by the time we get the letter."[13]

Sidenbladh says of planning commissioner Yngve Larsson:

He was a very dynamic man. . . . He didn't wait for formal letters and things like that. He said, "Prepare a plan," and that was that. So, instead of a letter to the city planning office from the real estate department, the initial document would more likely be a letter from the city planning office saying, "Here is a sketch for a plan, and what do you think of it?" Helge Berglund succeeded Larsson as city planning commissioner. Although educated to be a lawyer, he was very informal. He was a sort of man who said, "Well, if you think this is right, okay, do it." And that was that. There was very little in writing.[14]

After the planning office prepares a preliminary master plan proposal, it goes to the planning and building board for approval in principle. If it is an important plan, the real estate board may already have approved it in principle. The city planning director then sends it out to municipal offices and other interested organizations for their opinions and comments.

The planning office solicits opinions and comments on the proposed plan from a wide range of municipal boards, agencies, and offices: real estate; streets; electricity, gas, and water supply; the transit company; fire protection; sport and leisure-time activities; schools; children's welfare; medical care; city beautification; social welfare; cemeteries; finance; and, whenever appropriate, the Stockholm Chamber of Commerce, the Co-op (a chain of cooperatively owned stores and markets), the National Telecommunications Administration, the National Board of Building and Planning, and Swedish Railways. The city planning director reviews the opinions and may accordingly adjust or modify the plan.

The director then sends the statements, along with a proposed plan map, a written description of the plan, and the legal rules and regulations he suggests adopting with the plan, to the building board for consideration. If the board approves the proposed plan, it sends it on the city council, where the central board of administration examines it. Although the central board of administration first screens and prepares all business to be transacted by the city council, a plan that gets this far is virtually certain to go before the council. Josef Stäck notes: "Because each commission is composed of people from all the parties, it's very seldom that an unacceptable plan reaches the central board of administration. Very seldom does anyone try to force a plan through the central board of administration and the city council."[15]

In preparing a planning question for the consideration of the city council, the central board of administration assembles a report containing a short outline of any earlier plans for the area under consideration, requests for the preparation of the present plan, statements of the real estate board and building board, solicited opinions, and suggestions for plan revisions to answer questions raised in those opinions. The city council then takes up the plan, discusses it, and usually adopts it. Application to the national authorities for plan approval and ratification, if necessary, can then begin.

The procedure for formal site development plans follows the same steps. In addition to solicitations of opinion and comment, however, the proposal must be publicly exhibited and announced. Also, notice of the proposed plan must be mailed to all property owners within the planning area, and their written replies, opinions, and objections must be examined by the city planning director. Further, once the city council adopts a site development plan, the council must send it to the national authorities for ratification. Upon ratification the proposals of the document become binding on the city and any affected citizens.

These formal processes have many steps and involve many participants (see Fig. 3.16). However, throughout these processes there is a continual interweaving of the formal and the informal. Stäck explains:

On this [building] law there has been built a tradition, a practice that a thing shall be done in this manner. But everyone knows there are ways to stop something if it is bad; the city council, for example, can stop a plan if a majority finds it bad. Also, it's possible to speak to almost everybody who has any say in the matter, so you know in advance how people will react, before the plan undergoes formal treatment. You never risk making a plan only to have it refused; you always work with an awareness of this. You take your sketch and ask, "Can I show you something? What would you say if a plan like this should come to you?" For example, if a city planner has a feeling that the conservatives would oppose a plan proposal, he can make a simple sketch and present it to a man who he knows is linked to the right wing. He asks him, "Would you oppose such a plan?" He will discuss it with his friends or ask the planner to present his ideas to a meeting of his organization.[16]

Practical planners spend many evenings before various political organizations, explaining ideas, looking for reactions, and getting a feel for what is acceptable and what is not. They also stay in touch with individual influential Stockholmers on an informal, nonpartisan basis. With this foundation, when plans are formally discussed, there are few surprises to cause disagreement. Stäck continues:

That does not mean that everything always goes perfectly: we are not working under a pure market system, and we have some difficulty getting ideas from the people we are planning a development for. Though they are the people who are going to live there, they can't know that, so how can they suggest anything? When we . . . publicly exhibit a plan, we hear no reactions. But when it's built five years later, and we ourselves know that it is old-fashioned—though we do better now—then the newspapers tell us it is no good. . . . We never find out by waiting to see if people rent it or not, because they always rent it. The housing shortage is a problem, but it's a political problem.[17]

The city planning office director, who is directly responsible to the building board, is the link between the planning office and the planning and building control board. However, the office is divided into several sections. Each section head can communicate directly with the board because, as a civil servant, he is independently responsible to the city for his actions. Each major post has a formal job description and well-defined duties and powers, but it can be safely said that the office functions mainly because people cooperate; such an organization could not work otherwise.

Figure 3.16
Timetable for construction of moderately large residential area.
   Source: Stockholms Stads Stadsplanekontor, *Generalplan för Stockholm 1952* (Stockholm: Stockholms Stads Stadsplanekontor, 1952), p. 410.

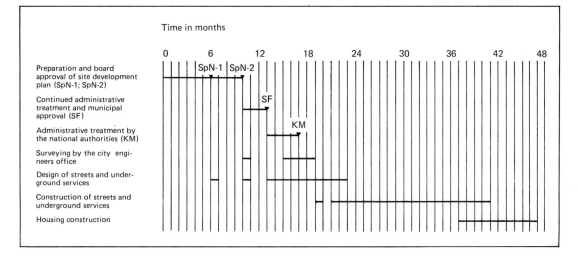

The National Labor Market Board

Of the various factors hampering the early creation of employment opportunities in Vällingby and Farsta, the most obvious was one of national policy. Initially the state refused or delayed permission to relocate or expand industrial facilities, particularly small industries and workshops, even for relocation at Vällingby Center. This discouraged potential employers, who either stayed where they were or relocated outside Stockholm. There were also changes in planned land use. A major effect of the delay was to reduce considerably the application of the Vällingby Walk-to-Work principle, as housing was already occupied or committed by the time industry moved in.

Until the late 1950s, the National Labor Market Board strictly regulated the use of capital, materials, and labor.[18] The board had several means of influencing urban development.

One was a general consultation that had to take place between a city and the board before the city could embark on urban expansion. This usually consisted of conferences between the city authorities and the director of the local office of the labor market board. The board supported Stockholm's policy to develop Vällingby and Farsta as Walk-to-Work suburbs. And while the national government did not take the initiative, it at least accepted the validity of Stockholm's proposals.[19]

Another means was the labor permit, introduced in 1941, which was required before labor for any new construction could be obtained. The major effect of the permit requirement was to delay construction rather than to influence its character directly. According to Stockholm labor board representative Bengt Svensson, this was the case with the construction of Vällingby Center when the board refused a 1948 labor permit request.[20] While this had no apparent effect on the actual development, construction was delayed until 1951.

Also, a labor-board-administered industrial location policy existed. Because of the hous-

ing shortage in the Stockholm area, the board directed industrial expansion to other parts of Sweden, even though local plans required it at Vällingby Center.

The labor market administration had a general principle for employers—commercial or industrial—which it applied at Vällingby; it was to refuse permission for construction that would create a need for additional new employees. Organizations whose new premises would not require additional labor got building permit preference. This principle applied even to employers tied to the Stockholm region who could not relocate. Svensson notes, however, "There were no absolutely hard and fast rules. It was more the development of a practice. They received a 'no' for the construction of new premises in Vällingby if it meant a large expansion in the number of employees."[21] If it was purely for the sake of rationalization—new machinery and such—in order to increase production without any significant increase in its labor force, an organization might receive permission.

During the whole period of development of the Vällingby area, the rules themselves remained unchanged, but after Blackeberg, Råcksta, Grimsta, and Vällingby their practical application underwent modification. Svensson recalls, "By the time Hässelby Strand and Hässelby Gård were developing, the situation in the capital market and—even more important—in the materials market was much better, so much so that the regulations simply were not applied. . . . During the construction of Vällingby Center and the surrounding housing, it was forbidden to build for industrial uses, but later it was possible to complete the planned industrial construction."[22]

The rules continued in effect during the development of Farsta too, and again their severity regarding building materials and capital were somewhat softened. The degree of application was mainly a reflection of the availability of labor: there was no quota system[23] and no intent—whatever the effect—to force industry away from the Stockholm area.

Informal Procedure

Complementing the formal framework of rules and regulations is a set of informal techniques, widely available but most useful perhaps to those with contacts. Jan Herbert Martin explains that the easiest way to discuss problems among the municipal staff from other offices is over coffee in the lunchroom.[24] Former city planner Carl-Fredrik Ahlberg states that he often took problems directly to the commissioner.[25] Many in the administration, particularly at the level of office section chief or planning group captain, discuss problems with their equal numbers in other municipal offices.

S. Albert Aronson, manager of the city-owned building and management company AB Svenska Bostäder ("AB" is equivalent to "Corporation"), points out the advantages of inside information: as a member of a variety of municipal boards he knows the activities, desires, and intentions of each. In such a position, he feels he is able to gauge the broader needs of the city; when he prepares a program for the municipal development company, he begins with a better than fair idea of his chances of success.[26]

Former engineer Arne Bergqvist's familiarity with the practices of the municipal real estate office, experience with the development of Vällingby, professional relationships with many municipal officials, and full working knowledge of plans to develop Farsta made him invaluable both to the private builders and to the private development combine AB Farsta Centrum.

Between the formal and the informal lies the written request for consideration and written comment, used when one municipal board wants to know what other boards think of its ideas. It is a concrete reply to proposals. The replies are often highly diplomatic in tone, sometimes concealing motivations, possibly even agreements that staff members of a board have already reached, though not necessarily deliberately.

In all these ways views are exchanged, preferences are expressed, and solutions are worked out through prior discussion without disturbing the public façade of dynamic democracy.[27] The commissioner looks over his staff members' shoulders, trying to follow and perhaps guide their activities. When conditions require higher-level agreements, he presents their efforts to the politicians, then relays political positions back down the line. The professional planner must take political factors into account, of course, but the general acceptance of the need to solve urban development problems and the technical and budget limitations they impose assure him of a high degree of control. It is he who must propose workable solutions, and it is at his level that the pivotal, though often informal, trade-offs are worked out.[28]

The Vällingby Principle[29]

Prior to the planning and development of Vällingby and Farsta there had been considerable discussion in city reports and professional journals regarding the physical structure of new suburban development. However, the city council had never firmly advanced a binding set of even general principles, much less detailed guidelines. The council extended only a general commitment to offering a pleasant and convenient way of life, a practical consequence being the Walk-to-Work principle, which would not require the city to enlarge municipal facilities for commuter transportation.

Establishment of the principle clearly illustrates the willingness of the administration to attempt to carry out a generally accepted, worthwhile, and noncontroversial idea. Unfortunately, other circumstances involved in the development of Vällingby and Farsta doomed the experiment.

Although the city council never officially insisted that the Walk-to-Work idea be put into effect, it permitted the planners and administrators to try it. The real estate office succeeded in reaching an agreement in principle with the housing exchange to give housing priority to applicants who had jobs in the development area.[30] On April 1, 1952, the real estate board requested the housing exchange board to express its opinion regarding the proposal; the latter board approved it on April 28. (Before this, the priority system had been a discretionary power of the exchange used only on a case-by-case basis.)

Preference was also given to essential employees of businesses and institutions that intended to establish premises in Södra Spånga—particularly in Råcksta-Vällingby. These employees were divided into three groups of decreasing priority. The first consisted of Stockholm residents who had housing in the city to place at the disposal of the housing exchange. The second group were residents who did not have housing for the housing exchange. The third group were non-residents of Stockholm.

From 1953 to 1958 the housing exchange filled 2,050 priority requests for 330 businesses (only about 10 percent of them for areas other than Vällingby and Farsta) and was obligated to satisfying about 670 more during 1958 and 1959.

By 1957, however, a reaction against the Vällingby principle had developed among housing applicants in general. This was the result of a combination of increasing demand and the apparent worsening of the housing situation as reflected by an increase in waiting time.[31] When the housing exchange board approved the Vällingby principle in April 1952, the normal waiting time was three years for a two-person household with no exchangeable dwelling unit, twenty-six months for a family with one child, and twenty-one months for a family with two children. The principle appeared at the time to be quite fair. By the beginning of 1958, though, a two-person household without an exchangeable unit was waiting five years and eight months, a family with one child three years and six months, and a family with two children three years and three months, roughly double the waiting time in 1952.

As Table 3.2 shows, the city's population increased 6.21 percent between the end of 1951 and the end of 1957. More than 50 percent of the increase was influx. In late 1951, 7.88 percent of the population was registered on the housing exchange waiting list. By the end of 1957, it was 13.58 percent. During the same period, the dwelling stock increased 12.81 percent, an increase greater than the increase in population but not enough to keep up with the demand. Contributing to this condition was the combination of population influx, an increasing trend for young unmarried people to live alone, earlier marriages, a higher divorce rate, and increased longevity.

By April 1958 the Vällingby area contained some fifteen industrial organizations, of which

Table 3.2
Comparison of Increase in Population, Housing Applications, and Housing Stock (Stockholm, 1952–1958)

1.	a. Population[a]	b. Excess of influx (1952–1958)[a]	c. Applications at housing exchange[b]	d. Housing stock[c]
2. 1952	752,193		59,311	274,202
3. 1958	798,913		108,520	309,340
4. Change (3–2)	46,720	23,605	49,209	35,138
5. Change (4:2)%	6.21	3.13	82.96	12.81
6. (b4:a4)%		50.52		
7. (c2:a2)%			7.88	
8. (c3:a3)%			13.58	

[a]Stockholms stads statistiska kontor, *Statistical Yearbook of Stockholm 1967* (Stockholm: Stockholms stads statistiska kontor, 1967), Table 36, p. 52. Data from the end of the preceding year.
[b]*Ibid.*, Table 156, p. 173. Data from the end of the preceding year.
[c]*Ibid.*, Table 146, p. 158. Data from the beginning of the year.

Arenco and IBM were the largest; a large municipal building and management organization, AB Svenska Bostäder; a considerable number of commercial organizations; and a variety of municipal offices and public institutions. Additional organizations were scheduled to assume occupancy in the near future, including the National Power Board and several large industrial organizations.

In a 1956 real estate board investigation of thirty of the Vällingby area's larger organizations, it was discovered that of about 1,600 employees, at least 1,100 were residents of the area; about 70 percent of those who worked in the Vällingby area also lived there, a reasonably certain result of the Vällingby principle.

As stated, one of the intentions of the Vällingby principle was to help solve the housing problem for personnel of industries moving to the area during the area's early development. Official memoranda point out, however, that industries planning to locate in the Vällingby area in 1958 made few housing priority requests for their employees. They add that the area's population appeared to have reached a point that would allow local labor recruitment; and with the opening of the extension of the rapid transit line, commuting was possible. [32] The authors of the memoranda further insist that by 1958 conditions had so changed that the general priority accorded by the Vällingby principle no longer seemed very important.

The real estate office claims that these new conditions, along with the Vällingby principle's inequities expressed by the housing exchange, convinced it to withdraw the general application and in the future apply it in new city districts on its pre-Vällingby principle case-by-case basis. During April and May 1958, the real estate office and the housing exchange office discussed the question; the real estate board officially dropped general application on May 13, 1958.

Official memoranda notwithstanding, resident-employment data have clearly shown that the experiment was unsuccessful, though "failure" has never been admitted. Indeed, most municipal officials have publicly denied that the results were less than they expected. Others, like Jan Herbert Martin, see the matter in a different light. As head of the industrial section of the real estate department, one of Martin's chief duties was to interest people and industry in moving to the new suburbs. He recalls that within the city administration, there were conflicting goals, and to planning director Sidenbladh's contention that there is still plenty of unoccupied land at Vällingby, Martin replies:

He is exaggerating. The argument is this: I say he gives me too little land, and he always says that I still have land left. That is not the point; it is not what is left that matters but rather what this or that part of the city needs. We can never agree on this. The planning director is living in a climate of pressure because of the housing situation. He must produce houses; he cannot be interested in promoting industry because that just increases the demand for housing. What he wants, naturally, is to reduce the pressure and see to it that as many industrial concerns as possible, especially the larger ones, go elsewhere. [33]

As to the ultimate effects of this policy conflict, Martin insists that because of too much emphasis on housing at the expense of employment, job opportunities are developing too rapidly downtown, too slowly in suburban Stockholm. He estimates that for every 100 employable residents of the central city, there are 179 employment opportunities; for every 100 such residents of the suburbs, there are only 45 openings. "It is not until you get to cities beyond Stockholm's borders that the situation is practically balanced." [34] With specific reference to Vällingby, Martin states:

The situation has not developed as we thought. We had intended to have local employment opportunities equal to half the number of employable residents. . . . Actually, we have only about 9,000 jobs available there. . . . We put a great deal of money into the promotion of Vällingby, but we simply could not get industry to move there before or even while the housing was being constructed. Industry didn't believe that in five years we could create a city for 60,000 people, and they didn't want to risk being stuck in a badly equipped satellite. But ten years after the housing was completed, industry came in very willingly.[35]

More recent statistics (see Table 1.3) make Martin's estimate of 9,000 local job opportunities seem rather low, but the same figures bear out his conclusion. The city's failure—for whatever reasons—to induce industry to locate early in Vällingby's development produced precisely what the planners were trying to avoid: a largely commuter-oriented suburb, though still a considerable advance from the dormitory suburb. By the time industry began moving in and providing local employment opportunities, the chronic housing shortage had precluded a sizable enough turnover in dwellings to make the Walk-to-Work idea a meaningful one. That the city discarded the principle suggests its limited effectiveness in an increasingly mobile urban society. Granted, the city had never bound itself to Walk to Work as official policy, but official reasons for having discarded it fall somewhat short of satisfying.

4

Vällingby and Farsta: The Development Process

Before the turn of the century, a number of suburbs had begun to develop outside the city of Stockholm. In 1876 the Stockholm–Västerås railroad opened for traffic. To the northwest the town of Sundbyberg began developing along this line during the late 1870s. The well-to-do residential suburbs of Djursholm and Saltsjöbaden, also connected to Stockholm by rail, were expanding, attracting the more affluent from the city. In 1902 the town of Nynäshamn was founded to the south of Stockholm.

At the turn of the century, Swedes in great numbers were emigrating to the United States.[1] To counter this the city of Stockholm instituted a program designed to provide inexpensive home ownership on municipally owned land. In 1904 Stockholm purchased land at Enskede and Bromma, in 1912 at Farsta. Extension of municipal boundaries followed land purchases. Stockholm incorporated Brännkyrka (including Enskede) in 1913 and Bromma in 1916. The city's ownership of land at the Vällingby Development Area in Södra Spånga dated from the purchase of Råcksta Gård in 1927 and Hässelby, with surrounding farms, in 1931.

The 1930s and the depression brought migration to Stockholm from other parts of Sweden. At the end of the 1930s, forecasts pointed to a cessation of population growth in Stockholm. In 1945 Professor W. William-Olsson summed up the situation as follows: "[It was thought that] the population of Stockholm, which at the end of 1939 totaled 710,000, would during the coming 30 years increase to 900,000. . . . [and that] in the immediate future, the increase would probably be great but . . . toward 1970 would successively decrease so that it would eventually remain static."[2] However, new population studies in the early 1940s showed previous growth estimates to be too conservative, and by the end of the war, some experts were anticipating that the population of Greater Stockholm would exceed one million before 1960.[3]

During the 1930s, the housing supply in Stockholm had been plentiful. With the coming of World War II new production slowed, ceasing altogether about 1940, and the city began to suffer a housing shortage. At almost the same time, the national government, through rent control and long-term, low-interest loans, stepped up its policy to encourage new housing construction. To assure that housing construction received a fair share of labor, capital, and materials, in especially short supply in the building industry, the national government began requiring labor permits in 1941.

As in most large cities, Stockholm's housing and industrial development are closely related to the transportation system. The first systematic transportation study for Stockholm took place during 1906–1907. During the following years, a number of proposals to improve the transit system were made and discussed in the city council. In March 1931 the city council ordered the construction of an underground trolley car line beneath Södermalm, in south central Stockholm, to run from Skanstull to Slussen. The recommendation for it was the result of a study by a special transportation committee, which the city's central board of administration had set up in 1930. Committee membership included the city's planning, real estate, streets, harbor, and transit company directors, with commissioner Yngve Larsson as chairman. By October 1933 the line was in service. In 1934 the transportation committee presented its final, comprehensive report.

After further investigations, on June 16, 1941, the city council decided in principle to plan and construct a subway connecting the central business district with both the near western and near southern suburbs. On November 22, 1944, AB Stockholms Spårvägar (the city-owned transit company) sent to the central board of administration a new proposal based on recent population studies. The proposal called for revision and expansion of the transit system to increase its capacity. With the full support of the real estate office, on June 18, 1945, the city council accepted the proposal, which also recommended

lengthening station platforms to accommodate eight-car rather than six-car trains. Additional discussions in 1945 led to the eventual construction of two independent transit systems, each with two tracks.[4]

Earlier, small neighborhoods of detached single-family homes, each on its own parcel of land, or three-story apartment dwellings had developed amid narrow streets, served by suburban trolley car lines and neighborhood shops. By the 1940s it had become possible, not to say necessary, to undertake suburban development on a scale greater than ever before. Much of this development was the result of efforts by real estate director Axel Dahlberg. (City planning director Albert Lilienberg, a civil engineer, was more concerned with downtown traffic planning.) As director of the real estate office, Dahlberg administered the use of Stockholm's land and housing policies. He also had considerable influence on actual planning, normally the province of the city planning office. (It should be noted that until 1940, real estate, city planning, building, and architecture were all part of the same administrative division; it was not unusual, therefore, for real estate to be involved with city planning.)

Planning competitions in the early 1940s and subsequent development at Gubbängen, Årsta, and Hökarängen produced a number of innovations. For example, because these areas were fairly large, there were proposals to provide each of them with its own complex of cultural, social, and commercial facilities in a community center, an idea that ushered in a new stage in planning.

In 1940, in a reorganization of the city administration, Yngve Larsson, a Liberal, became planning commissioner. Previously, Larsson's division had been restricted to public works. Now, it took over planning from commissioner Harry Sandberg, a Social Democrat, who also lost building and architecture, which became a separate division.

Larsson was then working on two major problems, transit and central business district redevelopment. He wanted a city council decision to build a transit system that would sweep around in a semicircle through central Stockholm as it connected western and southern Stockholm. The real estate director, Axel Dahlberg, father of Stockholm's garden suburbs, wanted a straight-line transit connection between the western suburbs and the center of Stockholm. Larsson's plan was the one the city council accepted in 1941.

As to the other major problems, Larsson favored a proposal that had come from outside the usual channels, a plan quite different from that of his planning director, Albert Lilienberg.[5] Larsson then asked Lilienberg to have the planning office develop the plan, but Lilienberg refused. So Larsson bypassed Lilienberg and set up a planning group within the office of streets to develop the plan. Lilienberg resigned shortly afterward, before reaching retirement age. In June 1945 the city council again approved the plan Larsson favored.[6]

In 1944 Larsson hired Sven Markelius as city planning director, a post Markelius held for ten years. Much of the planning and design at Vällingby was the product of Markelius's inspiration. Göran Sidenbladh, Carl-Fredrik Ahlberg, and traffic expert Sven Lundberg soon joined him in the planning office.

On May 9, 1944, Larsson proposed the development of a master plan for Stockholm. His proposal had the support of both the central board of administration[7] and the city council.[8] The city planning commission delivered a preliminary work plan to the board of commissioners on November 8, 1944, and the city council quickly approved it. This resulted in a report containing a short but comprehensive statement of goals and directions for further research and discussion. The report, dated June 1945, was entitled *Det framtida Stockholm—Riktlinjer för Stockholms generalplan* [*Stockholm in the Future—Principles of the Outline Plan for Stockholm*].[9] It deals with the prospects for satellite towns and some of the requirements of such towns: a satellite town must be geographically separate from and external to a large mother city;

there must be good transportation between satellite and city; and the satellite must have a suitable ratio of local employment opportunities to housing to avoid being simply a dormitory suburb.

Guidelines for city district development are also set forth in *Stockholm in the Future*.[10] In social composition every city district would form a Stockholm in miniature. Each would have an optimum number of residents for the planned social and cultural services. (Between 10,000 and 15,000 total population is the maximum for a moderately large Stockholm secondary school to serve.) Each would have its own communal facilities: there would be at least one school, day nurseries, laundries, a post office, a library, a movie theater, a restaurant or coffee shop, a community hall, and shops. To illustrate the proposal, the then projected plan for Årsta Center was included in the report (see Fig. 4.1). The authors of *Stockholm in the Future* also emphasized the importance of centrally located premises for retail, social, educational, and service uses in the community. In nonplanned residential areas, the post office, the cinema, the library, and the shops tended to be widely scattered, a condition that the report cautioned future planners to avoid.

When it became obvious that the city was going to develop the rather large area of Södra Spånga, there was speculation that the city might use the new planning concepts that evolved from the Gübbangen competition and the Årsta Center proposal—a city district–based suburban community combining neighborhood development with a community center to form a distinct unit around a projected transit station. In 1946 the signal came from Larsson to prepare development plans for Södra Spånga as quickly as possible. Markelius, unwilling to divert his Ahlberg-Sidenbladh-Lundberg-von Hofsten group from master planning, got extra money to hire architect Fritz Voigt specially to work on the area. Markelius and Voigt made the first sketches, which Markelius presented in lectures to a variety of social and political clubs and societies. The idea was news, and discussion began outside the planning office.

From the beginning Markelius and Voigt favored developing suburban communities along a transit line, like pearls on a string. Real estate director Dahlberg opposed the idea. Larsson invited Dahlberg to sessions he held to convince him that he was wrong, but Dahlberg persisted in his opposition.

The Vällingby Development Area in Process

With the passage of the 1947 building law, the master plan became a recognized instrument. On June 10, 1947, the national government decided that providing adequate housing was a municipal responsibility; in the same year Stockholm purchased AB Svenska Bostäder and made it a public-owned developer-management company. In fall 1948 the city commissioned the municipally owned housing company, AB Familjebostäder, to build apartment houses at Blackeberg. During the same year, however, the National Labor Market Board refused to grant the aforementioned application for a labor permit for the construction of a center at Vällingby. County opposition to the incorporation of Södra Spånga had ended with an agreement reached toward the end of 1947. On January 1, 1949, Stockholm incorporated Södra Spånga.[11]

Proposals and plans for Södra Spånga, dated 1940 and 1946 (see Figs. 4.2, 4.3), had already appeared. On February 25, 1946, the city planning board approved in principle a land use plan, which served as a basis for future planning work. The plan proposed three city districts of equal size: (1) Blackeberg on the east with 10,000 residents; (2) Råcksta in the middle with 12,700; and (3) Loviselund (now Hässelby Gård) on the west with 14,300. Each district was to have a small community center. This was followed by the plan of 1948, which the city planning board approved in principle on April 20, 1949; it, too, served as a basis for further planning. The most important documents, however, were to be the 1949–1950 master plan[12] (see Fig. 4.4) and the 1952–1954 master plan for Södra Spånga. The 1949–1950 document was presented to the city council in report form.[13]

In 1950 city planning director Sven Markelius asked the architectural consulting firm of Backström & Reinius for their assistance in preparing detailed site development plans for a center at Vällingby. Carl-Fredrik Ahlberg, director of the Greater Stockholm Regional

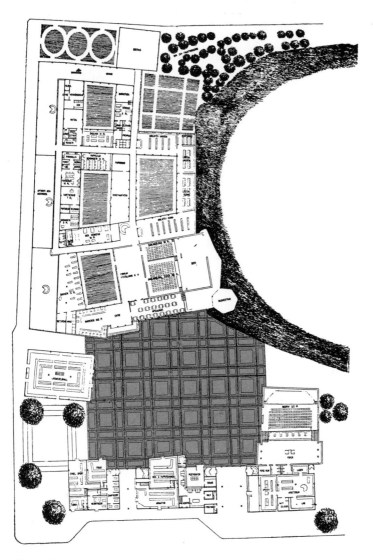

Figure 4.1
Projected plan by architects Eric and Tore Ahlsén of community
center for Årsta city district (about 23,000 inhabitants).
   Source: *Det framtida Stockholm—Stockholm in the Future*
(Stockholm: Stockholms kommunalförvaltning, 1946), p. 59.
   The most important buildings are grouped around the plaza
(bottom center). These include a market hall, shops, post
office, pharmacy, cinema, and a restaurant. In the other
buildings there are assembly rooms that serve as a theater, a
library, and premises for woodworking and handicrafts. At the
top of the plan is a children's nursery and a garden.

Figure 4.2
Sketch plan, 1940.
Source: Archives of the city of Stockholm.
This 1940 plan for the Vällingby Development Area has
numerous smaller dwellings occupying the bulk of the site.

N

1000   2000
feet

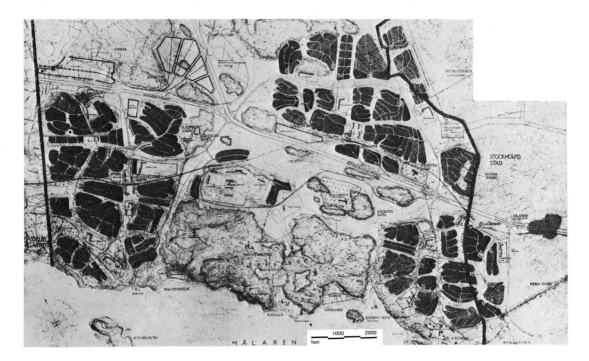

Figure 4.3
Spånga-Hässelby land use plan, 1946.
  Source: Archives of the city of Stockholm.

LEGEND

▭	MULTISTOREY APARTMENTS		⌂	NURSERY
▦	ROW HOUSING		⚡	TRANSFORMER STATION
⋯	DETACHED SINGLE-FAMILY HOUSING		ᙍ	POWERLINE
▦	INDUSTRY		⌇	ALLOTMENT GARDENS
▦	TRUCK FARMING		✝	CEMETERY
				RAILROAD
	PARK AND OPEN-AIR RECREATION. EDGE OF WOODED AREA.			SURBURBAN RAILWAY (TRANSIT LINE)
	SHOPPING CENTER			ATHLETIC FIELD
	CULTURAL CENTER			BALL PARK
	PRIMARY SCHOOL		●	PLAYGROUND
	SECONDARY SCHOOL			FIELD FOR CELEBRATIONS AND FESTIVALS
	SECONDARY SCHOOL TRADE SCHOOL			BOAT HARBOR
	COMMUNITY HALL		≋	OPEN-AIR BATHING
	HOSPITAL			BOAT STORAGE
	HOME FOR THE AGED			RIDING STABLE
				RIFLE RANGE
				BOUNDARY OF MASTER PLANNING AREA

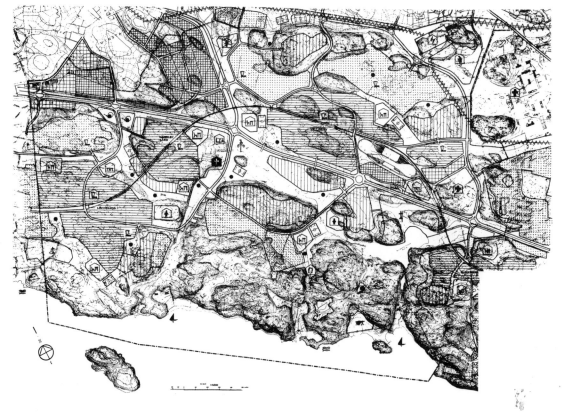

Figure 4.4
Master plan map G 5:50 for Södra Spånga, 1949–1950: the
basic planning document for the Vällingby Development Area.
Source: *Utlåtanden*, 1950, no. 382.

Planning Office since 1952, recalls the planning office hope that Backström & Reinius might also design the individual buildings, as at the time it was not yet certain that Svenska Bostäder would construct and manage Vällingby Center: "I think we had an agreement with the real estate office that they would try to arrange that whomever they leased the land to in the center, Backström & Reinius would be the architects. That, of course, was more uncertain. It wasn't definite that they should have that job, but they have, in fact, designed most of the buildings in the center."[14]

During the same year city councilman Gösta Agrenius proposed to the city council that the Södra Spånga development's housing and community center arrangement encourage the development of local employment opportunities and retailing.[15] He also emphasized the need for inducements to attract employers.[16]

On October 26, 1950, Yngve Larsson, representing the central board of administration, forwarded to the city council a master plan for Södra Spånga.[17] On December 4 the master plan was approved by the city council; it was the first master plan Stockholm approved under the new national building law. The 1950 master plan report for Södra Spånga included a land use map (Fig. 4.4) that the city planning office had prepared in 1949. The report noted that the master plan and the site development plans for Blackeberg proposed the development of a large community outside the ten-year-old area of villas and small cottages in Ängby, along the extended tramline 11, leading west from central Stockholm. The report recommended housing most of the population in multistory apartment buildings, though such a disposition was contrary to earlier thought that population density should decrease as the distance from the city center increased. The report explains the new position as a consequence of population growth in Greater Stockholm, at the time much greater than earlier calculations anticipated. As there was no regional plan and no machinery for intermunicipal economic and administrative cooperation to solve the housing problem, it was decided to use the major portion of the city's land for the densest possible development within accepted planning norms. This was the position of the master plan investigation and the city planning office regarding the grouping of suburban communities in city districts.

The master plan investigation also dealt with structure and size; to equip each city district with its own buildings for commerce and culture would require grouping its housing in functional units and providing each with a different type of center. The plan proposed building the city districts around suburban railroad stations. Each would have a central cluster of multistory apartment houses not more than 500 meters from the center and an outer ring of one-family houses of different types not more than 900 meters from the center. The proposed residential population for Södra Spånga was 42,000: 69 percent in multifamily apartments, 17 percent in row houses, and 14 percent in detached, single-family homes.

A Södra Spånga rapid transit system, with an extension of the Ängbybana tramline west from central Stockholm, had always been the backbone of the plan. Other ideas included connecting the Swedish Railways station on the Västerås line to a projected transit station at Sundbyberg.

Regarding the balance between working areas and living areas, studies of Södra Spånga indicated that the only definite employment sources would be the hospital and health institutions at the Bromma border and the industrial park in Johannelund. Larger industrial areas would require railroad spur connections, which seemed impossible to provide within the planning area.

However, the report indicated there were good employment possibilities outside the planning area. Lövsta, in the municipality of Järfälla, had a reserve of industrial land, and the large area around the railroad station at Spånga also seemed suitable for industry. The housing supply in the vicinity of Spånga station was small, so some of the people working there would have to live in Södra Spånga. With a distance between home and job of 1.5 to 3 kilometers, it seemed that most people could bicycle to and from work, but the report nonetheless recommended establishing a bus line connecting with the railroad.

For many years plan proposals treated Grimsta Wood as a recreational reserve. This was the position of the Stockholm beautification council in a 1935 article in *Stockholmstraktens natur- och kulturminnen*; a document entitled "The Regional Plan of 1936 for Stockholm with Surroundings" treats Grimstaskogen, too, as a natural reserve. But in 1950 there was a proposal to use 33 hectares (81.5 acres) of Grimsta Wood for residential construction for about 3,000 inhabitants, who would be served by a bus line from Vällingby. The proposal provided the area with a school and an athletic field; near the school, land was reserved for a children's care institution. However, the transit company, Stockholms Spårvägar, calculated that the bus line would thereby suffer an annual loss on the order of 150,000 kronor ($30,000), which contributed to a feeling of uneasiness toward the proposal.

By 1951 the National Labor Market Board had agreed to grant a labor permit so work could begin on Vällingby Center; in June 1951 the city commissioned AB Svenska Bostäder to design it.

The same year Stockholm city council chairmen Carl Albert Anderson, Yngve Larsson, and Albert Aronson, among others, stated before the city council, which since the election of 1950 had been under the control of the Liberal-Conservative coalition (known as the Bourgeois Majority), that the city ought to develop semi-independent satellite towns within its administrative boundaries.[18] The planning, they said, should make maximum use of the Walk-to-Work idea, one byproduct of which would be to reduce rush-hour commuting and improve the traffic system economy. It would also markedly increase a new city district's chances of attracting employers: if workers were sure of finding suitable housing near their jobs, business could be assured of a readily available labor supply. They urged that the development of Vällingby and similar city districts should provide that: (1) construction of premises for industry, handicraft, business, and other community services would go forward in tempo with housing construction; (2) people who worked in the city district would have local housing preference; and (3) construction of detached and row houses at the periphery of the city district would develop at the same rate as rental apartments.[19] But no action was taken in the report from the real estate commission of November 20, 1951, the debate in the city council, or the report of the central board of administration.

The minutes of the discussion in the city council,[20] however, reveal a wide range of understanding regarding new suburban development, including one councilman's definition of a typical development as a self-supporting city district of about 60,000 inhabitants. The meeting closed with Larsson's reference to von Hofsten's 1943 Gubbängen report, which had for the first time used methodical analysis to examine the actual allocation of private and public land use in planning documents. Larsson believed that Vällingby could be a new urban model, offering far greater promise than the existing dormitory suburbs.

Gösta Agrenius's 1950 proposal eventually received a reply from the central board of administration's chairman, Yngve Larsson, in a report of October 6, 1952;[21] the reply included statements from the city planning commission, the real estate commission (including a special representation of retailing interests by Gösta Bohman, secretary-general of the Stockholm Retail Trade Federation), the street commission, and the board of commissioners. The statement of the board of commissioners refers to the 1950 master plan for Södra Spånga and the Vällingby site development plan of 1951. One is further referred to the forthcoming "master plan book" of 1952 (which was never adopted) for positions on the intensity of construction in general. The city council neither debated nor voted upon the contents of the report.[22]

An answer to the 1951 Anderson-Larsson-Aronson city council remarks on satellite towns appeared on June 5, 1952, in a report from the central board of administration[23] signed by Yngve Larsson and Gösta Wennström, real estate commissioner. The report pointed out that the city planning commission was having difficulty coordinating commercial and residential construction, primarily because it was still having trouble acquiring the necessary labor permits from the national government. The report added that Stockholm's housing exchange had already approved new priority principles for the distribution of apartments in the Råcksta-Vällingby area.

To stimulate interest in Vällingby, an exhibit was held to inaugurate the opening of the transit station in October of 1952, just after people began moving into the area. Preparations for the exhibit resulted in two useful by-products: brochures using the ABC slogan (Arbeta, work; Bo, living; and Centrum, center) designed to appeal to potential employers and residents,[24] and crash-designed illustrative maps (see Figs. 4.5–4.8) that later actually served as foundations for detailed planning and construction.

On October 20, 1952, the city planning commission sent the real estate commission a new map projecting changes in and expansion of the master plan for Södra Spånga. It designated the hills and woods of Grimsta as cultural and recreational areas. Another change did away with construction of single-family homes because of the higher cost of feeder bus service; to offset this, it proposed increasing multistory construction at Grimsta and Hässelby. The revised plan also called for increasing the housing density in the Vällingby Development Area by having 88 percent (instead of 70 percent) of the population in apartment houses. The previous density standard of 220 to 300 people per hectare (90 to 120 people per acre) would now rise to 320 per hectare (130 per acre), and the total population of the Vällingby Development Area would increase by about 2,000 (from 42,000 to 44,000). On February 25, 1954, the revised master plan, with the support of the central board of administration, went to the city council and was approved.

On November 11, 1954, Vällingby Center, with two department stores and some forty shops, was inaugurated. Another thirty shops, a youth center, a public library, two restaurants, and various social institutions followed in 1955. Opening in 1956 were the medical center, the community hall, a church, and a cinema. By that year construction in all parts of the development area was well under way. (For a comparison of the Vällingby Development Area in various stages of completion, see Figs. 4.9–4.12.)

By this time the tracks of the transit line extended west as far as Vällingby station. There were stations at Blackeberg and Råcksta and a large yard for storage, makeup, and repair in Råcksta immediately southeast of Vällingby Center. West of Vällingby the right-of-way was clear through Johannelund, Hässelby Gård, and Hässelby Strand; some viaducts had been constructed, but no track had been laid. Transit service to Hässelby Gård began in November of 1956; the Hässelby Gård–Hässelby Strand section opened in November of 1958.

In 1962, AB Svenska Bostäder undertook a major expansion of Vällingby Center. New construction focused on additional retail sales areas and a multistory parking garage. Ceremonies marking completion of the Vällingby Center expansion were held in 1966.

Figure 4.5
Råcksta-Vällingby location map.
  Source: Stockholms stads fastighetsnämnd, *Råcksta-Vällingby. Ett Arbeta-Bo-Centrum* (Stockholm: Stockholms stads
fastighetsnämnd, 1952), p. 2.

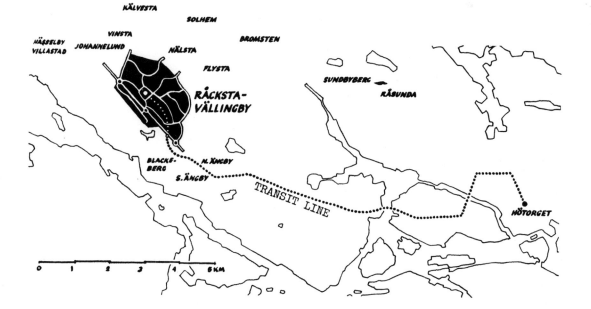

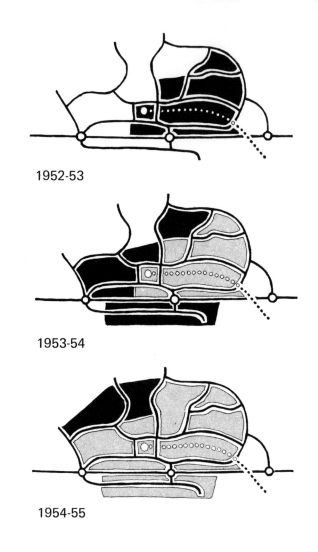

1952-53

1953-54

1954-55

 under construction

completed

Figure 4.6
Råcksta-Vällingby, stages of planned development.
  Source: Stockholms stads fastighetsnämnd, *Råcksta-Vällingby. Ett Arbeta-Bo-Centrum* (Stockholm: Stockholms stads fastighetsnämnd, 1952), p. 3.

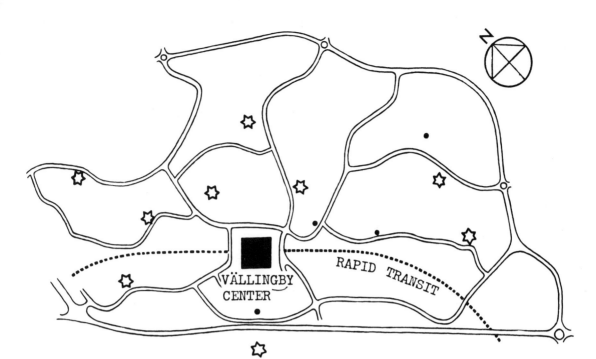

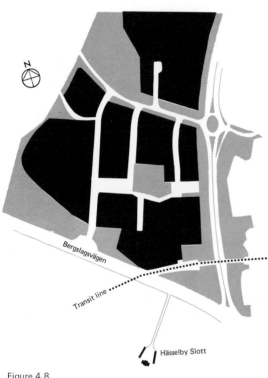

Figure 4.7
Neighborhood shopping centers at Vällingby: schematic diagram.

Source: Stockholms stads fastighetsnämnd, *Vällingby. Företagens Framtidsstad* (Stockholm: Stockholms stads fastighetsnämnd, 1952), p. 15.

Neighborhood shopping centers (stars) are located in the residential neighborhoods in a wide ring around Vällingby Center. They are complemented by single shops (black dots).

Figure 4.8
Johannelund industrial area.

Source: Stockholms stads fastighetsnämnd, *Vällingby. Företagens Framtidsstad* (Stockholm: Stockholms stads fastighetsnämnd, 1952), p. 23.

Johannelund industrial area consists of 200,000 square meters primarily for those industries that require premises separated from residential construction. Improved sites are available under long-term lease.

Figure 4.9
Site of Vällingby Development Area in 1950.
Source: Geographical Survey Office of Sweden.

The area is at this time almost entirely undeveloped. The site borders both sides of the main road, Bergslagvägen (the almost straight white line running diagonally across the photograph), from the traffic circle at the northeast corner of Blackeberg (in the lower right) to the end of the developed main road at the northwest corner of Hässelby Gård (in the upper left). Counterclockwise from the southeast (bottom right), the site includes Blackeberg, Råcksta, Vällingby, Johannelund, Hässelby Gård, and, on the shore of Lake Mälar, Hässelby Strand and Grimsta. Rolling areas of the site, particularly Hässelby Gård, Hässelby Strand, Grimsta, and Blackeberg, are heavily wooded. Flat land is used for agriculture. The site is crisscrossed by narrow, winding county roads.

At Blackeberg, streets have been laid out, graded, and partially paved; there is no other disturbance of the natural vegetation. Housing construction is not yet underway. For the transit line from central Stockholm on the east, a tunnel runs beneath northeast Blackeberg; both portals are visible. There is a clear right-of-way for the tracks west of the western portal, extending north from Blackeberg across Bergslagvägen into Råcksta.

Development surrounds the entire site. Norra Ängby and Södra Ängby (southeast) have many detached single-family homes. From the air, the formal pattern of the buildings, paths, and gardens of the Beckomberga mental care hospital in Beckomberga (due east) is clearly visible. The detached single-family homes in Flysta and Nälsta are on the northeast. Vinsta, on the north, consists of wooded areas, farms, and hothouses. West of Hässelby Gård and Hässelby Strand are the detached single-family homes of Hässelby Villastad, whose northern portion (cut by a railroad branch line) has areas under cultivation and hothouses.

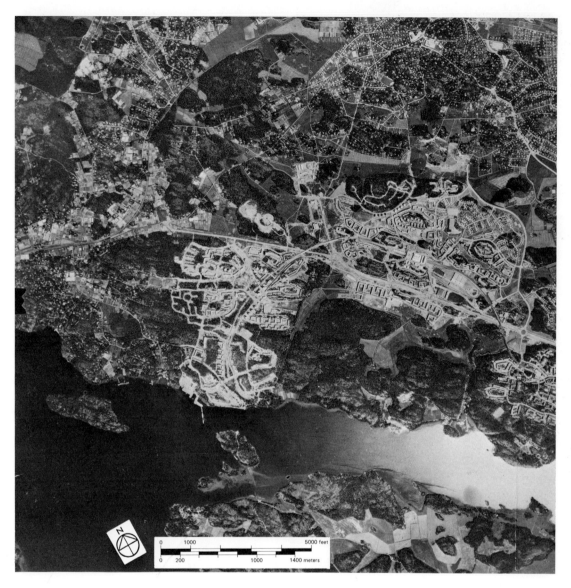

Figure 4.10
Site of Vällingby Development Area in 1956.
   Source: Geographical Survey Office of Sweden.
   Photo extends from the eastern border of Blackeberg on the right well into Hässelby Villastad on the left.
   Bergslagvägen, the main road leading to the site, has been improved. Traffic circles have been built at intersections. There are perimeter roads and paths and underpasses for pedestrians and bicycles. At Blackeberg, construction of housing, streets, and Blackeberg Center has been completed. In Råcksta, housing, streets, greenbelts, pedestrian paths, and the transit yard have been completed. As at Blackeberg, there is little construction in progress. The large site owned by the national government east of Råcksta station in the southeast corner of Råcksta is as yet undeveloped.
   Housing at Vällingby is almost completed. Streets are ready, and only one area, at the northern corner of Vällingby, is without houses. Construction has been completed at Vällingby Center, and parking areas are visible immediately north of the center.

The construction of streets and housing at Grimsta is finished. In Johannelund, only a few large industrial buildings have been constructed.
   Streets and multistory residential construction at Hässelby Gård is complete, and work continues on Hässelby Gård Center and in residential areas in western Hässelby Gård, where streets have been constructed amid the trees, but not all building sites have been cleared.
   Streets and some multistory housing have been completed at Hässelby Strand, and work on other residential housing is in progress. As in the other city districts of the Vällingby Development Area, very little natural vegetation has been disturbed.

Figure 4.11
Grimsta, Råcksta, Vällingby, Johannelund, and Hässelby Gård in 1964.

Source: Geographical Survey Office of Sweden.

Additional housing has been completed at Råcksta, including five multistory apartment buildings, in the lower right, near the traffic circle, where the administrative offices of the National Power Board are located. On the strip of land between the transit yard and the road, Bergslagvägen, several sales and service buildings have been erected.

Single-family housing in northeastern Vällingby has been completed, and the center itself is undergoing expansion. The northwestern edge of the deck across the transit tracks has been moved to form a taxi and bus depot, replacing a similar plaza on the northeastern side of the center, where additional shops have been built. The multistory parking garage is farther northeast of the center.

Transit line tracks and station and additional industrial buildings at Johannelund have been completed.

In northern Grimsta there are workshops and other commercial buildings on a strip of land south of Bergslagvägen. Additional multifamily housing has been constructed in southern Grimsta just south of Bergslagvägen. A running track and other sports fields have been completed in Grimsta Wood.

Figure 4.12
Map of Vällingby Development Area indicating additional
facilities in place in 1965.
  Source: Generalstabens Litografiska Anstalt, Stockholm,
1965.

one thousand feet   *incorrect!*

—————— railway

—Ⓣ— transit line with station

—·—·— city limits

– – – – city district boundary

✶ police station

Ⓐ post office

♪ telephone, telegram office

The Farsta Development Area in Process

In the 1940s there was some apartment
house construction in Gubbängen and Hökarängen, and a small area of one-family homes
was built in Sköndal. Geological investigations at the Farsta site and preliminary
planning had begun as early as 1948 (see Fig.
4.13). With these exceptions, however, very
little happened at the Farsta site until 1953.
At this time the city planning office knew
when the transit line would reach the southern
suburbs, and it began planning for Farsta,
Larsboda, and Farsta Strand. (Although the
transit line was open as far as Hökarängen by
the fall of 1950, it did not extend all the way
to Farsta until the fall of 1958.)

In 1950 the only developed city districts of
the Farsta Development Area were Gubbängen, Hökarängen, and western Sköndal.
Larsboda, Farsta, Farsta Strand, and Fagersjö
were almost entirely undeveloped, except for a
few older cottages.[25] The land was heavily
wooded, with small agricultural areas.

On November 24, 1957, the city opened the
transit system link between Slussen and
Hötorget, connecting Stockholm's southeastern and northwestern transit lines. By
1958 considerable construction was under
way in Farsta, including a road network and a
number of multistory apartment houses surrounding the center, and work was about to
begin on the Farsta Center site.[26]

There was considerable variety among maps
of the Farsta Development Area prepared
during planning and construction; a comparison of two of them published in 1958 (see
Fig. 4.14) and 1959 (see Fig. 4.15) indicates
the extent of differences, for example, in the
location of the Farsta Strand transit station,
the buildings and streets at Farsta Center,
the streets and housing in the northern part
of Farsta Strand, and the spur tracks for the
Stockholm-Nynäshamn railroad in Larsboda.

During 1958 and 1959 the preliminary
results of economist Lars Persson's investigation of Vällingby Center became available,
although they had little impact on the planning of Farsta Center. His final report, *A
Shopping Center and Its Customers*, appeared
in 1960.

In April 1958 the private combine AB Farsta
Centrum was awarded the leasehold to the
Farsta site. During the same month the company signed the large chain stores Tempo and
Co-op for space at the Farsta Center and
began excavation on July 1. The prestigious
Stockholm department store Nordiska Kompaniet (NK) held out until April 1959, when it
committed itself to space for a large branch
store. By January 1962 the first employees of
the Swedish Board of Telecommunications
were at work in their new offices in Farsta.
(For a comparison of the Farsta Development
Area in various stages of completion, see
Figs. 4.16–4.22. For a chronological development pattern of the southern and western
suburbs, see Fig. 4.23.)

Figure 4.13
Site plan of Farsta published in 1948.
  Source: Sven Markelius, "Synpunkter på moderna bostads-
planer," in Stadsbyggnad: Svenska Kommunal-Tekniska
Föreningens Stadsbyggnadsvecka IV, 1948, p. 78.
  For a population of 11,000, an internal system of parks with
pedestrian paths to the center, schools, transit station, and
so forth, is planned.

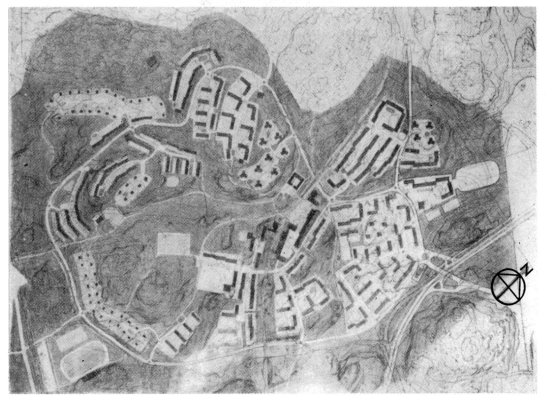

Figure 4.14
Site plan of Farsta city district.
  Source: AB Farsta Centrum, *Farsta* (Stockholm: AB Farsta
Centrum, 1959).

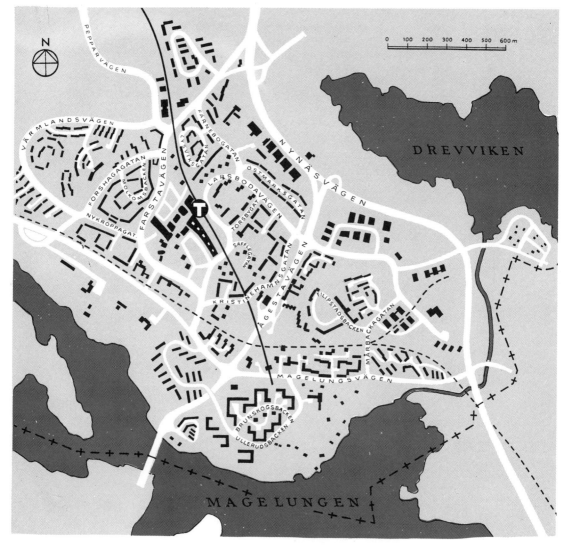

— + — city limits   - - - railroad

——— rapid transit   transit station

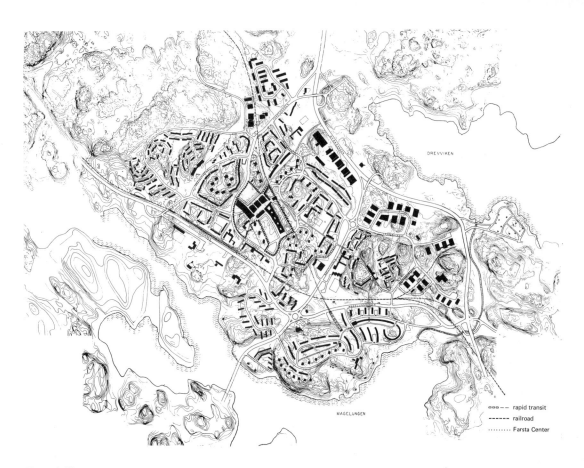

Figure 4.15
Plan of Farsta.
  Source: Giorgio Gentili, "The Satellite Towns of Stockholm,"
Urbanistica, No. 24–25, September 1958.

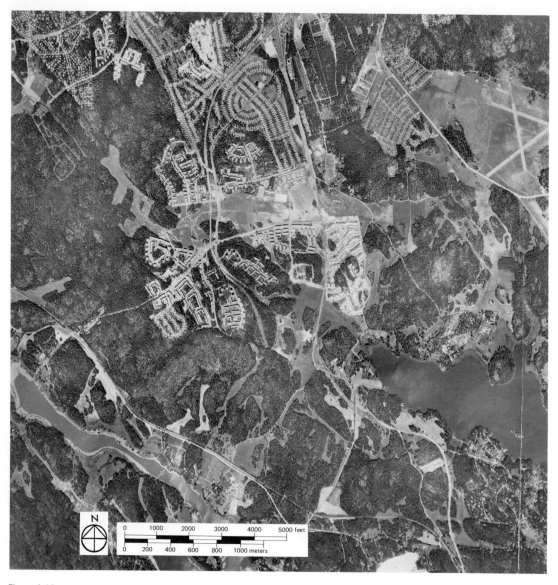

Figure 4.16
Farsta Development Area in 1950.
Source: Geographical Survey Office of Sweden.

In 1950 the only developed city districts of the Farsta Development Area were Gubbängen, Hökarängen, and western
Sköndal, Larsboda, Farsta, Farsta Strand, and Fagersjö, with
the exception of a few older cottages, were almost entirely
undeveloped. The land was heavily wooded, although small
areas were in agricultural use.

North of the site, there is residential development, primarily
single-family detached homes in Stureby, Svedmyra, Bagar-
mossen, Gamla Enskede, and Tallkrogen (where streets have
been laid out in concentric semicircles).

Sections of the main road, Nynäsvägen, running north-south
between Stockholm and Nynäshamn, are being improved. In
Farsta and Larsboda, land has been cleared to widen and
straighten a portion of the winding alignment. A major road,
Magelungsvägen, winds across the southwestern and southern
portions of the site through Fagersjö and Farsta Strand, parallel-

ing the Stockholm-Nynäshamn railroad track. The railroad,
closely following Farsta Strand's northern border, made stops
at Farsta station on the Farsta–Farsta Strand border and at
Södertörns Villastad on the Larsboda–Farsta Strand border.

South beyond the Hökarängen station, trees have been
cleared just into the Farsta city district for an extension of the
transit line's right-of-way.

At Gubbängen, the construction of streets, housing, and
schools is complete. A wide, treeless greenbelt extends across
the entire southern portion of the city district and contains the
Gubbängen School. The only area under construction is Gubbängen Center, immediately east of the Gubbängen transit
station. The site of the center is split by the north-south road,
Lingvägen. Just south of the center, a wide road, Majrovägen,
terminates abruptly at the end of the residentially developed
area.

Housing and streets are complete at Hökarängen, and there is
little construction in progress. A road, Pepparvägen, which
eventually will extend south to Farsta, now ends in the woods

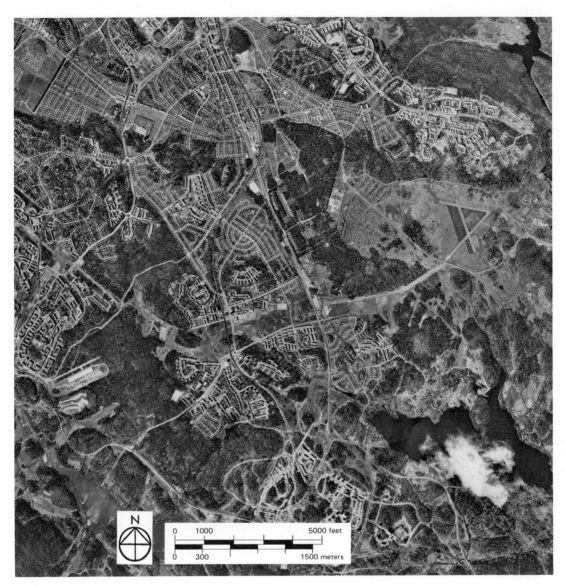

N

| 0 | 1000 | | 5000 feet |
| 0 | 300 | | 1500 meters |

just south of the residential areas. Hökarägen School has been finished, but neither Park School nor Skönstaholm School has been built. No work has yet begun on Hökarängen Center.

In western Sköndal there is an area of detached single-family homes and some streets. In southwestern Sköndal, on the estate of a Church of Sweden organization, are some older buildings. The estate is crisscrossed by a few narrow, winding roads; otherwise, Sköndal is almost wholly undeveloped.

Farsta is still almost entirely covered by trees, and there is no evidence of development or construction, except the clearing for the realignment of Nynäsvägen.

Larsboda and Farsta Strand are dotted by older homes and cottages along the shore of Lake Magelungen. There is no evidence of other development or construction, and large areas are covered by trees.

Except for a few cottages on the shore of Drevviken, Larsboda is also covered by trees, and here again there is no evidence of development or construction.

Figure 4.17
Farsta Development Area in 1958.
Source: Geographical Survey Office of Sweden.

There is further development in all the city districts except Fagersjö. No major changes appear in the alignment of Nynäs-vägen, although an intersection of the Hökarängen-Sköndal border has been improved.

The transit line right-of-way is clear well into Farsta, although not as far as the site of Farsta station at Farsta Center. At Gubbängen, the center and two schools are finished. No additional housing has been added, and there is little evidence of other construction. Additional housing, two schools (Park and Skönstaholm), and the center have been added at Höka-rängen. Pepparvägen has been extended south and is now a connecting road to Farsta. In Larsboda there is now both residential and industrial construction in progress, and in Farsta Strand a few multistory apartments are going up.

Figure 4.18
Farsta Development Area in 1959.
  Source: Geographical Survey Office of Sweden.
  Farsta is the only city district in the Farsta Development
Area where discernible change has occurred. Gubbängen,
Hökarängen, and Fagersjö (still undeveloped) show little or
no change. In Sköndal local streets and residential construction
have been added. In Farsta Strand the alignment for some local
streets has been cleared. In Larsboda a few multistory apartments have been constructed, and development has occurred
on the site for Larsboda school. At Farsta local streets have
been improved, the number of multistory apartments has
increased, and there are two new schools. Farsta Center's site
has been cleared, and buildings there are under construction.

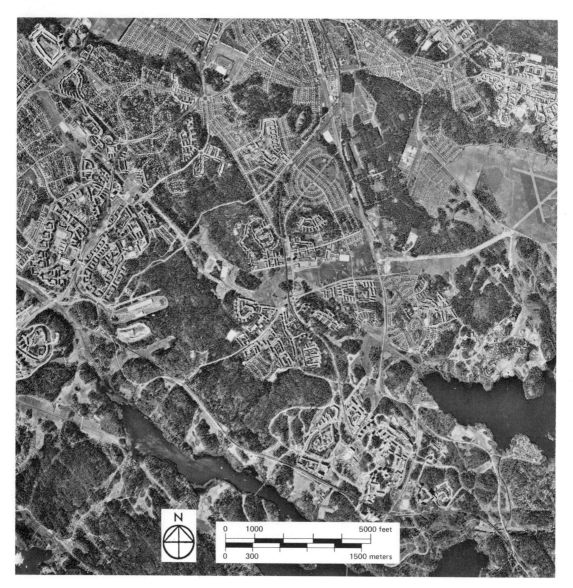

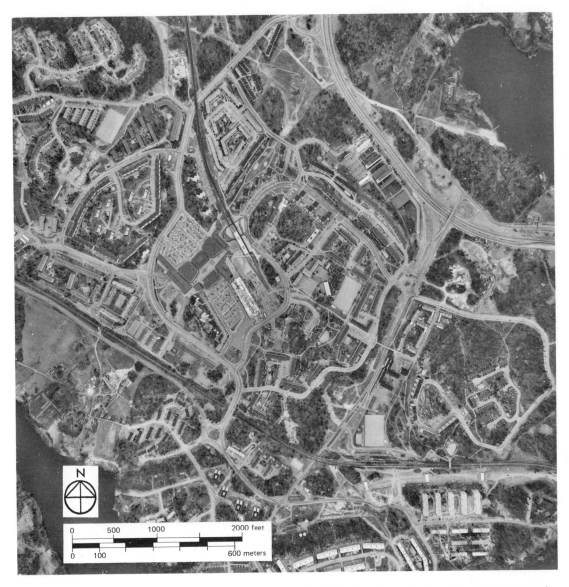

Figure 4.19
Farsta and parts of Fagersjö, Sköndal, Larsboda, and Farsta
Strand in 1964.

Source: Geographical Survey Office of Sweden.

Farsta, Farsta Strand, and Larsboda have been considerably
developed, although there are still a few signs of construction in
progress. Nynäsvägen has been realigned and widened, although only half the divided roadway is open through Larsbod
New grade-separated intersections have been constructed at
Farstavägen and at Ågestavägen. A right-of-way has been
cleared, and pedestrian underpasses have been constructed
across eastern Farsta Strand for the new east-west highway,
Magelungsvägen.

Sidings have been added on the Stockholm–Nyäshamn railroad line at the Södertörns Villastad station. Local streets and
through roads at Farsta have been extended and improved.
Additional single-family and multistory housing are completed, and two new schools have been added. The core and
open parking areas of Farsta Center are now in use, and an

office building is under construction at the southeast corner of
the center. The research laboratories and administrative offices
of the National Board of Telecommunications are now in use,
just west of Nynäsvägen.

In Larsboda, additional multistory housing and the Larsboda
School have been constructed. The local street pattern in Farsta
Strand has been expanded, considerable single-family and
multistory housing has been completed, and a school is under
construction.

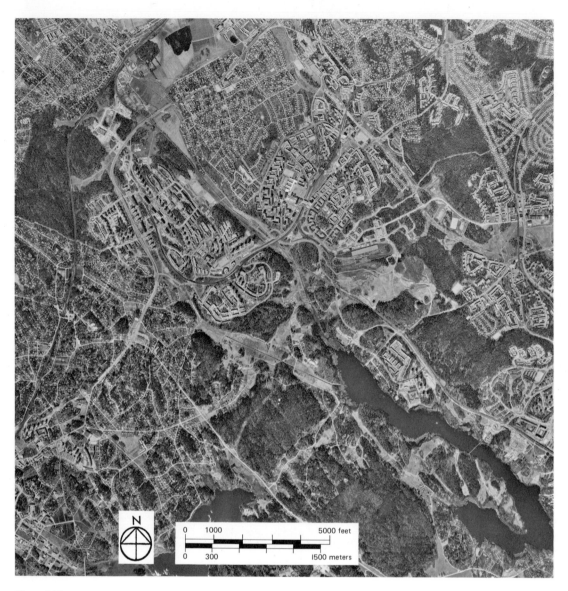

Figure 4.20
Fagersjö and parts of Gubbängen, Hökarängen, Farsta, and
Farsta Strand in 1965.
Source: Geographical Survey Office of Sweden.

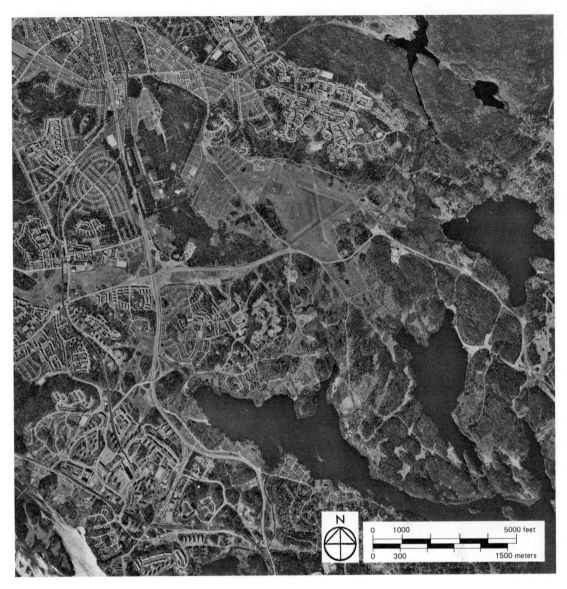

Figure 4.21
Gubbängen, Hökarängen, Sköndal, Farsta, Farsta Strand, Larsboda, and part of Fagersjö in 1965.
 Source: Geographical Survey Office of Sweden.
 Considerable changes have occurred in Sköndal and Fagersjö, a few in Gubbängen, Hökarängen, Farsta, and Farsta Strand, but almost none in Larsboda. Örbyleden road is now complete from northeastern Sköndal west through Hökarängen, and the large, grade-separated intersection has been finished on the Nynäsvägen road. A viaduct to carry Magelungsvägen over the alignment of the projected extension of the transit line from Farsta to Farsta Strand has been constructed. There are two new buildings at Gubbängen Center, and several additional multistory apartment houses have been erected at Hökarängen. Single-family and multifamily dwellings have been added at south central Sköndal and at Farsta Strand; the retirement community at Sköndal is being enlarged, and the Magelungen School at Farsta Strand is now finished. The office building at Farsta Center has been completed, and at Fagersjö, multifamily housing. Fagersjö School, and a network of local streets have been built.

Figure 4.22
Map of Farsta Development Area indicating additional facilities in place in 1965.
   Source: Generalstabens Litografiska Anstalt, Stockholm, 1965.

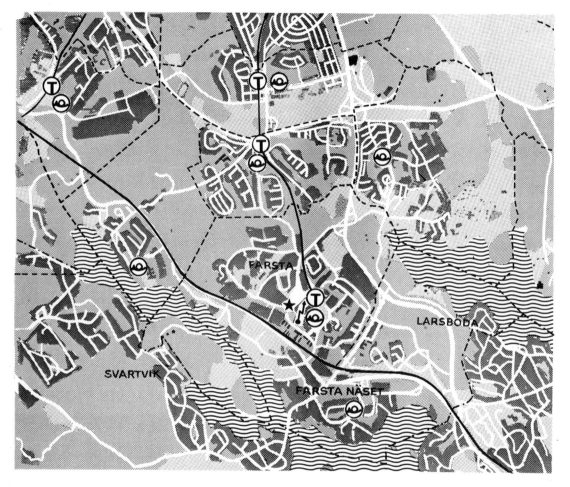

one thousand feet

━━━━━━━━ railway
—Ⓣ— transit line with station
—·—·— city limits
— — — — city district boundary
★ police station
🅐 post office
♪ telephone, telegram office

Figure 4.23
Suburban residential development by city district, center development, and transit system extensions in western and southern Stockholm suburbs.

Prepared by Miss Clare C. Cooper, 1966. Source for selected centers: Stockholm Chamber of Commerce, *Swedish Shopping Centers*, 2nd ed. (Stockholm: Stockholm Chamber of Commerce, 1965).

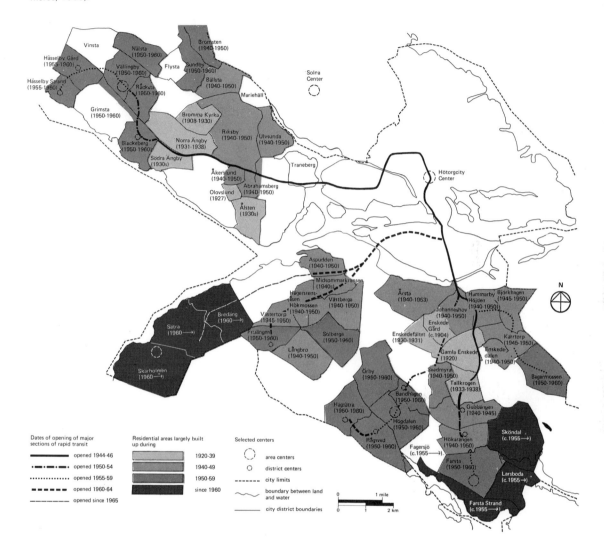

5
The Community Center

If the transit line is the backbone of Stockholm suburban development, the community center is its heart. Shopping centers in only the most casual sense, they offer goods and services ranging from coffee and dry cleaning to statuary and adult education. Like every other element of Swedish metropolitan planning, they have known individual failure as well as success. However, what is probably the most arresting aspect of the center as an institution is that it has, through a happy confluence of foresight and legitimate self-interest, realized its chief aims without becoming burdened with the avoidably unattractive qualities so common to its counterpart in the United States.

Classes of Centers

Swedish planners have distinguished between four different classes of centers: regional or A, area or B, district or C, and neighborhood or D (see Table 5.1). A word about each will perhaps put those of the area class, such as Vällingby and Farsta, in clearer perspective.

Regional (A) Centers

The largest center is the A, or regional, center. This type is mentioned only in passing, however, as it now seems that instead of there being A centers, a number of the B centers will be enlarged to take on the role originally conceived for regional centers:

  Data compiled at some B centres such as Vällingby and, above all, Farsta have shown that, if they are conceived on a large enough scale and provided with the necessary parking space, such units can exert an attraction upon both customers and stores sufficient to make them serve as regional centres. . . . The scope of the real regional centres would thus be reduced, and the competition for the trade of shoppers buying commodities other than prime necessities would instead take place between the large B centres and the shopping districts of the City [downtown Stockholm].[1]

Area (B) Centers

By 1949 it was clear that the city district, with its resident population of approximately 10,000, was inadequate to support a center with a complete range of shopping facilities. Planners therefore decided that within each group of three or four districts, one would have such facilities, drawing support from a primary clientele of 12,000 to 15,000 and a secondary clientele of at least 60,000.[2] This center would serve both those living in the immediate vicinity and those in neighboring districts whose own centers did not provide such variety (see Table 5.2).

  There are seven such centers in the Greater Stockholm area. The first, of course, was Vällingby, which serves Hässelby Strand, Hässelby Gård, Råcksta, Grimsta, Blackeberg, Norra Spånga, Norra and Södra Ängby, Bromma Kyrka, and parts of Nockeby, Ålsten, Riksby, and Åkeslund. The others are Solna, serving Solna, Sundbyberg, Mariehäll, Ulvsunda, and Traneberg; Högdalen, serving the inner southern suburbs, including the older areas of Örby and Stureby and the newer areas of Bandhagen, Rågsved, and Hagsätra; Farsta, serving Tallkrogen, Gubbängen, Hökarängen, Sköndal, Fagersjö, Larsboda, and Farsta Strand; and the recently completed centers, Täby in the north and Skärholmen in the southwest. The seventh center, Hötorgscity, is a redeveloped pedestrian shopping precinct in the center of Stockholm, serving people who work and live in the central city.

  As Table 5.2 shows, there is considerable variation in sales area, ranging from 12,000 square meters at Högdalen to 28,000 square meters at Farsta. There is a similar variation in the average size of shops, going from 200 square meters at Högdalen to 700 square meters at Farsta.

  Aside from serving as shopping centers, the B centers also function as cultural and social centers. Table 5.3 shows the cultural, social, and community facilities common to most B centers. An exception to this is Solna Center, which opened recently in an older area that already had such facilities.

District (C) Centers

The neighborhood shops of the new suburbs had their origins in the single shops of the garden suburbs of a generation before. Similarly, facilities of the district center were foreshadowed by the small groups of shops clustered around stops on the western transit line, around which formed such suburbs as Nockeby, Höglandet, and Ålsten.

  District centers must meet four requirements: an available primary clientele of 12,000 to 15,000, proximity to a transit station, shops to meet most basic and some specialized shopping needs, and suitable parking facilities (see Table 5.4).

  A C center contains an average of twenty to thirty shops, which include not only food shops but also, say, a hairdresser, florist, clothing store, pharmacy, bank, restaurant, and post office. It would not contain department stores, or such specialized stores as

Table 5.1
Types of Shopping Centers in Greater Stockholm

Type of center	Basic clientele	Selling area (sq. ft)	Examples
A (regional) center	150,000–400,000	More than 323,000	—
B (area) center	50,000–120,000	129,000–323,000	Vällingby, Solna, Farsta, Högdalen, Hötorgscity
C (district) center	8,000–15,000	27,000–54,000	Hässelby Gård, Hässelby Strand, Blackeberg, Fruängen, Bandhagen, Hagsätra, Rågsved, Gubbangen, Hökarängen
D (neighborhood) center	4,000–7,000	Less than 16,000	(numerous)

Table 5.2
Details of Selected Area Shopping Centers of Greater Stockholm[a]

Center	Primary clientele (500-m radius)	Secondary clientele (5-km radius)	Sales area (sq. m)	No. of shops	No. of dept. stores	Sales area of dept. stores	Parking spaces	Year opened
Vällingby[b]	26,000	80,000–120,000	20,000	90	2	9,700	1,250	1954
Farsta[c]	30,000	100,000–170,000	28,000	40	3	13,300	1,950	1960
Högdalen[d]	24,000	100,000	12,000	60	2	3,750	800	1960
Solna Centrum[e]	25,000	60,000	20,000	80	2	NA	670	1962
Hötorgscity[f]	300,000[g]		27,000	80	2[h]	NA	2,150	1962

[a]Source: Svenska Dataregister AB, *Sweda News*, No. 52 ab (Stockholm: Svenska Dataregister AB, November 1964). Figures for Täby and Skärholmen were not available at the time.
[b]Built by AB Svenska Bostäder (company owned by city of Stockholm).
[c]Built by AB Farsta Centrum (group of five private building companies).
[d]Built by AB Familjebostäder (company owned by city of Stockholm).
[e]Built by Carl A. Lilliesköld AB (private company).
[f]Built by a number of different municipally owned and private companies.
[g]Number of persons passing through fifteen exits of two adjacent underground stations daily.
[h]But five others in immediate neighborhood.

Table 5.3
Community Facilities at Four Area Centers of Greater
Stockholm[a]

	Vällingby	Farsta	Högdalen	Solna Centrum
Cinema	X	X	X	
Assembly hall	X	X	X	X
Theater	X	X		
Library	X	X	X	X
Youth center	X	X	X	
Church(es)	X	X	X	
Day nursery		X		
Child and maternity care center	X		X	
Medical center	X	X	X	X
Dental clinic	X	X		X
Premises for social welfare offices	X	X	X	
Labor exchange	X	X		
Post office	X	X	X	X
Old people's home	X			
Hospital	X		X	
Hotel	X			X
Town hall			X	
Police station	X	X	X	

[a]Sources: Stockholm Chamber of Commerce, *Swedish Shopping Centres* (Stockholm: Stockholm Chamber of Commerce, 1965); Svenska Dataregister AB, "The Five Biggest Stockholm Shopping Centers," *Sweda News*, No. 52 ab (Stockholm: Svenska Dataregister AB, 1964); and AB Farsta Centrum, *Farsta* (Stockholm: AB Farsta Centrum, 1959).

Table 5.4
Details of Selected District Shopping Centers of Stockholm[a]

Center	Primary clientele (500-m radius)	Total area (sq. m)	Sales area (sq. m)	No. of shops	Parking spaces	Distance from inner Stockholm (km)	Builder[b]	Year of construction (approx.)
Blackeberg	10,000	14,000	2,900	30	50	12	(a)	1950
Hässelby Gård	15,000	33,000	3,400	25	120	18	(b)	1955
Hässelby Strand	10,000	12,000	2,150	20	60	20	(c)	1958
Bandhagen	10,000	10,000	2,900	29	60	8	(a)	1958
Rågsved	12,000	18,000	2,500	20	140	12	(c)	1959
Hagsätra	15,000	40,000	9,500	34	225	15	(d)	1960

[a]Source: A. Scarlat, *The Development of Shopping Centers in the Stockholm Area* (Stockholm: The Swedish Institute, 1963), pp. 5–7.

[b](a) AB Familjebostäder—company owned by city of Stockholm.
  (b) Hyreshus i Stockholm AB—company owned by city of Stockholm.
  (c) AB Stockholmshem—company owned by city of Stockholm.
  (d) AB Hagsätra Centrum—private company.

those selling furniture, jewelry, photo equipment, books, or wines and liquor. The center would have such facilities as a youth club, day nursery, medical clinic, and cinema.

The district center generally provides between 50 and 150 parking spaces, though later centers of this type have more, keeping pace with increasing car ownership.[3] The transit station is located on one side of the shopping center, the station exit leading directly onto the plaza shopping area.

Most of the shops face onto pedestrian malls and squares and have a private, comfortable atmosphere. The other shops face the street approaching the center; through them passersby catch a glimpse of the inner pedestrian area. Often visual integrity is further enhanced by breaking the center's fairly limited parking area into a number of small units and providing underground approaches to loading bays.

Pedestrian underpasses beneath the streets leading to the centers ensure a safe approach on foot. As the centers themselves are pedestrian precincts, some of them with temporary child-care facilities, shoppers can do their errands in quiet ease.

Neighborhood (D) Centers

Providing small groups of three to five shops, or even isolated single shops in the areas farthest from a district (C) center is hardly a new idea in Stockholm. In the area of self-built cottages developed in Norra Ängby, a small row of shops provided for the day-to-day needs of local residents. In the garden suburb of Enskedefältet, a single shop was placed at each corner of the long green mall that forms the central spine of the area.

Postwar planning applied this concept to the outer, low-density areas of the new suburbs. Because few people seemed willing to walk more than 200 or 300 meters to a district center, residents in such areas were provided with clusters of neighborhood shops—in an approximate ratio of one shop for every thousand people in the vicinity. Occasionally, single shops in the more distant areas of one-family, detached houses further supplemented the C center.

However, the development of more elaborate facilities at the C centers and the increasing use of the car caused shoppers to bypass the local shops and do both daily and specialized shopping in the district shopping center. After some of the neighborhood shops closed, planners began using a walking distance of 500 meters as a standard for locating neighborhood shops in outlying districts, at least in areas where a shopping center was likely to compete with them.

Vällingby Center

As a B center, Vällingby Center serves the entire surrounding suburban area. In 1966 the development area housed some 55,000 inhabitants, all within a 3-kilometer radius. On June 12, 1951, the city commissioned the municipal development management company, AB Svenska Bostäder, to develop Vällingby Center. Construction began the same year, and the center opened formally on November 14, 1954 (see Fig. 5.1). About 24,000 square meters were devoted to shops and stores and another 23,000 square meters to offices, health services, social institutions, and assembly rooms.

In February 1962, AB Svenska Bostäder began an enlargement of the center, which it completed in March 1966 (see Fig. 5.2). The expansion, which removed the familiar plaza on the northeast side of the center, consisted of five projects: (1) a building containing a residence hotel for medical personnel, a police station, and shops; (2) a department store with shops and offices; (3) a building for shops; (4) a multistory parking garage for 600 cars; and (5) an extension of the underground delivery system. Shop floor space nearly doubled, office floor space rose by 45 percent, and storage and other secondary space increased. The two existing department stores more than doubled their retail sales area, and about twenty new shops opened (see Table 5.5).

The center has more than fifty retail shops as well as restaurants, banks, beauty parlors, coffee shops, and laundromats. Institutional services include a post office, offices for health insurance payments, dentists, and doctors, and recreational facilities, including a cinema, a community meeting hall, youth clubs, and a library. There are also a number of large private offices in the center, contributing to the number of jobs available locally.

A large portion of Vällingby Center is on a platform above the rapid transit line (see Figs. 5.3, 5.4). This puts the center in the heart of the city district and provides residents with convenience to both transportation and the services at the center. It also eliminates the traffic barrier that a surface transit station would have caused. Since the center was planned primarily, though certainly not exclusively, for people who live within walking distance, housing is assembled around it. There was no need to accommodate its location to parking facilities and access routes.

There has been, however, a change in demand for parking space and also for shopping facilities at Vällingby and the other larger centers, underlining the importance of allowing for future expansion. During the planning of Vällingby, for example, it was presumed that almost all shoppers would come either on foot or by rapid transit, so only 470 parking spaces were provided. However, an inquiry in 1957, only three years after opening, revealed that about 30 percent of the shoppers were coming by car, 36 percent on foot, 27 percent by public transportation, and 7 percent by bicycle.[4] In 1964 the 600-car parking garage was constructed on the northeastern edge of the center, and there are now 650 parking spaces outside, a total of 1,250 spaces.

Table 5.5
Space Distribution at Vällingby Center[a]

Space distribution by major use

Major use	Sq. m	Sq. ft
Retail shops (including storage)	31,557	339,676
Bank, pharmacy, hairdresser, barber, laundry	8,005	81,165
Restaurant, coffee bar	4,467	48,082
Hygiene	2,161	23,260
Hobbies and educational work, cultural institutions	4,187	45,068
Offices (including storage)	19,963	214,879
Various storage and administration rooms	3,280	35,305
The Lutheran State Church of Sweden	1,940	20,881
Parking structure	23,529	253,263
Residence hotel for medical staff	2,856	30,741
Totals	101,945	1,097,325

Space distribution by retail trade

Trade	Total space		Percentage of total space
	Sq. m	Sq. ft	
Department store	14,984	161,286	47.5
Foods, fruit, fish	2,136	22,991	6.8
Clothing	7,946	85,529	25.2
Furniture, radio-TV, sporting goods, electrical appliances, hardware	3,734	40,192	11.8
Dye and drug stores, household goods, infirmary supplies, perfumery, flowers, tobacco	1,439	15,489	4.5
Watches, photography, jewelry, optometry.	602	6,479	1.9
Others	716	7,706	2.3
Totals	31,557	339,676	100.0

[a]Source: AB Svenska Bostäder, *Vällingby* (Stockholm: AB Svenska Bostäder, 1966), p. 24.

Figure 5.1
Site plan of Vällingby Center, published in 1956.
   Source: *Byggmästaren*, 1956, No. A3, p. 60.
   The plaza, between the transit station and the central shop
building, is free of vehicular traffic and connects directly with
the footpath network that extends throughout the entire
district. The center is scaled to allow normal shopping crowds
to fill the plaza and shopping streets with life and activity.
Festivals, public meetings, and other functions of this type
take place in the greenbelt to the northeast of the center
(upper right-hand corner).

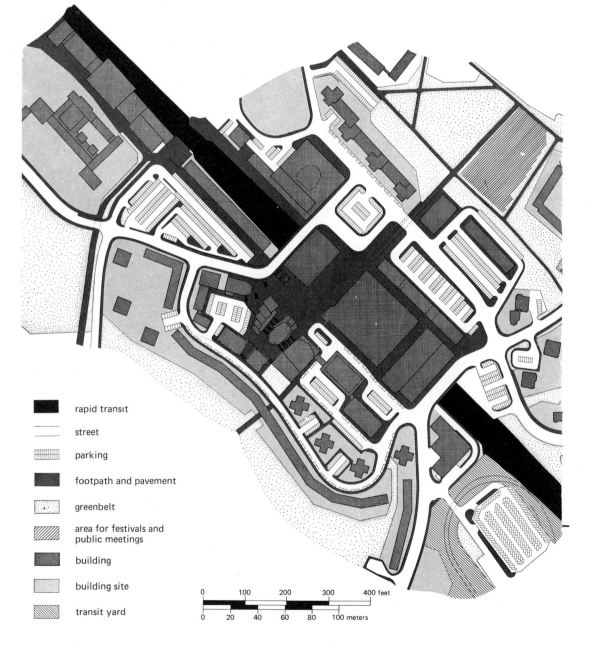

rapid transit

street

parking

footpath and pavement

greenbelt

area for festivals and
public meetings

building

building site

transit yard

0	100	200	300	400 feet

0	20	40	60	80	100 meters

Figure 5.2
Vällingby Center.
  Source: United Nations Department of Economic and Social
Affairs, *Planning of Metropolitan Areas and New Towns*, Docu-
ment No. ST/SOA/65, 1967, p. 99.
  Transit station, department stores, and shops are incorporated
into a system of pedestrian streets with the transit line beneath.
Parking facilities are at approaches to the center and in a parking
garage on the northern side. Multistory housing development
is on both long sides of the center.

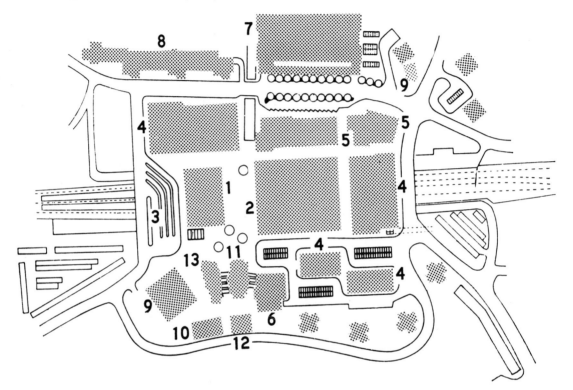

1	transit station	8	apartment building
2	commercial building	9	churches
3	bus platforms and taxi stands	10	library
4	commercial buildings	11	cinema
5	stores	12	youth center
6	residence hotel	13	community hall
7	600 stall parking garage		

Figure 5.3

Plan of Vällingby Center.

Source: AB Svenska Bostäder, *Vällingby* (Stockholm: AB Svenska Bostäder, 1966), pp. 14—15.

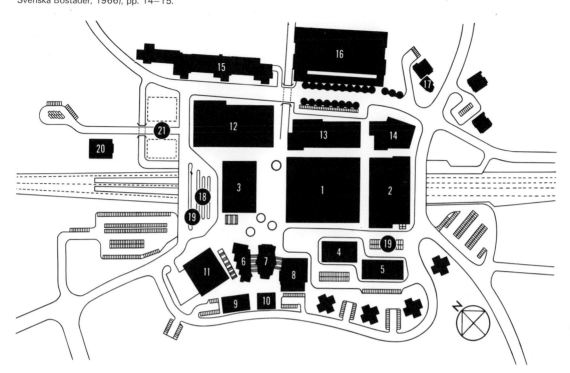

1 Department store. Other shops and services include clothiers and accessory shops, pharmacy, radio-TV store, furrier, florist, restaurant, record store, cafeteria, jeweler, furniture, groceries, watchmaker, banks, paint and cosmetics, shoes, beauty parlor, study rooms, and offices

2 Post office, travel agency, laundry, fruit store, hardware store, barbershop, yarn and knitting accessory shop, glove shop, men's store, electrical appliance and radio-TV shops, telephone-telegraph office, grocery stores, restaurant, offices

3 Rapid transit station, newspaper stand, coffee bar, haberdashery, bank, dry cleaning, gloves and bags, shoes, men's and women's hairdresser, home economics advisor, confectionery and delicatessen, perfumery, lingerie shop, rehabilitation office, other offices

4 Newspaper agency, coffee bar, ladies' wear shop, social welfare office, temperance office, employment office, car dealer

5 Newspaper agency, optician, cigar store, grocery, handbag shop, barber, dental and medical centers, maternity and pediatric clinic, hall for free church

6 Community hall

7 Cinema, travel agency, dancing school

8 Resident hotel for medical center staff, police station, shoe store, florist

9 Public library, study rooms

10 Youth center

11 Church, parish hall, youth club, parish offices

12 Department store, pet shop, yarn and knitting accessory shop, photography shop, offices

13 Men's store, sporting goods shop, book and stationery store, baby and sanitary articles store, fish market, perfumery, milliner, photography store, hot dog stand, bank, liquor store, local social insurance office, beauty parlor, ladies' wear store, dentist, club rooms

14 Glass-china-toy store, home textiles, grocery store, ladies' wear shop, dressmaker, newspaper stand, ballet school, offices

15 Household appliance store, ladies' wear store, car dealer, laundry

16 Parking garage, filling station, cafeteria, radio-TV store, household appliance store

17 Church, youth center

18 Bus stands

19 Taxi stands

20 Private medical center

21 Building planned for offices, artisans, and craftsmen

Figure 5.4

Section through Vällingby Center.

Source: AB Svenska Bostäder, *Vällingby* (Stockholm: AB Svenska Bostäder, 1966), p. 14.

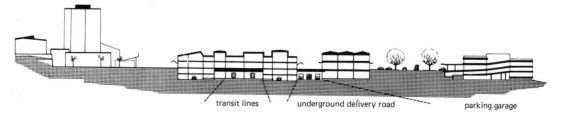

transit lines   underground delivery road   parking garage

Farsta Center

The Private Sector Responds

The chief distinction between Vällingby Center and Farsta Center is, of course, that the latter was undertaken as a venture of private enterprise. So elemental a departure from former procedure occurred neither casually nor without opposition, and the public and private maneuverings that brought it about are worth some attention.

After seeing the commercial success of Vällingby Center, a group of private builders sought to induce the city to entrust the projected Farsta Center to their care. Not only did they succeed in this goal; they did so at a minimum of financial risk. They argued that since Vällingby had been a public project, it was only fair that Farsta should be private. The decision favoring the private group, however, seems to have had more to do with politics than fairness.[5] The more conservative Bourgeois Majority (the Liberal-Conservative coalition) controlled the city government at the time and was naturally inclined toward development by private enterprise.[6] The reader should bear in mind that while the two interested city boards, those of planning (which had merged with the building board the year before) and real estate, had Social Democrats as chairmen, the Liberal-Conservative coalition, as the group in power, held majorities on each of them.

On March 24, 1956, the city planning office delivered to the real estate office a preliminary site development plan proposal for Farsta Center. On April 7 the real estate office recommended that the real estate board approve the plan in principle with the provision that the planning office work with the real estate office in developing the final plan. On April 10 the real estate board tabled discussion of these questions, taking them up again on April 24.

At that time, the chairman, commissioner Gösta Wennström, proposed that the board approve the real estate office's recommendation and also appoint a five-man development

committee to coordinate construction. Vice-chairman Gunnar Hjerne then announced that prevailing economic conditions compelled him to recommend that the city's municipal building companies reserve all their resources for housing. He further recommended that if qualified private organizations were willing to undertake the construction of Farsta Center, they should receive the commission. Finally, he proposed that the board instruct the real estate office to conduct preliminary discussions with any such qualified and willing organizations. Hjerne's proposals passed by a close party-line vote: Hjerne, Gösta Bohman, Artur Nordin, and Jan-Otto Modig (all from the Liberal-Conservative coalition) were for them; Wennström, Carl Gustaf Göransson, and Aronson (all Social Democrats) were against them. This vote was the key to putting Farsta Center into private hands.

The real estate board also decided to approve in principle the preliminary plan proposal for Farsta Center. To the five-member development committee the board appointed Social Democrats Wennström and Ewald Johannesson and coalitionists Hjerne, Nordin, and Bohman. Bohman was also chief spokesman for the Stockholm Retail Trade Federation.

The real estate director Torsten Ljungberger pointed out to the board that he had already been approached by three different organizations interested in developing Farsta Center: HSB i Stockholm on April 6; Byggmästares i Stockholm gemensamma byggnadsaktiebolag on April 17; and the participating organizations in AB Farsta Centrum—Bygg-Oleba, Olle Engkvist AB, Byggnads AB Projektor, John Mattson Byggnads AB, Nya Asfalt AB, AB Skånska Cementgjuteriet, and Svenska Industribyggen AB—on April 19. To no one's surprise, Social Democrats Wennström, Göransson, and Aronson went on record that it was too early to discuss which organization should receive the commission to develop Farsta Center.

On October 12, 1956, the real estate office reported that at the direction of the development committee, it had concluded an agreement commissioning AB Farsta Centrum to plan the development of the Farsta Center area.

The decision favoring private builders illustrates Stockholm's pragmatic attitude toward public-private affairs; it satisfied the private sector, avoided the appearance of municipal nepotism, and represented an immediate economy to the city by allowing public resources to be used elsewhere.

Civil engineer Arne Bergqvist was employed by both the building and real estate offices between 1948 and 1954. During the latter years his duties included work on Blackeberg and Vällingby. He resigned in 1954 to become chief of the technical department of Svenska Byggnadsentreprenörföreningen (SBEF), a national association of general contractors and house builders. Later he became manager of AB Farsta Centrum. At SBEF Bergqvist had an opportunity to familiarize himself with the workings of the Swedish building market and the activities of private building contractors. In 1955, when Bergqvist and his boss, Sten Källenius, learned of the plans for Farsta Center, they became convinced that private enterprise ought to plan and build it, and they made preparations for asking the city for the opportunity. In December 1955 they discussed this question with Gösta Bohman, assistant managing director of the Stockholm Chamber of Commerce and secretary-general of the Stockholm Retail Trade Federation. They agreed that without firm financial backing it would be fruitless to go before the city with any kind of proposal.

They then went to Bertil Odelfelt, assistant managing director of Svenska Handelsbanken, one of Sweden's largest banks. Accompanying them was Erik Thyreen, director of Näringslivets Byggnadsdelegation, the commercial and industrial trades building delegation, which was a lobbying group established by such large organizations as the industries' association, the wholesalers' association, the chamber of commerce, the bank association, and the insurance companies' association, to protect their interests in building and plan-

ning. They told Odelfelt they were convinced that if they could get the commission to plan Farsta Center, they would probably get the right to do the construction as well. Källenius says of this thinking: "We learned this from Mr. Aronson's pattern at Vällingby; he worked piece by piece also. When you have a clever competitor, you do things just the way he does; you just make sure you do it better."[7] Odelfelt adds: "We knew there would have to be a combine of some of the large building contractors, who would form some kind of a group and undertake the planning at their own risk. If the plan was acceptable to the city authorities, the group would have the sole right to build the center."[8]

To get help in forming the group, Odelfelt asked Colonel Agne Sandberg, president of AB Skånska Cementgjuteriet, Sweden's largest construction company, and also a board member of Handelsbanken, to join the conference. He agreed, and together they decided definitely to form the combine. Odelfelt recalls:

I told them that the planning could cost as much as 300,000 kronor [$60,000] and that if it wasn't approved, the money was thrown away. They estimated that the construction itself would probably cost something like 55 to 60 million kronor [$11 to $12 million]. I told them that we at Svenska Handelsbanken would grant building credits up to 48 million kronor [$9.6 million]. I think that was the exact amount I guaranteed on the condition that their plans be approved. First, of course, they would have to get department stores like Tempo, Åhlén & Holm, and NK to commit themselves. I said the bank would take one of the buildings and that the Co-op would probably want one. They got their commitments and were thus able to go before the city authorities in a sound position.[9]

Källenius says: "The bank got interested because the members of the building group were leaders in the contracting business—Skånska Cementgjuteriet, for example, whose managing director at that time was the vice-president of SBEF. And, of course, there was money, skill, and integrity behind these companies."[10]

Odelfelt explains his bank's motives in backing the Farsta project: "It is our job to see that building credits are granted. We also thought the center was quite a sound idea; aside from the building credits, which we earned money on, by the way, we wanted to help private enterprise because the bank's customers are mostly from private enterprise, even though we have building credits with municipal companies, too."[11] Källenius adds: "We went to them and said, 'You'll have to finance this either for the city or for us, and we are in business with you. Isn't it better for you to stick to your own clients? When the city comes in, they don't ask you—they tell you. They tell you what they need, and you put the money on the table.'"[12]

Bergqvist, as manager of AB Farsta Centrum, was able to get the real estate board's permission to allow the building group to prepare the site development plan, but for the moment that was all.[13] Says Bergqvist: "It wasn't possible politically to get more. Gunnar Hjerne and Gösta Bohman had to work hard enough for us just to get the planning job. The others wanted to have a planning competition, and a new vote was called."[14]

Källenius comments:

With the political situation in this town, you know from the start how the voting will come out. They always make sure that every party has all its representatives there when they are voting. So we knew from the beginning that it would be five to four. A party majority in the city council means a majority in every division, every committee, every department; there is never much arguing once the party decides something. And they like to take questions bit by bit, so it came as no surprise when at first they gave the group only the planning. The Liberal-Conservative majority was the reason it was a private project. If the Social Democrats had held the majority, Farsta would have been built by Mr. Aronson and Svenska Bostäder.

To encourage our members to participate in the Farsta project, I told them that they had to fight for the future, that they must show the people they were able to do things.[15]

Bergqvist agreed, saying: "You must show

you can do something well for its own sake, not just for the profit."[16]

But Bergqvist and Källenius both felt they were taking a risk since, except for the example of Vällingby, they could not know for sure that Farsta would be a good investment. Källenius continues:

We didn't know at all how to finance the building of all those shops because we didn't know if merchants and department stores would put a single penny in it or if they would attract customers if they did. We knew something about Vällingby, but there was nothing else like it in the whole country. Obviously it was a very big risk. For people like these contractors, who plan economic questions very carefully, it takes a lot of talking to get them to take such a risk, especially since there were other, safer opportunities available to them. Now that it is operating, it's turned out to have been a good business proposition for everyone concerned, especially for the people. Of course, there wasn't any real cause for concern. What with the housing shortage, we knew that the housing would have to be filled up. And the people living there, earning money, would have to buy things.[17]

In the summer of 1956 the city commissioned AB Farsta Centrum to design the center. The site development plan was ready a year later, and detailed design began soon after. In the spring of 1958 the city awarded the company a leasehold, construction began July 1, and the first buildings went up the following January. The commercial buildings were finished in the early fall of 1960, and Farsta Center was officially inaugurated on October 23. The remaining buildings were completed by December 1961.

Makeup of the Center

Farsta Center (see Figs. 5.5, 5.6), serving southern Stockholm, is convenient to three major traffic routes: a main north-south highway from Stockholm to Nynäsham (with six lanes to Farsta), the southern branch of the rapid transit system, and the Stockholm–Nynäshamn railroad. There are good east-west road connections. The trip to downtown Stockholm takes about twenty-five minutes by rapid transit.

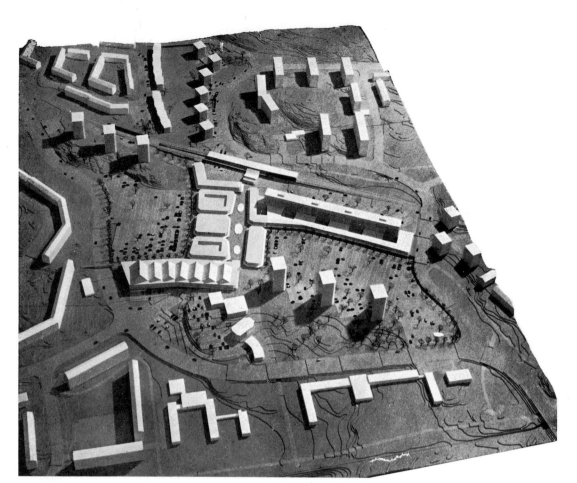

Figure 5.5
Model of Farsta Center and surrounding area.
  Source: Giorgio Gentili, "The Satellite Towns of Stockholm,"
Urbanistica, No. 24–25, September 1958.

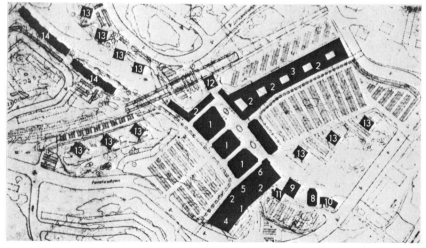

1	Department stores and shops
2	Shops
3	Offices
4	Theatre
5	Cinema
6	Restaurant
7	Medical Centre
8	Church
9	Library
10	Civic Hall
11	Youth Club
12	Underground railway station
13-14	Dwellinghouses

Figure 5.6
Plan of Farsta Center.
  Source: Giorgio Gentili, "The Satellite Towns of Stockholm,"
Urbanistica, No. 24–25, September 1958.
  Department stores and shops have been grouped around an oval pedestrian precinct enclosed at one end by the rapid transit station (building 12). Transit lines are on an overhead viaduct. Parking is at street level on both sides of the center. Housing development and schools around center are situated along pedestrian ways and separated from vehicular traffic.

In addition to the department stores and some forty smaller shops, the center offers a post office, cinema, restaurant, theater, community hall, public library, medical building, and banks. The sales area of the stores is some 21,000 square meters. (See Table 5.6.)

The center is on one level and extends, as a platform, across a valley running through the site. This decked-over valley contains truck tunnels and delivery services. The center has a total area of 80,000 square meters including parking.

The center is laid out like a marketplace. All pedestrian paths lead to the long central promenade, which is enclosed by the department stores and shops. All buildings are two stories tall, but there has been no attempt to keep the cornices on the same level; their façades give the marketplace a walled-in effect. The buildings have no backs, but rather display windows on all four sides, which can be seen by pedestrians as they approach the center.

Each of the three main department store buildings is distinctive in appearance. The façade of the Co-op's Kvickly Department Store is relieved by heavy shadowing and the use of aluminum plate. The artificial stone façade of the Tempo building has a lattice work pattern. The NK store is clad in light gray granite, the central building on the west side in teak.

Buildings A, B, C, and F in Figure 5.7 are the department stores, with sales areas at street level and on the floors immediately above and below. The developers achieved considerable flexibility at reasonable cost with a simple prestressed concrete structure. Except for lower basements in buildings A and B and certain parts of F (which were poured on site), these buildings have only three commercial floors, one below and two above the level of the square. They are of three-story, precast, prefabricated, reinforced concrete columns and precast, prestressed concrete beams. Prefabricated concrete planking completes the structural skeleton.

The natural park at nearby Lake Magelungen is the center for summer recreation. Here Farsta residents can swim, fish, go boating, or walk nature trails. Winter leisure activity has an outlet in the community center's five club rooms and theater. The community center also contains a youth center, which has a variety of rooms for children's and teen-agers' indoor activities. There are several hobby rooms, phonograph and photograph rooms, a drama and ballet school, a practice kitchen and beauty parlor, a handicraft workshop, a canteen with soft drinks, coffee, and cake, and a gymnasium for sports and dances.

Unlike Vällingby Center, which serves the 60,000 or so people of its nearby neighborhoods, Farsta Center was planned to attract customers from the entire southern and southeastern suburbs of Stockholm. For its combined primary and secondary clientele of between 150,000 and 200,000 people, there are over 2,000 parking spaces in lots around the center and in a small, obviously inadequate garage; and this raises an interesting point. Vällingby planners were quite unaware of the massive increase in personal car ownership soon to take place, and they failed to take it into account in their planning. By the time Farsta was under development, the move toward car ownership was under full steam, and planners allowed for it. Yet it is Vällingby, with its indoor garage and small outdoor parking areas, that has solved the problem with maximum convenience and minimum blight; Farsta, which had the benefit of greater planning experience, is left with a rather sizable eyesore (see Fig. 5.8).

Table 5.6
Space Distribution at Farsta Center[a]

Use	Area			
	Square meters		Square feet	
Sales areas				
Department stores	13,000		139,930	
Shops	8,000	21,000	86,111	226,041
Offices, staff rooms, and warehousing				
Department stores	11,000		118,402	
Shops	8,000	19,000	86,111	204,514
Offices, library, national health office		1,600		17,222
Offices for medical service and dental service		3,300		35,520
Community hall, theater, youth center		2,600		27,986
Police station		1,200		12,916
Church premises		700		7,534
Restaurant, cinema		1,700		18,298
Workshops		2,000		21,527
Service and delivery road		7,400		79,652
Garage		6,500		69,965
Totals		67,000		721,181

Building volume	Cubic meters	Cubic feet
Totals	370,000	13,066,439

[a]Source: "Farsta Centrum," *Arkitektur*, 1961, No. 3.

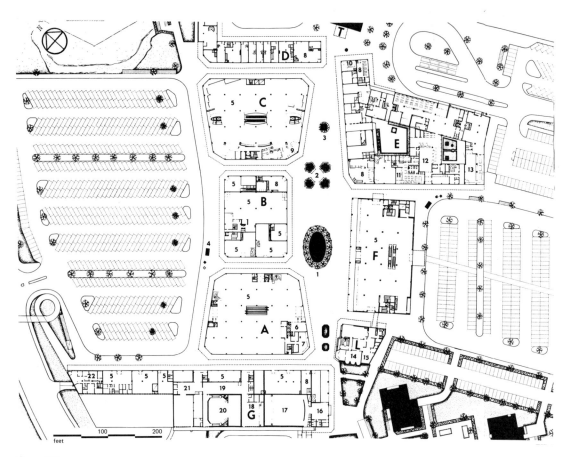

Figure 5.7

Farsta Center ground floor plan.

Source: "Farsta Centrum," *Arkitektur*, 1961, No. 3.

A Tempo department store

B Shops, library, and offices

C Kvickly department store

D Shops, offices, and church

E Shops, post office, pharmacy, medical and dental consultation rooms, mothers' welfare center, public dental service,
and social welfare service

F NK department store

G Cinema, community hall, youth center, shops, offices,
police station, car repair workshop, and premises for small
industries

L Restaurant

1. pond,   2. fountain,   3. planted tree,   4 parcel delivery
office,   5 sales,   6. confectionery,   7. storage,   8. bank,
9. cafeteria,   10. news and ticket office,   11. pharmacy,
12. post office,   13. liquor store,   14. restaurant,
15. restaurant kitchen,   16. cinema,   17. cinema foyer,
18. assembly hall,   19. vestibule,   20. theater,
21. youth center,   22. police station.

Figure 5.8
Farsta Center parking lot.
  Source: Stockholms stads gatunämnd and Aktiebolaget
Stockholms Spårvägar, *T-banan i ord bild* (Stockholm:
Stockholms stads gatunämnd and Aktiebolaget Stockholms
Spårvägar, 1964), pp. 50–51.

6
Selected Individuals and Organizations

Countless individuals and organizations shared in the development of Vällingby and Farsta. This chapter examines a number of them, with the aim of producing a cross section of the pressures and currents that affected the makeup and quality of the two suburbs, from early planning to final execution. Presented are representatives of each of the major areas of influence—public, professional, and private—and the highly varying degrees of success they had in achieving equally varying goals. Not all have been chosen for their farsightedness, wisdom, or effectiveness. Indeed, one or two appear for quite different reasons (again the intent is to offer a cross section), and if their roles were of a less positive sort, they are no less enlightening for an understanding of the development process.

Yngve Larsson

Doctor of philosophy and long-time local and national politician, Yngve Larsson began his major public service in 1924 when he was appointed commissioner of what was then known as the city's public works and traffic division. However, his personal influence was not felt until the 1930s, when the central board of administration began giving him important assignments in traffic construction projects.

One of his first undertakings in this area was the development of the large traffic intersection and canal lock at Slussen connecting Lake Mälaren and the Baltic. Larsson also shares credit for the large Western Bridge, the Traneberg Bridge, and many transit extensions.

Until the reorganization in 1940 (see Fig. 3.1), Larsson was not formally connected with city planning, although he was chairman of the special commission for the subway and the central city redevelopment.

Of course the master plan embodied these things, but I wasn't officially involved with it then. Ostensibly I was cooperating in a friendly way with my colleague, Harry Sandberg, commissioner of planning and real estate, but as a matter of fact, I was intruding on his job. Take the cloverleaf construction; apparently it's a job for the town planner, but it isn't easy to see where the job of the planner ends and the job of the construction engineer begins. It just seemed natural that public works should be responsible for the big traffic constructions.

With the construction of the lock and intersection at Slussen came the decision to build the transit system. It's very important to know that the subway under Södermalm was planned and built as only one part of a future system that would eventually connect the southern and northern parts of the city and the western suburbs to central Stockholm. There had to be changes, of course. The transportation load in the planned development of the southern and western suburbs became much heavier than expected. Fortunately, in 1945 we decided to build the stations to accommodate eight-car rather than six-car trains.

People were also thinking about developing suburbs along the transit line—not simply adding blocks to blocks or building garden cities as in the twenties, but creating largely independent communities. These ideas were current among architects at the end of the thirties and were developed in Great Britain during World War II. The big Abercrombie plan for London had a decided impact on Swedish architects and planners in the forties. [1]

In 1943 Erland von Hofsten, Larsson's secretary, published preliminary research for building just such suburbs. [2] "We made a research study for a southern suburb called Gubbängen. It didn't turn out according to our ideas of those days, but we quite definitely intended it to have not only housing but social, commercial, and educational facilities, and employment opportunities as well." [3]

In the early 1950s Larsson met Alf Johansson, national housing board commissioner during the 1940s and 1950s. Johansson suggested that Larsson investigate whether a sense of community was developing in the newly inaugurated Årsta Center area. In 1954 Larsson asked sociologist Gunnar N. Åsvärn to undertake such a study. The results showed that while there hadn't yet developed much of a community feeling, it was still a sensible way to build a community. Even before the study was completed, however, the failure to develop community feeling had led to the more functional motivations embodied in the master plan for Stockholm of 1952. Larsson explains functional motivation as "simply a matter of people having their shopping and social facilities near where they live." [4]

Albert Lilienberg was still planning director when Larsson took over as planning commissioner in 1940. Like Larsson, his chief interests had been transportation improvements and the redevelopment of the central city. Larsson freely admits the general debt a whole generation of urban planners owed to Lilienberg's 1928 Stockholm Master Plan, but is equally frank in disagreeing with him on specifics:

We cooperated, of course, but Mr. Lilienberg had his ideas, and I had mine. And in the end, ideas other than Mr. Lilienberg's prevailed.

The ABC ideas were easily accepted by the local politicians. As far as I can remember, there wasn't much debate in the town council. ABC gave a locality a certain sense of itself, and while we use the word "democratic" pretty freely, ABC did seem to express the democratic idea.

My philosophy as commissioner was to let the director and the staff get on with it. Markelius had two young architects of outstanding capacity—Sidenbladh and Ahlberg. Of course, I stayed in close touch with the team, and we debated any important matters, especially if they had political overtones; after all, I was a politician responsible to the city council, a political body, but Markelius was the real planning chief. The director must feel that he is in charge of the technical work. Markelius and I had a very good relationship. During the winter of 1945–46, I was an almost daily visitor at the office simply because I was interested. But my job was to be an intelligent listener; the way the plans were made was strictly up to the architects and their chief. [5]

Once the ideological groundwork for Vällingby had been laid and accepted, the office staff took over. In cooperation with the real estate office, Markelius and the city planning office made a master plan for Södra Spånga, which they submitted to the appropriate boards and offices for comments. Markelius made certain changes and then presented the plan to the city planning commission, which approved it. Larsson then appeared before the central board of administration to present the plan.

That is the commissioner's chief job: to get proposals through the various boards, the central board of administration, and the city council. There was little debate because the planning people and the real estate people had the full confidence of the city council. Everyone thought they were doing a good job and said, 'Gentlemen, please go on.' . . . Even after 1946 I was still very much interested in their work, but I was no longer the commissioner— just an ordinary town councillor—so I had no personal influence on the work going on under Helge Berglund. Of course, when they needed support for their plans in the city council, I did whatever I could. [6]

This was of no little importance, for Larsson was the leader of the opposition Liberal Party in the city council, and at that time the Liberals were the most active group among the opposition parties.

In the elections of 1950, the Bourgeois Majority (the coalition of the Conservative and Liberal Parties) gained a clear majority, and Larsson was chosen chairman of the central board of administration. With his colleague and political ally, John Bergvall, as commissioner of finance, he was able to exert considerable influence on planning; he was especially helpful in seeing to it that Berglund got the money to carry out the plans for the transit system and the central city redevelopment. Larsson notes: "And he carried them out because he had the political resolution to do what he set out to do. . . . His contribution was not in debates: he was given to action, not talk." [7]

One reason why Larsson's name is mentioned so often in connection with Vällingby and Farsta is that he was planning commissioner while the projects were in the concept stage. For both the public and the private citizen, it was Larsson who held the brief for these ideas.

Axel Dahlberg

Although there was no direct opposition to the development of Vällingby and Farsta, there was a trouble spot in the city administration. During the 1940s, a conflict arose between the real estate director, Axel Dahlberg, and a number of city officials, including his own superior, Harry Sandberg, the commissioner of real estate. As mentioned, from the mid-twenties to the beginning of the forties, much of the city planning was actually done, not by the planning office, but by Dahlberg, who favored low-intensity residential development for the outlying suburbs. His plans provided only a minimum of local shopping and service facilities and would have forced residents to rely on those of the central business district. Architect Carl-Fredrik Ahlberg recalls: He was used to having his way in all development problems. . . . He started the development of multifamily houses on city-owned land outside central Stockholm. He also started the building of one-family houses, which owners built themselves with city help. . . . He was an important man, but as I said, he wasn't used to accepting ideas from other people. [8]

Toward the end of his career Dahlberg's ideas were running precisely counter to those of the city planners. A former commissioner, Joakim Garpe, has suggested some possible reasons for this: Dahlberg was getting old, new ideas were appearing, and the size of Stockholm was becoming a problem. [9] Statisticians, demographers, and politicians began to see that the population of the Greater Stockholm area would eventually reach 1,500,000, not the 900,000 predicted earlier. Dahlberg-style suburban garden villages could not possibly accommodate such numbers.

Dahlberg's ideas were not the only problem. In the early 1940s, the Social Democrats grouped themselves around either the radically inclined finance commissioner, Zeth Höglund, or the more conservative real estate

commissioner, Harry Sandberg. Dahlberg and Sandberg didn't get on together at all well, and there was steady conflict between them. [10] Dahlberg finally "left" his job after being charged with failure to obey orders from the real estate committee. Höglund then offered Dahlberg the post of finance board representative on a special committee of directors and commissioners concerned with planning for the Vällingby Development Area. Bertil Hanson states, "He was delighted to accept, the better to be able to continue his fight for single-family homes." [11] And as Göran Sidenbladh surmises:

This gave Dahlberg the chance to take revenge on Sandberg. . . . Even if you had an okay from the real estate side, you had to go to Axel Dahlberg to find out what the finance board's position was. Following the preparation of Fritz Voigt's preliminary plan proposals for the Vällingby area, we began to work in detail. Blackeberg was first, and there were many discussions about that. . . . We had to overcome a lot of opposition in the administration, especially from Dahlberg, who was an adviser to the finance board. He was against separating pedestrian and car traffic, and he wanted a different route for the transit line. . . . He also wanted another kind of land allocation. We worked with planned units of blocks of apartment houses in the central area, surrounded by one-family houses; he wanted all the apartment houses in one place and all the one-family houses in another place. I can't tell you how many alternate plans we made before the existing plan for Blackeberg was adopted. . . . Axel Dahlberg had different ideas for everything we planned for Södra Spånga. . . . As for greenbelts, Dahlberg believed they were just nonsense; he wanted to develop them into areas of one-family dwellings. [12]

Hanson puts it this way:

At this same time Swedish architects took notice of foreign thought in architecture and planning, and were stimulated by it. Commissioner Larsson himself was among those well versed in the Abercrombie plan. Vällingby would be, it was said, a "satellite city"— a self-contained urban center beyond the existing central urban area. It would have homes of all shapes and sizes—one-family homes, row houses, small apartment build-ings, and high-rise apartment buildings. There would be parks, playgrounds, and open spaces. There would be special walks for pedestrians. There would be a central shop-ping center. And there would be places for business and industry, so that residents could work conveniently near their homes.

This was the picture the representatives of the city planning office presented to the com-mittee. Commissioner Larsson found it com-mendable. Only Mr. Dahlberg disapproved. . . .

This veteran advocate of residential develop-ments consisting largely of single-family homes was unsympathetic to the new ideas. He wanted to fill the urban landscape with cottages and gardens. He thought high-rise apartment buildings abominable, and he had no use at all for parks. He spoke out for his ideas, arguing that they represented what ordinary people wanted, but he seemed old-fashioned to modern architects; as they pointed out, he was not an architect anyway, but a civil engineer, and they wanted to get on with the task of bringing into being a com-munity in which well-designed modern con-structions predominated.

The differences were to be resolved in the committee, the answers depending on reason-able and amicable discussions between the experts about the tentative plans on the draw-ing boards. They divided the area under con-sideration into four sections. In what was later described as the "compromise," two sections were set aside for development as the majority would have it (i.e., for a satellite city), and two as the dissenter, Mr. Dahlberg, would have it. He accepted this arrangement and signed his name to the committee's un-animous recommendation. [13]

So the 1950 master plan for Södra Spånga had large areas of one-family and terrace housing (much to Markelius's discontent) simply because otherwise Dahlberg, represent-ing the finance board, would have vetoed it.

In a December 1949 report to the city plan-ning board, Markelius presented a site devel-opment plan proposal for an area north of the Råcksta transit station. In making the proposal, he pointed out that during the pre-paration of this plan Axel Dahlberg had often been consulted by the planning office. As Dahlberg would not approve the plan, it was

agreed that the planning office would pre-pare an alternative proposal under Dahlberg's direct supervision. [14] On December 14, 1949, the board approved the planning office pro-posal and recommended a suspension of work on Dahlberg's alternative.

The accountant's office then requested the council to make another comparison between the proposals. In an attachment to the request, Dahlberg criticized the city planning office proposal and added that his own proposal had never gone out to the various boards for opinion and comment as had the city plan-ning office proposal. [15] On January 20, 1950, Markelius criticized certain of Dahlberg's re-marks concerning the Råcksta site develop-ment plan. On January 25 the planning com-missioner, Helge Berglund, sent both the Dahlberg and the planning office proposals to the real estate board. That same day the city planning board approved the planning office proposal. Dahlberg's proposal was attached to the approved proposal, but for information only.

Dahlberg left municipal service shortly after-ward, and subsequent plans for the Vällingby Development Area show progressively less of his influence.

Sven Markelius

Yngve Larsson makes the following comment:

Planning Director Lilienberg was approaching pension age when I became commissioner. I was convinced that the next director had to be an architect rather than an engineer like Mr. Lilienberg. Conditions called for a prominent architect, trained in planning and thoroughly abreast of the latest ideas. Only a few candidates fulfilled these requirements, and Sven Markelius was the best. [16]

Markelius was city planning director from 1944 until 1954. He is generally credited as being the major creative force in the development of Stockholm's new suburban communities. On becoming city planning director, Markelius was confronted by two massive problems: housing for a rapidly increasing municipal population and the forthcoming redevelopment of the central business district. These two problems made a master plan an absolute necessity. Architects Ahlberg and Sidenbladh, and von Hofsten from the Stockholm statistics office joined the planning office, and the staff was rapidly expanded from about 35 to some 150.

Larsson's victory over Dahlberg in determining the subway alignment through downtown Stockholm gave the planners whatever impetus they might have needed. They began in 1945 with what Markelius calls a preliminary exercise: the little book *Det framtida Stockholm* (reprinted as *Stockholm in the Future*), a program for a master plan for Stockholm prepared with the help of Sidenbladh and von Hofsten, which was circulated among influential public and private citizens for comment and opinion. It was this document that, after countless enlargements and delays, eventually led to the 1952 master plan for Stockholm.

Markelius's office was under continuous pressure from the real estate office to produce site development plans, particularly for the western suburbs. This created some difficulty because, while Markelius was known as a fine organizer of ideas, he was very slow in producing working plans; he liked to ponder them before rushing into plan production. It was therefore necessary for his staff to assume a great deal of the responsibility for translating his ideas into concrete proposals. As the staff gained experience, it continued to develop and modify his ideas in such a way as to gain acceptance both from him and from the various boards that had to approve them.

Regarding Markelius's working methods, a colleague Carl-Fredrik Ahlberg comments:

He took very little active part in planning the first area, Blackeberg. . . . When he saw a sketch, he simply said, "I like it" or "I don't like it." If he said, "I don't like it," you went back and tried again. That was the way he worked on Blackeberg. With Vällingby he was more personally involved. I remember very clearly the time he called in traffic engineer Sven Lundberg and me and told us to start working on the neighborhood immediately. Then we went at it, the three of us. That's the only time—when that happened—that we really worked as a team with Markelius making the very first concept. It was just for an hour or two, but much of Vällingby's character was born that day. . . . Of course, I had many plans to discuss with him, and in the Vällingby case we discussed everything thoroughly. Sometimes he walked around the office looking at what was going on, and we would discuss things still on the architect's drawing board. But usually we took the plans to Markelius when something important came up because he was the only person to whom a group chief felt an official responsibility. Of course, I very often talked with Commissioner Berglund about things, too. . . .

Interdepartmental discussion was more formal. We had regular once-a-week meetings that brought together the head of the research section, the head of our roads and traffic section, myself and some others from the street building office, and people from the real estate office, too. Those meetings were just below the director level; we met to discuss the plans that were going on in all the offices. Then, of course, you sometimes had to go to outside people to discuss things, for example, with Gösta Bohman at the Retail Trade Federation. . . . As for taking the political temperature of the time to see if our plans would be acceptable to the different committees, we tried to do that for him. After all, Markelius was an architect, not a politician or an administrator. [17]

As to the origins of Markelius's planning innovation, building executive Åke Grauers says:

He probably got his greatest inspiration from England. They were involved with "green towns" long before the Second World War. . . . Markelius was the planning chief when these new ideas were introduced in Sweden, particularly in Stockholm. . . . Markelius was receptive to the English thinking on the development of satellite towns of 50,000 to 100,000 residents around London, at some distance from the central city but connected to it by a high-capacity mass transportation system. These self-sufficient satellite towns were intended to provide housing and employment opportunities but still have easy contact with London. . . . Vällingby, too, was to employ the same people it housed. [18]

Markelius himself minimized the influence that the British New Towns idea had on the development at Vällingby: "The fundamental reason is that the English New Towns were genuine satellite towns, but Vällingby and the other suburbs were to have a much less independent function." [19] He explained his views: "I studied the New Towns, of course, and with great interest, but the solution in Stockholm had to satisfy the special conditions of Stockholm. I have no feeling that Vällingby is copied from the New Towns, even though they were planned at about the same time and there are some general ideas they have in common." [20] When it came to detailed planning, however, particularly the separation of pedestrian and vehicular traffic, he freely admitted the influence of the American pattern exemplified by Clarence Stein's Radburn.

Markelius's ideas met constant opposition. At Blackeberg, for example, he had pressed for traffic separation through green areas, which would have made it possible to walk to schools, bus stops, and the transit station without having to cross any major roads. The opposition, led by Axel Dahlberg, objected to it on the grounds that it was unnecessarily expensive and that it would be dangerous for unescorted women at night.

At Vällingby, however, most of his ideas were accepted. [21] And at Råcksta (see Fig. 6.1), vehicular access and parking are completely relegated to one side of the meandering row housing, while the buildings opposite face a large vehicle-free green space where children can safely play. There is also a system of pedestrian ways to the school, the shopping center, and the transit station.

High-rise construction came naturally to the suburban centers. It permitted a concentration of dwellings around the center, supplied a local clientele for the shops, and gave commuters a short walk to the rapid transit station. In a sketch (Fig. 6.2), Markelius presents his concept for the physical disposition of major activities in the new suburban community. On one side of the rail transit line is the center, surrounded by dense high-rise apartment construction. The larger shops are here, close to the rapid transit station. After a separating green space, there is an outer zone of row houses and detached single-family homes on larger lots. There are a few clusters of local shops in the outer zone for daily purchases. Schools are in the green space. On the other side of the transit line are areas of light industry.

It goes without saying that Markelius did not always succeed in putting his ideas into effect. Even when he did, he was not always satisfied with either the results or the planning techniques that produced them. [22] However, if the size and intricacy of the problems he had to find solutions for are considered, it seems clear that the meeting between Markelius and Stockholm suburban planning was a profitable one.

Figure 6.1
Site plan for housing area in Råcksta.
    Source: Sven Markelius, "Stockholms Struktur," *Byggmästaren*, 1956, No. A3, p. 62.
    Complete traffic segregation. Streets and parking on the periphery. A central greenbelt on land unsuitable for buildings with central foot and cycle paths, grade-separated from streets, connecting local shops, nursery school, and other services and leading to schools, the area center at Vällingby, and the transit station. Playgrounds for small children are located in the immediate vicinity of the housing and are visible from apartment windows. The site plan aimed at an effective contact between dwellings and playgrounds but has been realized to only a limited degree.

Figure 6.2

Conceptual sketch of suburban development area.

Source: Sven Markelius, "Stockholms struktur," *Byggmästaren*, 1956, No. A3, p. 65.

An area of multistory housing around a center and transit station. Row and detached housing farther out. Originally published in "Stadsplanefrågor i Stockholm," *Byggmästaren*, 1945, No. 18.

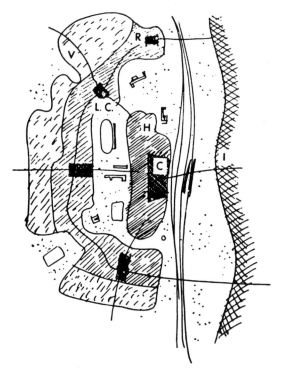

C   center
H   multi-story housing
R   row housing
LC   local center
V   detached single-family housing
I   industrial area

S. Albert Aronson

Aronson occupies a singular place in Stockholm public affairs. Since its inception, he has been chief executive of Stockholm's housing development and management company, AB Svenska Bostäder; he has simultaneously held posts on the city council, the central board of administration, and the boards and committees of finance, real estate, and city planning. While Aronson's situation is not uncommon in smaller Swedish municipalities, it is unique in Stockholm. He believes that this combination of powers benefits both the company and the city: "If I didn't think it was good for the city, I would certainly give up some of my positions. . . . We gain efficiency, save time; and deal with proposals much more rapidly. My personal contacts are tremendously useful. . . . The intimate knowledge I have of the politicians' movements gives me a good idea of where there is maneuvering room. In city planning work, success very often requires sailing between Scylla and Charybdis. There are always different currents, some of them dangerous; if the channel is well marked in advance, you reduce the risk of losing the ship."[23]

On February 16, 1944, AB Svenska Bostäder was established by Baltzar Lundström as a private organization, under the jurisdiction of the city, for the management of cooperative housing, and Aronson, a former journalist turned politician, was appointed chief executive. World War II helped bring about Stockholm's purchase and expansion of the company. Jan Herbert Martin, former planning office secretary, states: "About 1940 building activity came to a standstill, and in 1941, not one house was built in the whole country. . . . The housing situation deteriorated immensely in the first years of the war. The shortage grew from year to year until just after the war, when the city finally decided to do something about it."[24] A national social housing investigation in 1946 indicated the acuteness of the housing shortage, and on July 2, 1947, Stockholm purchased all the shares in AB Svenska Bostäder, declared it a nonprofit municipal housing company, and determined that it should build as well as manage housing for the city.

AB Svenska Bostäder is responsible to the municipal real estate board, and the city appoints its board members and audits the books. Operating for many years on a capital of 7,350,000 kroner ($1,470,000), it was increased to 24,000,000 kronor ($4,800,000) after 1964; in 1965 it paid the city a 4 percent dividend on profits.

In 1950 the company took on a major task, the construction of 845 housing units in Blackeberg. When Vällingby projects were first being consigned, Aronson's only position, aside from heading AB Svenska Bostäder, was that of a newly elected city council member. He says of his activities:

Cooperation between the company and the municipal administration was excellent from the start. I'm sure this contributed to the very short planning period required for Vällingby. . . . Torsten Ljungberger [member and later director, 1954–1960, of the real estate office] was tremendously effective in getting such quick action on the Vällingby proposal. And naturally, we maintained close contact with the planners, not only Markelius but also his top administrator-planners and the architectural firm of Backström & Reinius. There was a synchronization that simplified things immensely. . . .
The city council established the development committee to direct the work, but it didn't even meet until after things were finished; some years later we had a meeting just to disband. . . . Neither the backers nor the detractors of Vällingby had rational explanations for their stands. We knew very little except that the small neighborhood centers of the late 1940s were unsatisfactory. There isn't much done on this scale with so hazy a rational basis. Certainly, for many of us, Lewis Mumford's ideas were very influential. *The Culture of Cities* [1938] was circulated widely during the late 1930s and early 1940s, but the enthusiasm it created for a multicored city remained latent for nearly a decade.[25]

A specific example of the advantages Aronson speaks of occurred during the construc-

tion of the transit line underneath Vällingby Center. The rapid transit line was the city's responsibility, the buildings were that of AB Svenska Bostäder. The planners wanted to combine the transit right-of-way and the buildings of the center to form a single architectural unit. One suggestion was to have the transit line in an open cut alongside the center. Aronson recalls:

I was sure we could find a solution. It was all owned by the same person. During construction we didn't have any formal agreement; we went right ahead and resolved the money problem afterward. We exchanged advantages and arrived at sensible solutions. . . . Through personal, informal agreements we put the center directly over the transit line. . . . Had we been a private company, we might have had one idea and the city another; the private company or the city might have refused to do anything at all without formal arrangements. . . . With us it wasn't necessary to figure to the last crown what each would pay because it all came from the same pot. It was like a bookkeeping question . . . between members of the same family.[26]

As a municipal company Svenska Bostäder has to balance its social responsibilities with its economic requirements. Aronson continues: "A nonprofit company must have a long-range view toward the management of its properties, for example, the Vällingby Center. We calculate with a predicted economic life. If it's too long, we risk losing money, and we mustn't do that. It can't be too short either; it would be a fine thing if a nonprofit company made a profit."[27]

However, the balance between the two extremes is difficult to attain, and the company tends toward a small profit to provide dividends and to accumulate capital to cover possible shortages. Further, as long-term money is rather tight, rapid amortization, at a pace often greater than motivated by economically useful life before write-off, has contributed to a forced capital accumulation.

During the first year, for example, the company suffered a large loss on Vällingby Center; by 1966, it was breaking even. If the inflation of that period had continued, the company would have shown a considerable profit. In that case, rather than trying to reduce prices by lowering commercial and retail rents, such profits would instead have been used to lower residential rents. Aronson explains:

After all, our primary responsibility is to rent dwellings at cost. However, the nonprofit idea is flexible—thank goodness, fine definitions have never been drawn. And, of course, one can change one's frame of reference regarding them when the need arises. . . . Because of their generality, laws and regulations require interpretation for each specific application. They were not written with Vällingby in mind. . . . A poor statute can be very useful with a good interpretation of it. And a good statute can lead to poor results if it is misinterpreted. There was wide cooperation in interpreting the statutes to fit Vällingby Center because people were anxious for it to succeed. We found solutions where there might not have been solutions if people had been lukewarm toward the project. [28]

Nordiska Kompaniet

Nordiska Kompaniet, commonly referred to as NK, is Stockholm's most fashionable department store. As such, it was eagerly sought as a client for Vällingby Center. The center's management, it will be recalled, had had initial difficulty in convincing merchants of Vällingby's potential, and NK's locating a branch store there would doubtless have had a desirable effect on other prospective clients. NK decided against Vällingby. For one thing, the relatively affluent, older western suburbs, where Vällingby was located, were already among NK's best customer areas. Also, NK had a long-standing nonexpansion policy. Finally, Vällingby Center was an unknown quantity, which even lacked parking facilities. That NK later decided in favor of Farsta Center was largely the result of the efforts of one man—Rudolf Kalderén.

Kalderén was with NK from 1926 until 1966. He became president in 1958, though he had been running the company since the retirement of its president in 1952. NK had already declined an early invitation to locate at Farsta, as it had with Vällingby, but soon after Kalderén took over he renewed contact with AB Farsta Centrum.

In December 1958, Kalderén engaged planner Gösta Brännström[29] to work up rough plans for an NK branch at Farsta Center. Unlike Vällingby, at Farsta Center there would be parking for 2,000 cars. And even though Vällingby had proved a huge success, Kalderén says: "I was still a little uncertain, and persuading the board of directors was not easy; Farsta was a distinct departure from earlier policy, one that meant a big, risky investment."[30] Brännström agrees:

At that point I do not think that even Mr. Kalderén was sure he wanted to go to Farsta, and it seemed to me that the board of directors did not like the idea from the very beginning. . . . It was not very carefully planned, which is, perhaps unfortunately, characteristic of Mr. Kalderén. He's the controller, but on something like this he is inclined to play hunches, saying that in one way or another there will always be money for a good idea. . . .

But everyone was looking at Vällingby. It was very successful. All the signs indicated that any given suburban center was likely to succeed. And since city planning was very orderly, one would know where the regional centers would be. Nobody could just buy a piece of real estate and build his own center. Instead, there was a plan. Everything indicated that the southern suburbs would grow, and the only large center in that area would be at Farsta. And Farsta Center's central mall would be completely closed in by the department stores. You were either in at the very beginning or you weren't in there at all. [31]

During March and April 1959, Brännström and his group were busy making plans with the assistance of New York architect Morris Ketchum, who specializes in department stores. Brännström continues: "We were not specialists in planning this type of suburban department store, and then NK has always been inclined to hire specialists—expensive outsiders. It's part of their image."[32]

It was late spring by the time NK formally decided to go ahead. The other stores planning Farsta locations were about a year ahead. NK needed a final design; it needed retailing policies to fit the Farsta clientele and a complete market analysis to base it on; it had to make arrangements for financing; and it had to do everything at the same time. Moreover, the executives and staff were inexperienced in that type of work. Brännström states:

Professionals might succeed in building a department store in fifteen months, but as a first venture it's pretty dangerous. This was the situation at the time the decision was made: The contract was signed, but there was no fixed price on the building; the building was not even laid out; we hardly knew what it would look like from the outside, much less the inside. . . . Yet we opened the store on October 23, 1960, right on time. It must be one of the fastest jobs of its kind. And we still have what we think is the best-planned store in the center when it comes to space utilization. . . .

We started with the leanest sort of simple statistics. . . . We had the projected area population and a tabulation of the number of members in each family and their average ages and incomes. But you couldn't base policies for a department store on those. There wasn't even a breakdown of the estimated turnover or a realistic projection of profit and loss for year one, year two, and so on. . . . Decisions were based on the general thinking of the time, roughly paralleling what was happening in the United States. [33]

Policies of the Stockholm Housing Exchange have produced a variety of income groups in the Farsta area, and, on the whole, its income statistics today are among the highest in corporate Stockholm. But at the time Farsta was being planned, the southern part of Stockholm had for many years been a low-income area. To be successful, a branch at Farsta would have to attract people from the entire southern area. NK statistics showed very few charge accounts in this area: people who lived in the southern area obviously weren't going downtown to shop at NK; but they might shop at NK if it had a nearby branch. Kalderén says: "The downtown store was at that time producing sales of about 6,000 kronor [$1,200] per square meter a year. At Farsta we only needed to plan on something like 3,600 kronor [$720] a year."[34]

After NK did decide to go to Farsta, there still was concern about its image. Was the Farsta store to have the same appearance and atmosphere as the downtown store? If it did, then the older one would no longer be unique. Kalderén states:

This caused much discussion among the board of directors. We knew at that time that the American department stores had made mistakes when they moved out into the suburbs. They had not presented the same image in the suburbs as at the main store downtown, and they found very quickly that this made people in the suburbs feel mistreated. This was very costly to the suburban stores. So we were absolutely convinced that in going out to Farsta with an NK store, we had to present as much as we could of the original NK image. . . . However, we didn't want the Farsta branch store to be a carbon copy of the downtown store with its massive, old-fashioned elegance. Times change, and we have to keep up with them. But we knew that if we could present a beautiful house, beautiful from the architectural standpoint, and give it not the same appearance but the same atmosphere as the downtown store, we would be accepted as NK outside downtown Stockholm.[35]

As mentioned, the buildings surrounding the oval Farsta Center mall are not symmetrical. The sides are not parallel, and corners are cut. Ketchum advised NK to try to get a building as nearly rectangular as possible and not too long or too narrow. NK was able to do so.

Unlike Vällingby, *private* builders carried out the entire Farsta Center development, but as they acted as subcontractors for AB Farsta Centrum, clients still had no choice of builder. One had to accept as general contractor AB Farsta Centrum, which operated on a cost-plus basis. NK, though, succeeded in putting certain limits on costs, but the two other main clients, Tempo and the Co-op, did not. However, Kalderén would have preferred having open bidding on construction. The land at Farsta Center belongs to and is rented from the city. Theoretically the client builds his own store; in fact, AB Farsta Centrum builds it to the client's order. NK had the choice of renting or buying. After consideration, NK decided to purchase. Kalderén says:

That was a sound choice because even though the final price far exceeded the original estimate, I'm certain that compared to the cost of future development, this will seem a bargain. . . . Although the Farsta store has been a success, one can still ask whether it was wise to expand without the necessary investment capital. That is a sound question, but we were late in our expansion program. We felt we had to run just to keep from lagging behind. Besides, you never know how long your freedom to act will last. While you're waiting to make up your mind, the costs of land and building increase. So whatever you build is actually cheap compared to what you build in the future.[36]

The Stockholm Retail Trade Federation

The Stockholm Retail Trade Federation, through sales research and intraorganizational communication, develops retail policy positions and lobbies for their acceptance by the local authorities; it also acts, when appropriate, as a professional adviser to the city and private builders. Its role at Vällingby and Farsta included influencing general planning decisions on retail trade, persuading the city to build a larger center at Vällingby than originally planned, and using its good offices to convince skeptical member retail organizations of Vällingby Center's commercial potential. The federation was founded in 1943 as part of the Stockholm Chamber of Commerce. It began as a working body for problems concerning shopping hours and retail planning, the latter having been its major activity since its inception.

A key figure in getting favorable decisions on federation proposals was Gösta Bohman. As a director of the chamber of commerce, he was its first secretary-general, a post he held for more than ten years. Bohman was also chairman of the federation's planning group. During Vällingby's early planning stages, the federation limited itself to making general suggestions to the city planning department. Later, though, it offered a concrete proposal for a shopping center of a specific area and recommended the types of stores and shops the center should have. However, as Axel Wennerholm, former managing director of the federation, puts it, "First we had to get the city professionals and the politicians to accept the idea. . . . We had to establish contacts with the people at the planning office and the building board."[37]

The 1946 plan for the Vällingby Development Area proposed the development of three city districts with roughly equal populations of up to 13,000 residents: Blackeberg, Råcksta, and Hässelby Gård. Each of these city districts was to have a small community center. Only later came the idea of creating the much larger Vällingby Center, which other neighboring districts in Södra Spånga might use for services not available in their own centers.

The Stockholm Retail Trade Federation, however, maintained that a consumer base of 20,000 to 25,000 persons within walking distance was required to support so large and well-equipped a center. As a result, the city revised its plans; the September 1949 master plan proposal recommended a combined Vällingby-Råcksta population of 21,000.

In spite of the acceptance of a large center at Vällingby, early planning proposed a net shop area of only 3,300 square meters. In April 1950, the federation again responded. Pointing to retail trade figures for the center at nearby Sundbyberg, it suggested that Vällingby Center would need considerably more than 3,300 square meters for retail space. It felt that Vällingby Center should at least equal Sundbyberg center's 11,815 square meters. And again the city accepted the federation's recommendation; the site development plan approved by the city council June 29, 1951, reserved 20,000 square meters for retail trade.

Bohman's activity on behalf of the federation in this instance had much to do with the city's decision. In letters to the city planning office Bohman called for larger retail areas and higher residential density to support the Vällingby Center, and he even had something to say about the design of store façades. Correspondence between the city administration and Bohman indicates that the study of downtown Sundbyberg definitely demonstrated that Stockholm was dragging its feet in developing a comprehensive program with suitable space requirements for Vällingby Center and that the administration was forcing him to defend the validity of the Sundbyberg figures and prove their pertinence to the Vällingby Center.[38] By reinforcing his initial arguments, Bohman gradually succeeded in gaining acceptance and support of his ideas and a corresponding diffusion of responsibility.

For its retail trade proposals in the 1952 Stockholm master plan,[39] the city planning office relied to a degree on the Co-op, the Swedish Retail Trade Federation, and the Stockholm Retail Trade Federation. Each of the organizations submitted its recommendations for the provision of shops in residential areas, specifying such things as minimum consumer base and floor space requirements for various types of retail stores. Bohman's Stockholm Retail Trade Federation is acknowledged to be the chief source of the information presented in the plan.

The second phase, getting retailers to accept shops at Vällingby, was even harder work. Axel Wennerholm recalls:

Shopkeepers felt they would be taking a great risk and said: "My business has been in the downtown area since my grandfather's time. What the hell, who is going to live out in Vällingby? I mean, just think of the name of it— Porridge Town." But retailers did accept shops there, and those visionary— or lucky— ones made a fortune. . . . And the ideas that formed the planning program for the Vällingby shopping center came not only from the federation but from the Co-op as well.

Even today we admit that intuition plays a definite role in planning. But at that time there were almost no statistics whatever. We didn't have enough hard evidence to make even a rough guess about future consumption. That we have today. . . . So, just as we had done for years, we'd say, "All right, you have so many customers in that area—so you'll have about the same number in this area. Well, that makes it three supermarkets." Why not just one big supermarket? There was too much money involved in the really big stores. Not even the Co-op, which has been very progressive in self-service supermarkets, had that kind of courage. . . . We were convinced, and now I think we were wrong, that the customers didn't want those enormous selling areas. . . .

We know today that to have a good shopping center you have to be near good transportation routes like the bus or subway, where you get a good flow of customers. Even if they don't buy when they're getting off, they at least get visual contact with the center. You also need to be near good road connections and have good parking facilities for the customers who drive. Everybody felt terrible about the lack of parking facilities at Vällingby.

We never dreamed there would be this auto explosion. Finally, you need good pedestrian lanes for people in the surrounding apartment houses. Housewives seem to prefer the smaller roundabout roads for walking to the center. . . . The center should have a central mall so people don't feel crowded. It's funny that good old Main Street, fairly narrow as at Högdalen and Vällingby, is the very best form for a shopping center. . . .

Maybe I'm too great an admirer of Mr. Aronson, but I am really convinced that future expansion of Vällingby Center was always in his plans. If it hadn't been planned, it would have been very difficult to create the unity it has today. Just look at the second stage with that new Tempo building—it closes the square in such a beautiful way. That was not the original idea, which had it a little further away so that the square opened toward the surroundings. There again, though, the retail trade federation said it must have that unity. And by moving the building a little, we closed the square, got rid of the winds, and made ourselves a nice, modern, medieval European market square.[40]

The Co-op does not belong to the retail federation; the cooperative movement forms one group and private enterprise retailing another. Wennerholm states:

They have their opinions, and we have ours. The city planning office sends plans both to the Co-op and to us for comment. . . . We answer independently, but in almost every case our answers are the same. . . .

When developing a program, the wise architect at the planning office would get hold of the planning committee of the retail trade federation and find out if there was anything new happening in retailing, something he might be able to use. The people at the federation would then tell him what they thought, giving their reasons and any helpful statistics. Just for example, figures showed that the larger stores were gaining on the medium-sized ones and that smaller shops were disappearing. This wise architect would then talk to the Co-op, too. He'd find they had the same opinion—and an even stronger one than we did because now the cooperative federation is closing all their smaller stores. . . . I think they are right, even courageous, considering the risks they take. Anyway, they told the municipal architect about their policies and

their needs, and we told him about ours. And the architect agreed if he was wise, and he usually was after a couple of years of experience. At first, he suspected us of operating only for our own interests against the Co-op, the consumers, and even society. But we were always completely straightforward. So after the first years of suspicion, the architect made use of our information in his plan, and his boss accepted the plan. . . . Nearly all the plans were good for the city. . . .

Decisions as to what kinds of shops the center would have were strictly up to AB Svenska Bostäder, and this is still the principle; the owner decides. . . . Looking back on the ratio of successes to failures, I think that they were fairly successful. There were, of course, some mistakes. Some shops at the center went under. A number of neighborhood shops and smaller neighborhood centers have also failed. Everybody thought the consumers would patronize those shops, too. It came as a surprise that the people reacted so favorably to the area center that it severely hurt the smaller shops and centers. This was particularly true at Råcksta Center, only one kilometer from Vällingby Center. Of course, it was a very silly center. You couldn't see it until you fell over it, but there I don't think that mattered. Even if it had been better planned, Vällingby would still have been too much for it. Vällingby simply offered too large a variety of activities for Råcksta to compete with. . . . One of the few things the federation disagreed with was the decision to have three department stores in the center. This meant having fewer specialty shops, which we feel is a commercial disadvantage.

The big job was Vällingby. Speaking comparatively, Farsta was easy for us. The concept of Vällingby had been accepted by planners, municipal architects, politicians, and retailers. And by that time, we had the regional plan for Stockholm, which proposed a center in Farsta very much like Vällingby's. . . . Everybody knew the idea was sound. It was a matter of doing something along the same lines.[41]

IBM

Svenska IBM AB (IBM Sweden) decided to expand its manufacturing and assembly operations and to consolidate a number of small manufacturing activities temporarily located in central Stockholm and by 1954 had moved some of its activities into a new building in Vällingby's Johannelund industrial area.

Sweden's high degree of overall technical competence had made it a natural choice for IBM International to fit into its European program. But the IBM Sweden product mix was based on the fact that IBM France and IBM Germany were already very highly specialized in electronics. They had got into electronics in the early stages of the game with the 650s, and they needed rather large resources to build complete systems. So it was logical that Swedish manufacturing got smaller units and components, such as the card-reading input and a smaller separate punch card unit. They were specific problems that could have been handled either in Italy or in Sweden. Bertil Hedin, IBM Sweden's director of finance and administration, states:

We cannot say that even the present product mix stems from a mission concept of manufacturing. In the long run, IBM Sweden has to have a mission for its future growth, and that's something that will go into our next five-year plan. We want to expand the activity, from a long-range viewpoint, into fields where we can offset our negative cost situation with quality and organizational efficiency. . . . We were not as sophisticated in 1953 as we are today. I won't say we are sophisticated now either, but now when we want another factory, we go through a hell of an exercise.[42]

The company has a five-year plan and a two-year plan, each based on sales forecasts. From these figures the load on the factory was calculated. Another prerequisite of any IBM Sweden factory venture was that it be expandable. At Johannelund the company went in knowing that it would be possible to get more space in the future; the building was, in fact, expanded in 1961. The contractor for the new building, Svenska Industribyggen Aktiebolag

(SIAB), constructed it to IBM's specifications and now rents it to their client. IBM includes in its payment the leasehold fee that SIAB is charged by the city. The location has proved satisfactory with respect to both personnel turnover and availability of essential parts, two factors generally solved only by a central Stockholm location. Floor space in 1959 was 4,000 square meters; in 1962 it was 6,300. Employees in this factory operation increased over the same period of time from 189 to 230. Hedin explains IBM's choice of Vällingby:

There were three major reasons. One reason was the relationship we had with SIAB that made it possible to have a factory tailored to us. Another was not having to invest the money, which at that time would have been difficult. IBM preferred at that time to invest its capital in machines rather than in buildings. The third reason was that Vällingby was an interesting area; by being one of the pioneers in the concept of housing and industry going hand in hand, we got good support from local government in housing and so on. . . . Through the Vällingby principle, IBM people had housing preference. That was eliminated after a while, but it was a big advantage for us to keep and attract good people. . . . A lot of the employees we already had on board at that time were helped by the housing exchange, and new employees, after they'd been with us for a while, also could take advantage of it. They got some new housing units, and there were also a lot of exchanges. . . . They gave up whatever they had, and usually there was a quality increase. So being rather early in the game, we had a very big advantage. . . . However short a time the agreement lasted, it was very helpful to us. . . .

One of our concerns is with the people we have. We cannot risk losing more than a certain number. We need a rather big population to draw from. We require a lot of technical skills, and the bigger the total population we can draw from, the better. If the manpower is available, we will be able to get it. . . . But it's not like making dynamos for bicycle lights. It's a rather sophisticated assembly operation. . . . We have to be in an area with good educational facilities, cultural surroundings, and attractive housing. . . . I don't think that the usual aspect you talk about in industrial location—having a pool of unemployed people

available for employment—has much importance for us. It's not the average person we
are after; it's the more advanced type, and
that makes a difference. [43]

AB Korphoppet: A Public Development Company

As economic growth had slackened during the
war, it was not until after 1945 that small
businesses in any great number began feeling
the need for additional space. To provide it,
the city took over a private industrial development and management company, AB Korphoppet, in order to complete the building
that the company had under way. Åke Grauers,
who had begun his career with the city real
estate office in 1937 and in 1939 had become
head of development in the office's newly
created industrial use division, was appointed
manager of the company in 1949.

Later at Vällingby, in accordance with its
policy to provide residents with local employment opportunities, including small industries,
the city allocated an area there for industrial
development. In this area Korphoppet erected
the first building for small industries, the Vagnhallen Building. The intention was that the
company should develop the entire area, but
while it has remained strong in management,
it constructed only the one building. Grauers
explains: "At that time the city was short of
funds, and there was so much else that de-
served priority. Perhaps more important, small
industry was succeeding on its own and was
acquiring a tendency to plan and build for
itself. So the city didn't have to provide nearly
as much as it had expected it would during the
1940s." [44] Korphoppet, in fact, built nothing at
Vällingby after the Vagnhallen building. [45]

Korphoppet borrows money on the open
market, mortgaging its properties in the usual
way, except when a building seems too expensive to be a safe prospect for full mortgaging;
in that case the city guarantees the excess and
stands the additional risk for an unsuccessful
project. However, Grauers states: "Korphoppet has been a good business. The city has
never had to provide capital, and the income
from real estate management has been completely sufficient to support the company." [46]

During the early 1950s the money market for
the building industry had not yet dried up, and

while it was still possible for a firm to get permission from the National Labor Market Board to relocate at Vällingby, industry was hesitant to move so far from Stockholm; the Johannelund industrial area had been established for a couple of years before anyone dared go there. By the time Farsta was being developed, in the 1960s, the combination of Labor Market Board restrictions and a regulated mortgage money supply made large-scale industrial development even more difficult.

Arenco was the first to take the step to Vällingby, and now the area is almost entirely occupied. Grauers says: "It is doubtful what would have happened if industry had not wanted to move out there. It is possible that the city would have built it up, using AB Korphoppet."[47] Grauers agrees with the consensus, however, that because industry did not go to Vällingby early, the Walk-to-Work idea was doomed. Those first industries that went to Vällingby had little difficulty securing nearby housing for their employees. And because housing was occupied as it was completed, industries going to Vällingby in later years found little left. Grauers contrasted this with the English New Towns, in which industry and housing were developed simultaneously.

Few industrial organizations chose to locate at Farsta. But Grauers believes that part of the reason for this is simply that times have changed. Owing to improved transportation—planned expansion of the rail rapid transit, the suburban Swedish Railways, and highways— industry has the freedom to locate in areas outside Stockholm. It no longer needs such proximity to housing areas in order to get labor; workers can travel longer distances in less time than before. A number of companies have moved outside the city limits to large, cheap, level sites where they can put up expandable, one-story plants but still be near the Stockholm labor market. Stockholm itself is becoming increasingly a city of offices; pure industry in the city proper is becoming a rarity.

SIAB: A Private Development Company

Svenska Industribyggen AB (SIAB) has participated in the development of both Vällingby and Farsta. At Vällingby it constructed the industrial buildings for Arenco and IBM, both in the Johannelund industrial area. Elsewhere in Vällingby it constructed a building and leased it to Thorsell & Lundberg until the tenant exercised an option to purchase. In addition, SIAB built some fifty one-family houses for a foundation managed by employees of the National Power Board. The members had secured the leasehold to a piece of land and were permitted to propose their own site development plan to the city. The leasehold association worked together with the Stockholm Savings Bank and with Ekkronan, the bank's housing development foundation, which arranged the financing. Then SIAB prepared a site plan, designed the houses, and constructed them.

Although SIAB will bid a job at a fixed price, the company director, Håkan Birke, comments: "About 60 to 70 percent of our production is for old customers on a cost-plus basis. But we guarantee from the beginning that the total cost shall not exceed a certain amount, so the owner can then calculate the yearly costs ahead of him."[48] The first stage of Arenco's plant at Johannelund was designed and built on a cost-plus basis.

Regarding IBM's decision to lease its building, Birke says:

The IBM people say that they need their money for their own business, and they want us here in Sweden to finance their building. We have very good connections with the finance institutions, and so as long as it is not on too large a scale, we can manage financing it and owning it. That is not at all inconvenient for us as long as it's not too big a portion of our total production. While inflation means that the structures actually increase in value, we cannot tie up too much of our resources because we need money for our own expansion. . . .

The real estate office was glad we came in with IBM because industries did not build out there as fast as the real estate office wanted. Besides, IBM was, I think, a very popular client. . . . The leasehold was given for eighty to ninety years, with the leasehold fee fixed for forty years. Later agreements provide for a fee adjustment after ten years, which means it's very cheap for us out there. [49]

Birke, Sven Dahlberg, and Carl Paulsson founded SIAB in 1945. Paulsson later withdrew because of bad health. The company expanded rapidly, designing and constructing industrial buildings throughout the country from 1945 until 1952. While this was a boom period for the Swedish building industry, SIAB was not able to compete so keenly in Stockholm; prior to 1951 it had done almost no residential construction in the city.

Birke says partner Dahlberg was one of the men who took the initiative in arranging the financing for AB Farsta Centrum to develop and construct Farsta Center. While NK and Tempo own their own buildings at the center, AB Farsta Centrum leases other buildings to Martin Olsson, for example; thus the participating companies in AB Farsta Centrum still have part of their investment tied up. While it may not be the best policy for a company like SIAB to have its money in such long-term propositions, Birke says: "You have to take whatever road is possible. If you want to build, you have to accept the disadvantages, though with the help of the banks it's not too inconvenient. . . . SIAB participated in Farsta and other projects in Stockholm because they were attractive. When I say attractive, I am speaking of our chances of getting the contracts. In a small country like Sweden the market is not very big, so any project we have a fair chance of getting is what I call attractive." [50]

Decisions on whether major projects are developed publicly or privately reflect the political climate of the moment, but not absolutely. Private, cooperative, and public organizations are all kept occupied, though to differing degrees, irrespective of which party or coalition is in power. This limited spoils system has made for a generally efficient use of capital.

Birke's company manages to get along and keep occupied no matter who has political power. "Whether the community is run by a Bourgeois Coalition or the Social Democrats usually doesn't make any difference. Those in charge try to do their best for the community, and it's very easy to get along with them." [51]

The simplest form of participation for the builder was to act as a construction contractor to a municipal housing company. Or he could develop residential properties himself, following a city site development plan but providing his own architecture, engineering, and financing.

As has been seen, though, the role of the private builder was an even more flexible one. At times he had to act as architect, engineer, planner, investor, and manager, as well as builder. This was most evident at Farsta Center, where the group of builders engaged in a broad spectrum of functions, ranging from preliminary planning to property development and management. It also included, at least potentially, property ownership and long-term financial commitment, though in most cases the buildings were sold or leased either before or soon after construction.

7
Mass Transit[1]

The decision to build a high-speed mass transit system connecting the western and southern suburbs to downtown Stockholm was vital to the successful development of Vällingby and Farsta. In fact, the system has had considerable influence on all subsequent suburban planning. The project met initial resistance from both technical and political quarters; disagreements arose even among those in favor of the system.[2] Eventual development required various levels of official approval, of course, but perhaps more importantly, it demanded active cooperation among a variety of city offices and departments.

AB Stockholms Spårvägar, the municipally owned transit company, planned, built, and operated Stockholm's transit system, including trolley cars, buses, and the rail rapid transit system.[3] From the city Spårvägar had a concession, for which it paid a nominal fee, to operate on rail rights-of-way and city streets. Its transportation monopoly permit, however, was a concession granted by the office of the governor of Stockholm, which officially determined schedules, fares, and bus stop locations.

The city paid for most of the transit system construction; Spårvägar paid for track, rolling stock, and signaling and station equipment. Spårvägar's technical director, Bror K. G. Hillbom, says that the city paid about half of the capital costs of the subway.[4]

Spårvägar kept itself informed on planning developments and was expected to make suggestions for additional services, at least in matters of surface transit. The city council, too, could suggest service changes and improvements. Hillbom states: "Any councilman can ask the city council to have us investigate a proposal on a matter of simple bus service. Subway questions are more complicated. Subways mean large capital investments, so the entire city government must be involved."[5]

The underground trolley between Skanstull and Slussen had been in operation since 1933, but it was not until 1939 that the central board of administration established a special transit delegation to review and consider route alignments for the transit system through central Stockholm that had been proposed following the submission of the transportation committee's full report in 1934. (For the proposals of the 1930 committee and earlier, see Figs. 7.1–7.5; for a recent plan of the system, see Fig. 7.6.) The delegation, which consisted of commissioners and municipal technical experts, presented its report in 1940. It said, in part: "In view of the anticipated increase in building construction and population, a considerable improvement in suburban transportation is necessary. The lack of a rapid mass transit system will hinder residential development in the outer suburbs. Connecting the transit lines of the southern and western suburbs to central Stockholm by subway will mean fast, convenient transportation between the suburbs and downtown, simplifying and contributing to residential development in the suburbs."[6] (See Figs. 7.7, 7.8.)

On June 16, 1941, the city council decided in principle to build a subway system connecting the southern and western suburbs. The city had originally intended to build the southern branch first; however, technical difficulties at Slussen[7] and the anticipated incorporation of southern Spånga in the west convinced city officials to start with the western branch.

The technical difficulties centered on finding space for a right-of-way between Slussen and Tegelbacken (see Fig. 7.9). The questions were whether or not the railroad line should remain there and, if so, whether the city should also build an expressway parallel to the railroad and transit line. Hillbom recalls:

It took some time before everybody could agree on the subway, the expressway, and the railroad. . . . There were aesthetic, economic, and all sorts of other problems involved. . . . The subway plans were very old; I think they were worked out in the late twenties and early thirties. . . . It was uncertain whether we should have a real subway with long trains and ticket booths or a high-speed streetcar system that would be underground only in the downtown area. The 1941 decision did not determine, for instance, if there should be ticket collectors on each car or only at the station, because all anybody saw were the existing streetcar lines and the Axel Dahlberg plans. . . . Luckily we couldn't start building in 1941 because . . . the war was on and we were short of materials and labor. Between 1941 and 1945 the city developed very rapidly, so when we really started building the subways, we knew we would end up with something quite different from what was decided upon in 1941. . . .

Yngve Larsson was in charge of both city planning and public works; so he had a great deal of power. . . . It was Larsson who proposed these plans. . . . Initiative also came from the real estate department. They had important figures on population. . . . We tried to work together in order to ensure that things would work in practice. For instance, we warned against rushing the development of housing in Vällingby until we had the capacity for it on the subways.

Along with capacity, we needed speed and dependability. Even in those days there were bottlenecks. Car ownership was very low then, but we could see it rising each year. . . . We were lucky to get in before the number of cars began to expand too much. People got used to using the subway from the beginning. . . . The subway, operating on its own right-of-way and separated from other traffic, would be faster and more dependable. Also, the subway would be more economical than surface operations; more speed means lower costs: the number of vehicles in traffic is less. And the subway allows rationalization because you require less operating personnel. A bus must have at least a driver; a train, moving over a thousand people needs only two men, and the ticket selling can be automated.[8]

In view of the large capital outlay and the maintenance costs that a transit system would involve, finance commissioner Zeth Höglund was hesitant about such a move during wartime. He offered instead a modified proposal, shifting some costs to Spårvägar and restricting construction for the time being to Slussen-Tegelbacken and Kristineberg-Fridhemsplan. In this way the suburban transit lines would reach the edges of central Stockholm, but not downtown. The city council, though, voted sixty-one to thirty in favor of extending the line all the way to the city center downtown, where it would connect with the western branch coming in under Sveavägen.

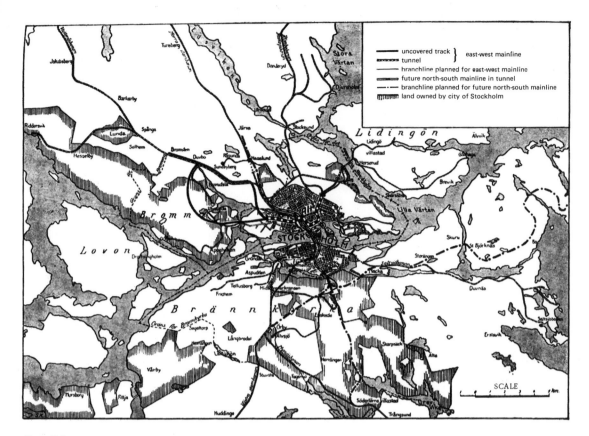

Figure 7.1
Transportation committee proposal for a suburban transit
system, 1910.
Source: Stockholms stadsfullmäktige. *Stadskollegiets
utlåtande och memorial—bihang*, 1934, Nos: 10A, 10B, and
10C. Report of the 1930 Års Trafikkommitté, "Lokaltrafikens
ordnande i Stockholm: Betänkande med förslag" (Stockholm:
Stockholms kommunalförvaltning, 1934), No. 10A, p. 33.

Figure 7.2
Transportation committee proposal for a suburban transit
system, 1921.
  Source: Stockholms stadsfullmäktige. *Stadskollegiets
utlåtande och memorial—bihang*, 1934, Nos. 10A, 10B, and
10C. Report of the 1930 Års Trafikkommitté, "Lokaltrafikens
ordnande i Stockholm: Betänkande med förslag" (Stockholm:
Stockholms kommunalförvaltning, 1934), No. 10A, p. 74.

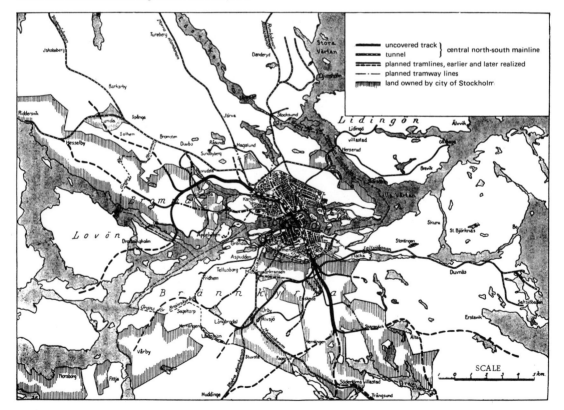

Figure 7.3
Suburban transit system proposed by planning director Albert
Lilienberg in 1928 master plan.
  Source: Stockholms stadsfullmäktige, *Stadskollegiets*
utlåtande och memorial—bihang, 1934, Nos. 10A, 10B, and
10C. Report of the 1930 Års Trafikkommitté, "Lokaltrafikens
ordnande i Stockholm: Betänkande med förslag" (Stockholm:
Stockholms kommunalförvaltning, 1934), No. 10A, p. 88.

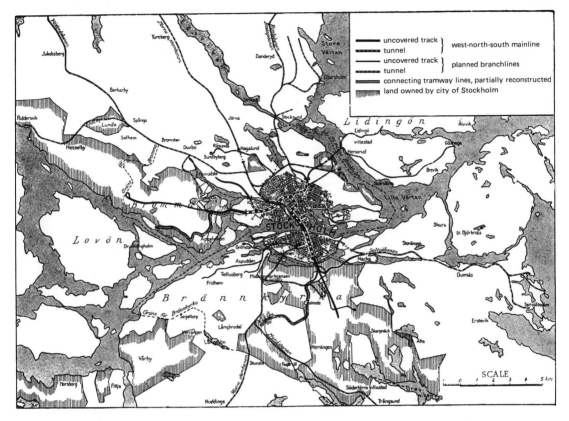

Figure 7.4
Transportation committee proposal for arrangement of local
transportation, 1930. General map indicating combination of
Bromma and Skanstull lines into local line through city center.
 Source: Stockholms stadsfullmäktige, *Stadskollegiets
utlåtande och memorial—bihang*, 1934, Nos. 10A, 10B, and
10C. Report of the 1930 Års Trafikkommitté, "Lokaltrafikens
ordnande i Stockholm: Betänkande med förslag" (Stockholm:
Stockholms kommunalförvaltning, 1934), No. 10B, Plansch
XI.

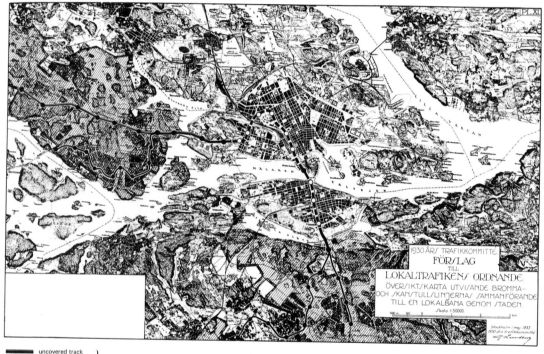

▬▬▬	uncovered track	⎫
▬ ▬ ▬	tunnel	⎬ trunkline, under construction ⎭
▬▬▬	uncovered track	⎫
▬ ▬ ▬	tunnel	⎬ trunkline, proposed ⎭

─────── existing connecting lines, new or partly
      reconstructed sections

▬▬▬▬ new connecting line, under construction

◄●▬ ▬●► stations on uncovered track and in tunnel

▨▨▨▨ land owned by city of Stockholm

Figure 7.5
Transportation committee proposal for arrangement of local
transportation, 1930. General map indicating future development possibilities of local transportation system.
  Source: Stockholms stadsfullmäktige, *Stadskollegiets
utlåtande och memorial—bihang*, 1934, Nos. 10A, 10B, and
10C. Report of the 1930 Års Trafikkommitté, "Lokaltrafikens
ordnande i Stockholm: Betänkande med förslag" (Stockholm:
Stockholms kommunalförvaltning, 1934), No. 10B, Plansch
XII.

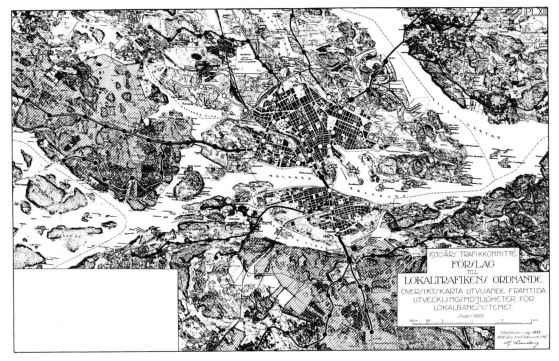

uncovered track ⎫ trunkline, under construction
tunnel   ⎭

uncovered track ⎫ trunkline, proposed
tunnel   ⎭

uncovered track ⎫ existing connecting lines, new or partly
tunnel   ⎭ reconstructed sections

new connecting line, under construction

uncovered track ⎫ new connecting line, suggested alignment
tunnel   ⎭

stations on uncovered track and in tunnel

land owned by city of Stockholm

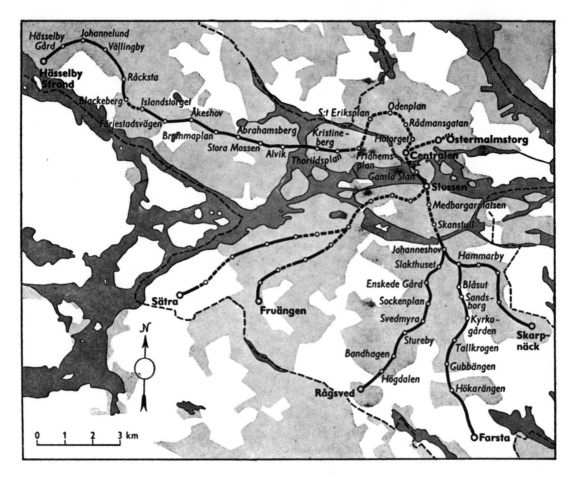

Figure 7.6
Stockholm's planned transit system in 1957; lines built to Hässelby Gård, Högdalen, and Hökarängen. Dotted line indicates tunnel.

Source: Stockholms stads gatunämnd and Aktiebolaget Stockholms Spårvägar, *Tunnelbanan i Stockholm* (Stockholm: Stockholms stads gatunämnd and Aktiebolaget Stockholms Spårvägar, 1957), p. 6.

Figure 7.7
Råcksta–Vällingby transit yard.

Source: Stockholms stads gatunämnd and Aktiebolaget Stockholms Spårvägar, *T-banan i ord och bild* (Stockholm: Stockholms stads gatunämnd and Aktiebolaget Stockholms Spårvägar, 1964), pp. 76–77.

Spårvägar's rolling stock fills a large yard constructed on a level piece of prime land, which a visitor to Vällingby can't miss. Although it was a lovely site, it was almost impossible to use economically for housing because of the subsoil of unstable clay. The car depot and tracks have a low load per square inch. According to an interview on May 4, 1966, with Spårvägar's technical director Bror K. G. Hillbom, "Everybody wants to have good transportation but nobody wants to have a car depot in the vicinity."

Figure 7.8
Transit viaduct at Blackeberg–Råcksta border.

Source: Stockholms stads gatunämnd and Aktiebolaget Stockholms Spårvägar, *T-banan i ord och bild* (Stockholm: Stockholms stads gatunämnd and Aktiebolaget Stockholms Spårvägar, 1964), p. 73.

Figure 7.9
View looking north across Norrström toward Tegelbacken.

Source: Stockholms stads gatunämnd and Aktiebolaget
Stockholms Spårvägar, *T-banan i ord och bild* (Stockholm:
Stockholms stads gatunämnd and Aktiebolaget Stockholms
Spårvägar, 1964), pp. 32–33.

Left to right: new bridge to carry vehicular traffic and railroad main line, existing railroad main line, transit tunnel construction shielding.

The system was to run from the southern suburbs north through the central part of Stockholm from Skanstull to Slussen, on bridges to Tegelbacken, under Sveavägen to Vasastaden and Odenplan, and then out to the Traneberg bridge and the western suburbs. It was originally planned as a single two-track tunnel with seven different branches. In the autumn of 1944, however, Spårvägar proposed building two separate systems, which would be joined between Slussen and the city center; it would have two sets of two tracks each, one above the other. This would accommodate traffic of both systems and do away with the need for the two systems to share trackage at any point.

Spårvägar's former chief engineer, Stig Samuelson (whom Hillbom credits as one of the company's key men in planning the subway system), recalls the situation:

It was decided in autumn 1945 to reserve space for the two undergrounds [subways] between the city and Slussen. Then all plans were geared to that. . . . At first it was not planned as a real underground; it was really a tramway [streetcar] in a tunnel. In 1944 we proposed to make it a real underground, not with 100-meter platforms but with 145-meter platforms. . . . Between 1941 and 1945, we succeeded in convincing people in and around Stockholm that it was necessary to build for three times the capacity that we had planned for in 1939 and 1940. By 1945 it was clear that Stockholm would need a real underground system with no connection with tramways or railways or anything like that—a whole system. We prepared the details for the cars, the signal system, the tracks, and all the different gradients and curves during the war.[9]

Once construction of the system was approved, Spårvägar seldom failed to get what it wanted. Hillbom states:

Most of the time, of course, there was good cooperation. Once the town planning authorities knew what we needed, there was very seldom any difficulty. . . . However, at Grimsta we found the walking distance between the housing area and the subway station a little too far. And as we didn't want to put in a bus line if it wouldn't get much use, Grimsta still

does not have bus service, and people have to walk about 900 meters. . . . Then we had this hilly area in Farsta Strand, which is rather densely populated. Now we must operate a bus line to the subway station. It is almost within walking distance, but there are so many families we must have a bus line.[10]

The Farsta subway line was originally planned as far south as Farsta Strand, but the extension was not definitely approved until 1968; it is now under construction.

Stockholm's subways are chiefly cut and cover. The city's geology of unstable clay and solid rock precludes deep-level tunneling. And as Samuelson puts it: "During the forties we were not as clear as we might have been about the escalators and lifts [elevators], and so on."[11]

The subway system is exceptionally quiet. Steep gradients and short distances between numerous stations require very high acceleration and good braking. The system takes passengers 15 to 20 kilometers from downtown in thirty to thirty-five minutes. Samuelson says: "That distance will comprise Greater Stockholm long into the future. . . . In any case, it would be impossible to reach all people with the underground. . . . For areas beyond 20 kilometers we have the suburban railways."[12]

To go by road from downtown to the southern suburbs requires crossing three bridges, to the western suburbs two bridges. These and the large suburban areas form traffic bottlenecks, and capacity there was the most difficult question. Samuelson continues:

With an underground system without connections to tramways or roadways, people could see at a glance how long a journey would be. By 1944—45 we could foresee severe congestion on the roads, especially at the bridges. . . . Now with the underground system, during the rush hour our two largest bridges, Tranebergsbro and Skanstullsbro, have about 75 percent of their traffic in underground cars and only 25 percent in automobiles. . . . We had made some proposals about that, but people were saying that conditions like those in the United States, with private cars overcrowding all the roads and bridges, would never come to Sweden. But I think we were very lucky to convince people to the contrary. . . .

The main difference between tramways and undergrounds is that the underground train can be 140 meters long and tramway trains could be only three cars long. . . . Also, the tramway lines were on their own tracks but still on the streets, and during—and for a long time after—the war there were many bicycles, scooters, and motorcycles. With the underground we achieved a completely grade-separated system, with safety, capacity, convenience, and speed. . . .

During the 1930s the arrangement was that the town planning department prepared the basic data for the underground; then Spårvägar prepared the details for them. The first system was a tramway system prepared by the town planning group under Yngve Larsson. The proposal to build two underground systems came in October or November of 1944. Mr. Larsson was very angry about that, and we had a lot of very hard discussions. He said that we were responsible for transportation questions and had nothing to do with population plans. But when other departments are not preparing the work as we think necessary, we have to do it ourselves. They were difficult discussions, but eventually Mr. Larsson was very glad that we acted as we did. [13]

At that time Larsson was commissioner of the streets and traffic division, of which Spårvägar was a part. As commissioner, he presided at Spårvägar's board meetings and kept himself fully informed of its doings. He recalled that the plan for the subway was clear even in the thirties. Samuelson, however, disagreed:

No, it wasn't. You see, when I came to the tramway company in 1938, we were calculating different alternatives; one was underground through town but on the surface with level or grade crossings in the suburbs and with conductors in the trains, not at the stations. . . . By 1945 it was quite clear that we must have the stations underground. . . . The lines just inside downtown Stockholm . . . were underground, but it was just a tramway; the platforms were only 100 meters long. . . . And neither the cars, ticketing operation, signal system, curves, nor tunnels were to underground standards, although the tunnel dimensions were quite good in the one existing

tunnel. We had to make only a small alteration to the tunnel under Södermalm. If that's what Mr. Larsson means, then he is quite right. But, you see, he is not talking technically, and he can't on these points. He was not quite clear about that. [14]

When Mr. Larsson learned of the proposal for two underground systems and longer trains that Spårvägar wished the city council to approve, he said that he was especially interested but that it was a problem for his own planners. . . . His planners had proposed one underground with two tracks and seven branches in one tunnel, and it was impossible. . . . We had to work in our own way with each department. The tramway department, the city planning department, the real estate department, and the street department—four different departments—were working with the figures and proposals. We had cooperation, but we also had hard discussions. From my experience, I would say it is very, very difficult—and sometimes dangerous—to have all planning done in one department. There is . . . technical planning, and there is also economic planning. By the time any transport question is put into a real proposal, it is a compromise. It is a compromise between economic, technical, and other questions. And when preparing a compromise proposal, it is necessary to have discussions; and to get discussions it is necessary for each department to study all the questions from its own point of view. [15]

The transit company's plan of autumn 1944 was accepted. It included a proposal to build two undergrounds and to lengthen the trains and platforms from 100 to 145 meters; it also contained design capacities, service areas, alignments, and projections of demand.

Appendix 1
Vällingby and Farsta Planning Documents

It is not possible to know how independent the administration was in beginning work with a plan, but interview data indicate there were frequent verbal contacts between the planning commissioner and leading employees of the city planning office. Further, the master plans ought to have given the administration guidance in the timing and direction of the detailed physical planning of an area.

The information in this appendix is taken from document files of the city. Not all the essential papers concerning a plan may appear in this record, and the time schedule may therefore be incomplete. However, the major features in the process of preparing development documents, described earlier, emerges clearly in each case.

The four planning cases studies are the Södra Spånga master plan, the Vällingby Center site development plan, the Farsta master plan, and the Farsta Center site development plan. The intention here is not to make a complete study of all the plan proposals for these areas from 1940 to the mid-1960s but to record some of the changes made in each area during the essential years of its planning. Site development plans, particularly for Vällingby Center, were greatly modified many times. The material includes identification of the plan with date of preparation and major features; and tables of the plans with commentary on the plan proposals, identification of the plan, the date of consideration, the name of the considering body, and a description of the consideration. The following code is used to identify the documents under consideration:

S—site development plan
Sf—site development plan (suburb)
G—master plan
Pl—preliminary plan
S 5 or G 5—map (the numeral indicating the size)
S 5:193—the group of figures following the colon indicates the order of the maps as they came from the city planning office

Vällingby Development Area

Master Plan Proposals for Södra Spånga[1]

The 1946 Plan   The proposal dated February 20, 1946, was prepared by the city planning office. The essential feature of the 1946 plan was the grouping of residential development around three centers: Blackeberg; Råcksta; and Loviselund, the common name of an area in the neighborhood of Hässelby Gård. By the time planning for this area was completed, only the name of Hässelby Gård remained. These areas would be served by tramline number 11, the Ängbybanan, which would continue to Hässelby Villastad and the industrial area at Riddersvik, southeast to Lövsta. The area between Råcksta and the Stockholm-Västerås railroad line would be served by an extension of a projected Odenplan-Sundbyberg transit line with stations at Flysta, Nälsta, and Vinsta.

Another of the populated areas would be situated southeast of Hässelby Slott. The area would include a hospital and other treatment centers. In the 1946 proposal two locations were chosen for high schools, one southwest of Hässelby Slott (which would become a cultural center) and another at Blackeberg Center. At Johannelund two industrial areas were proposed. Most of Grimsta Wood was reserved for recreation. However, the northeast corner of Grimsta was planned as a cemetery. The 1946 plan proposed the population and type of dwelling units found in Table A1.1.

Layout Plan for Spånga and Hässelby, February 25, 1948[2]   The 1948 proposal retained the three centers proposed in 1946, adding no others. The tramway alignment was altered somewhat, with Blackeberg station moved south. (The 1946 plan had located a maintenance yard for transit cars at Råcksta; the 1948 plan calls that area Vällingby.) The maintenance yard was relocated to an area between Råcksta and Vällingby stations. The major alignment of the tramway line was unchanged, and the stations at Hässelby Villastad and Riddersvik remained.

The direction of the transit line from Sundby-berg was altered. Stations were proposed at Spånga and Bromsten; the line would run parallel to the Stockholm-Västerås railroad. West of Spånga station the line would cross the Västerås railroad and run parallel to the railroad branch line to Lövsta. A large area north and northwest of Vällingby would be served by buses. As a result of the relocation of the Blackeberg tram station, most people within the plan area would live near it. (The 1946 plan proposal put about 4,600 Blackeberg residents at a considerable distance from the tram station.) In order to increase the number of people living south of Vällingby station, a portion of the main highway, Bergslagsvägen, was moved further south.

The location of certain social welfare institutions was changed, and new institutions were proposed: to the east of Råcksta station, a hospital, an area for a nursing home, and a children's home; at Vällingby station, a home for old people and a nursing home. (Earlier these had been planned for the northern portion of the Beckomberga hospital area.)

As a result of a municipal report concerning Stockholm's families,[3] the planning office proposed an increase in the proportion of detached and row housing. The number of people to live here is shown on Table A1.2. (Blackeberg is not included in the figures.)

A comparison with the 1946 plan indicates a proposed resident population of 38,900, an increase of 2,300 over the 36,000 proposed for the same area in 1946. The 1948 plan included Blackeberg; with it, the 1948 plan proposed housing 63 percent in apartments against 70 percent in the 1946 plan.

Plan Proposal G 5:18, February 18, 1949   This proposal was a development of the layout plan of 1948, with only minor changes. Site locations for social welfare institutions earlier proposed at Vällingby were slightly modified at the request of the municipal welfare director and the real estate office, and the proposed population of the area was further increased, as shown in Table A1.3 (Blackeberg is not included in the figures.)

Plan Proposal G 5:25, March 16, 1949

Bergslagsvägen, which had earlier been re-aligned to swing farther south of Vällingby, was again straightened out.

Plan Proposal G 5:26, March 16, 1949 More intensive development of Grimsta was now proposed. The cemetery was moved to the southwest of Råcksta marsh and replaced by apartment houses. South of Hässelby Slott the number of single-family homes was increased.

Plan Proposal G 5:31, April 12, 1949 The city planning office proposed that a larger portion of Grimsta be used for detached housing.

Plan Proposal G 5:32, April 12, 1949 Bergslagsvägen retained its original straight alignment. Dwellings were planned south of Bergslagsvägen. A portion of this area had earlier been intended for a cemetery. The cemetery was now moved from Råcksta marsh closer to Råcksta station. See Table A1.4 for a comparison of poulation projections in G 5:31 and G 5:32.

Plan Proposal G 5:50, September 29, 1949 This document shows little change compared with the earlier proposals. The alignment of Bergslagsvägen and tramline number 11 (Ängbybanan) was unchanged. Based upon an anticipated policy decision of the Swedish Railways, the city planning board regarded as sufficient having the last station of the tramline at Loviselund. However, the board did want to reserve an area for the line to the west. For the area between the Västerås railroad and the tramline (Ängbybanan), bus service was proposed. The construction of a line from Odenplan to Sundbyberg and then continuing down to Bromsten and Flysta northeast of Vällingby was still considered a possibility.

No major changes in social welfare institutions were proposed. On the north side of Råcksta and Vällingby a home for old people and a nursing home were suggested. Earlier these institutions had been located nearer Vällingby. The Grimsta area would remain reserved primarily for recreational uses (as in G 5:32).

Even if the planners and the city planning board were in agreement with the idea of having as many employment opportunities as possible, a study of Spånga indicated that the only sure jobs would be at the planned hospitals at Råcksta and Hässelby Slott, the nursing institutions at the boundary with Bromma, and the industrial area at Johannelund. At Lövsta and Vällingby Center, jobs would also be available and the employees could live within the planning area. However, the lack of a railroad made impossible the development of larger industrial areas in Södra Spånga.

See Table A1.5 for population and types of housing projected in the plan.

Plan Proposal G 5:222, March 27, 1952 Some small changes were made. The transit alignment was changed so that past Vällingby it went southward to Lake Mälaren. Two new stations were proposed: Hässelby Strand and Johannelund. The Hässelby Gård and Loviselund stations were moved westward. The planning board approved a suggestion to reserve an area for the transit line between Hässelby Gård and Hässelby Villastad. At this time no decision was made concerning the future of the railroad branch line to Lövsta and its possible use for passenger service.

The plan proposal reserved an area at Hässelby Strand for a combined power and heating plant. As a result of the new alignment of the transit line, more intense development of Hässelby Strand was planned. The loss of a portion of the Grimsta area for housing reduced the number of row houses and detached houses south of Bergslagsvägen (see Table A1.6).

Plan Proposal G 5:232, October 15, 1952 The proposed changes were minor: Hässelby Strand would have 400 inhabitants less than in G 5:222 (see Table A1.7). No other changes were made.

Chronology of the Master Plan for Södra Spånga (Fig. A1.1)

February 4, 1948. In a letter to the planning office, the planning commissioner instructed the planning office to make a preliminary layout plan for the whole of Spånga.

Table A1.1
Population and Housing Types in 1946 Master Plan Proposal

Area	Resident population	Percentage of resident population to live in		
		Apartments	Row housing	Detached housing
Blackeberg	10,000	—[a]	—[a]	—[a]
Råcksta	12,700	66	21	13
Loviselund	14,300	75	14	11
Totals	37,000			

[a]Not included in plan.

Table A1.2
Population and Housing Types in 1948 Master Plan Proposal

Area	Resident population	Percentage of resident population to live in		
		Apartments	Row housing	Detached housing
Vällingby	11,000	56	24	20
Hässelby Slott	6,000	56	44	0
Loviselund	11,900	62	15	23
Totals	29,000	58	24	17

Table A1.3
Population and Housing Types Proposed in Plan G 5:18, February 18, 1949

Area	Resident population	Percentage of resident population to live in		
		Apartments	Row housing	Detached housing
Råcksta	1,700	70	30	0
Vällingby	12,600	54	22	24
Hässelby Gård	6,400	58	42	0
Loviselund	11,300	73	13	14
Totals	32,000	62	23.5	14.5

Table A1.4
Comparison of Population and Housing Types Presented in Plan Proposals G 5:31 and G 5:32

Area	Resident population		G 5:31		
			Percentage of resident population to live in		
	G 5:31	G 5:32	Apartments	Row housing	Detached housing
Råcksta	1,700	1,700	—[a]	—	—
Vällingby	14,600	13,900	—	—	—
Grimsta	3,000	1,200	—	—	—
Hässelby Gård	4,700	4,700	—	—	—
Loviselund	11,000	11,000	—	—	—
Total planning area	35,500	33,000	60	24.5	15.5

[a]Not included in plan.

Table A1.5

Population and Housing Types Proposed in Plan G 5:50, September 29, 1949

Area	Resident population	Percentage of resident population to live in		
		Apartments	Row housing	Detached housing
Råcksta	3,050	mostly	—[a]	—[a]
Vällingby	17,800	66.5	15.2	18.3
Hässelby Gård	5,650	mostly	—[a]	—[a]
Grimsta	3,000	0	100	
Loviselund	12,350	84	16	
Totals	41,850	69.3	17.0	13.7

[a]Not included in plan.

Table A1.6

Population and Housing Types Proposed in Plan G 5:222, March 27, 1952

Area	Resident population	Percentage of resident population to live in		
		Apartments	Row housing	Detached housing
Råcksta	7,225	75.5	11.6	12.9
Vällingby (including part of Nälsta)	12,410	84.9	12.4	2.7
Grimsta (including part of Blackeberg)	3,570	92.8	7.2	0
Johannelund	120	—[a]	—[a]	—[a]
Hässelby Gård	12,950	89.5	10.5	0
Hässelby Strand	7,850	97.1	2.9	0
Total planning area	44,120	87.5	9.4	3.1

[a]Not included in plan.

Table A1.7

Population and Housing Types Proposed in Plan G 5:232, October 15, 1952

Area	Resident population	Percentage of resident population to live in		
		Apartments	Row housing	Detached housing
Råcksta	7,225	75.5	11.6	12.9
Vällingby	12,410	84.9	12.4	2.7
Grimsta	3,570	92.8	7.2	0
Johannelund	120	—[a]	—[a]	—[a]
Hässelby Gård	2,950	89.5	10.5	0
Hässelby Strand	7,450	96.8	7.8	0
Totals	43,725	87.2	9.6	3.2

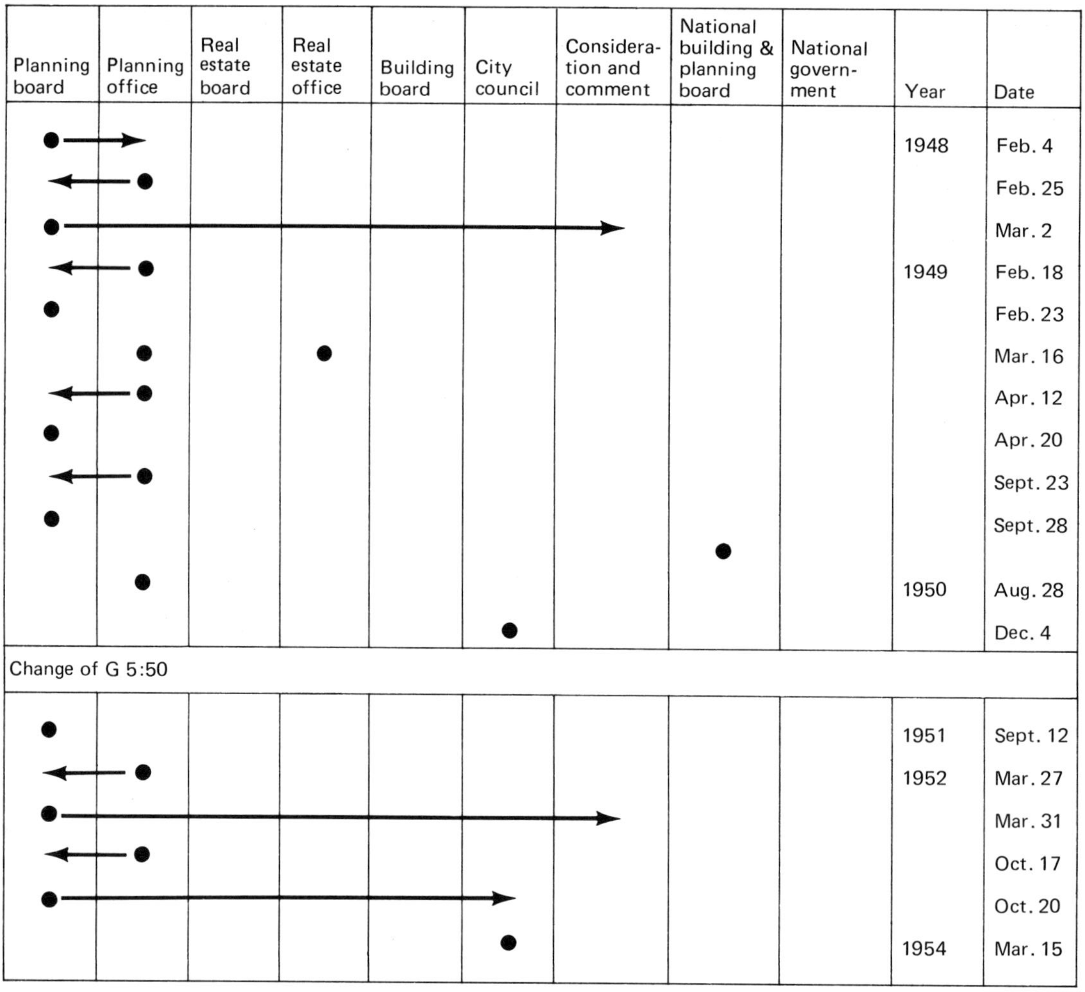

Planning board	Planning office	Real estate board	Real estate office	Building board	City council	Consideration and comment	National building & planning board	National government	Year	Date
● →									1948	Feb. 4
←	●									Feb. 25
● ——————————————————————→										Mar. 2
←	●								1949	Feb. 18
●										Feb. 23
	●		●							Mar. 16
←	●									Apr. 12
●										Apr. 20
←	●									Sept. 23
●							●			Sept. 28
	●								1950	Aug. 28
					●					Dec. 4

Change of G 5:50

Planning board	Planning office	Real estate board	Real estate office	Building board	City council	Consideration and comment	National building & planning board	National government	Year	Date
●									1951	Sept. 12
←	●								1952	Mar. 27
● ——————————————————————→										Mar. 31
←	●									Oct. 17
● ——————————————————→										Oct. 20
					●				1954	Mar. 15

Figure A1.1
A chronology of the master plan for Södra Spånga.

February 25, 1948. Sven Markelius of the planning office sent this plan to the planning board.

March 2, 1948. The layout plan was discussed in the planning board and circulated for consideration and comment.

February 18, 1949. The planning office outlined a proposal for a master plan for the south of Spånga (Map G 5:18). The plan was not intended to be sent to the national government for approval. Only the city council would be asked to accept it. [4]

February 23, 1949. At an ordinary meeting of the planning board, G 5:18 was discussed. [5]

March 16, 1949. At a meeting with the chiefs of the street, planning, and real estate offices, AB Stockholms Spårvägar, and the finance section of the city chancery, there was no approval of the proposal to reserve Grimsta Wood solely for leisure activities. Maps G 5:25 and G 5:26. [6]

April 12, 1949. An official report from the planning office proposed single-family homes for another 2,500 people in part of the Grimsta area. Maps G 5:31 and G 5:32. (Prepared simultaneously, but G 5:32 had less single-family dwelling coverage in Grimsta.) [7]

April 20, 1949. The planning board approved map G 5:32 in principle but did not decide what to do in the Grimsta area. [8]

September 23, 1949. After circulation for consideration and comment of the G 5:32 plan, the planning office concluded that the city administration had no major objections to the essential features of the plan. [9]

September 28, 1949. The planning board approved plan G 5:50 in its essential parts. The national building and planning board accepted the plan but disapproved of any master plan for Södra Spånga being decided upon before plans for the whole of Stockholm and a regional plan for Greater Stockholm had been prepared. [10]

August 28, 1950. In an advisory memorandum to the board of commissioners regarding the master plan for the south of Spånga, Markelius stated that the scope of the regional and master plans were of such a character

that they could not change the Spånga plan in any essential way. The work within the city administration had showed no important alternatives in the planning of Södra Spånga. Planning was increasingly spurred on by the rapidly worsening housing shortage. [11]

December 4, 1950. The planning board decided to change G 5:50, and several alternatives were presented. [12]

March 27, 1952. The planning office proposed a changed and enlarged master plan involving parts of Södra Spånga that were not site development planned; [13] changes of the traffic system at Hässelby Strand were dealt with. As compensation for a green area that would instead be developed at Hässelby Strand, the Grimsta area would have fewer one-family houses. This development resulted in a higher proportion of people living in rental apartments (from 70 percent to 88 percent of the total dwellings): Map G 5:222. [14]

March 31, 1952. The planning board approved G 5:222 and circulated it for consideration and comment.

October 17, 1952. After circulation for consideration and comment minor changes were made, and plan G 5:232 was presented in an official report from Markelius.

October 20, 1952. The planning board approved G 5:232.

March 15, 1954. The city council approved G 5:232.

Site Development Plans for Vällingby Center [15]

Plan S 6:399, November 14, 1950 The planning office proposed 79,700 square meters for Vällingby Center to be above the transit station and distributed as follows: shops—15,400 square meters; public buildings (church, cinema, community hall)—15,100 square meters; offices—33,000 square meters; and handicraft and service—16,200 square meters.

Some residential construction was planned to the northeast and southwest of this area, though most is in other planning areas.

At the north end of the center would be an exit from the transit station leading toward the shops. The tracks would lie immediately to the south of this exit in an open cut through the middle of the center. At the south end of the center plaza would be a large commercial building. On the west side of this building would be the main square. Across the square, facing the commercial building, would be public buildings, such as a church, theater, community hall, cinema, and restaurant. East of the commercial building would be a large number of offices and a street passing through the center. At the southeast part of the center, across the street, would be premises for handicraft activities. To the west of the station would be buildings intended for offices.

Plan Pl 3885, April 6, 1951 Two entrances to the rapid transit station were proposed. The first was unchanged. The second was located northwest of the center, at the northwest end of the station facing the high school.

Shop area was increased at the expense of pedestrian space, though principal features were unchanged. The center area of 98,900 square meters was then allocated as follows: shops—19,750 square meters; public buildings—15,650 square meters; offices—42,500 square meters; and handicraft and workshops—21,000 square meters. Total area had been increased by almost 20,000 square meters.

Plan Pl 3994, March 29, 1952 This plan dealt merely with some minor changes of the streets within the housing area.

Plan Sf 2:23, February 20, 1953 The plan proposed changing the basic structure of the square. Earlier, from southwest to northwest, buildings were placed as follows: theater, community hall, cinema, church, apartment houses. This plan proposed to place the community hall at the southeast part of the plan area and the theater, cinema, church, and a youth center at the north part of the square near the rapid transit station.

Plan Pl 4140, April 10, 1953 No essential changes were made.

Chronology of the Site Development Plan for Vällingby Center (Fig. A1.2)

May 10, 1950. Markelius sent to the directors' conference a memorandum summarizing the premises (shops, social institutions, and public buildings) needed at Vällingby. On the same date the planning board discussed this memorandum and an official report dated April 25, concerning the relationship between housing and employment opportunities in Vällingby.

November 14, 1950. Markelius presented the first plan for Vällingby, map S 6:399, which concentrated the buildings in order to have as many people as possible living in the area. Compared with the master plan, the population had increased to 22,000. The site development plan was to be flexible, allowing changes in the space between buildings. The plan would decide only the principal groupings of activities, the degree of development, and the basic architectural shape. [16]

November 29, 1950. The planning board approved plan S 6:399 and circulated it for consideration and comment. [17]

January 22, 1951. A report on plan S 6:399 was made by the real estate director, Jarl Berg, with the same content as the earlier report from the planning office. [18]

April 6, 1951. After circulation for consideration and comment resulting in minor changes, Markelius described the plan, map Pl 3885. [19]

April 11, 1951. The planning board approved Pl 3885. [20]

May 29, 1951. The real estate board approved all but one block of the plan. Wennström requested cooperation between the planning board and the real estate board in order to achieve the coordinated development of housing and employment opportunities. [21] The plan was exhibited by the building board, June 5 through 18. [22]

June 29, 1951. The city council approved the plan. [23]

October 9, 1951. The national building and planning board approved the plan, with some exceptions.

October 26, 1951. The national government gave partial approval to Pl 3885. [24]

February 13, 1952. The real estate office wrote to the planning office to change part of Pl 3885. [25]

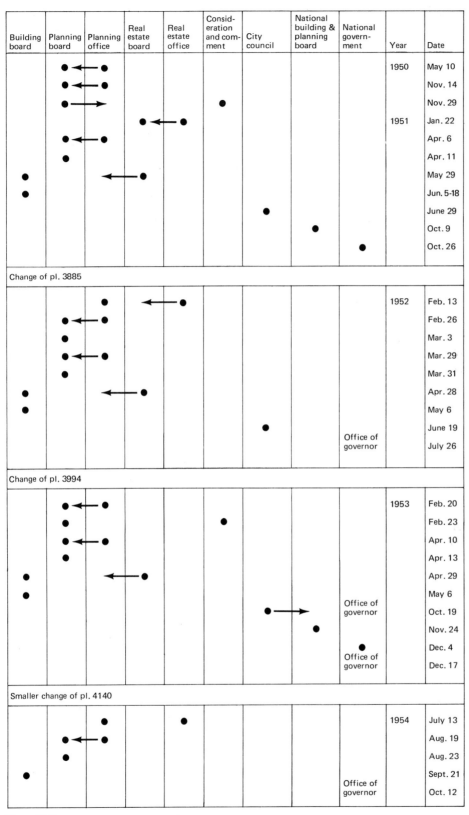

Figure A1.2
A chronology of the site development plan for Vällingby Center.

February 26, 1952. The planning office proposed a minor change in one block, increasing the area for one house.

March 3, 1952. The planning board approved the change.

March 29, 1952. Some minor changes were proposed in Pl 3885 to form plan Pl 3994 from Markelius.

March 31, 1952. The planning board approved Pl 3994 and rescinded the approval of March 3.

April 28, 1952. The real estate board approved Pl 3994, and it was exhibited by the building board, May 26 through June 9.

June 19, 1952. The city council approved Pl 3994.

July 26, 1952. The office of the governor of Stockholm approved Pl 3994.

February 20, 1953. Markelius proposed a change to the plan for some blocks around the Vällingby market plaza: map Sf 2:23. [26]

February 23, 1953. The planning board approved and circulated Sf 2:23 for consideration and comment.

April 10, 1953. After consideration and comment, the planning office presented map Pl 4140.

April 13, 1953. The planning board approved Pl 4140.

April 29, 1953. The real estate board approved the change, which would result in a new grouping of public buildings, earlier situated southwest of the market plaza in Vällingby. The plan was exhibited by the building board, May 27 through June 9.

June 16, 1953. The building board approved Pl 4140.

October 19, 1953. The city council approved Pl 4140 and sent it to the office of the governor of Stockholm.

November 24, 1953. The national building and planning board approved Pl 4140.

December 4, 1953. The national government approved Pl 4140.

December 17, 1953. The office of the governor of Stockholm approved the completed Pl 4140.

July 13, 1954. The real estate office wanted to change Pl 4140.

August 19, 1954. The planning office proposed a change of Pl 4140 in regard to minimum side yards.

August 23, 1954. The planning board approved completed Pl 4140.

September 21, 1954. The building board approved completed Pl 4140.

October 12, 1954. The office of the governor of Stockholm approved the Pl 4140 change.

Consideration and Comments on the Plan Proposals [27]

The document files show a greater number of critiques of master plan proposals than of site development plan proposals, the additional comments coming primarily from authorities engaged in welfare, health, education, and child care. In most cases the critics limited themselves to one or two pages, though the Stockholm Retail Trade Federation and the Stockholm Accounting Office wrote extensive replies. The document files indicate that most commenting authorities had frequent contact with the planning office during preparation of the plan proposals. This was especially true for the important "inner circle" authorities—those of the real estate office, the street office; AB Stockholms Spårvägar (the municipal transit company); the water, electricity, and gas agencies; the fire department; and the finance board's accounting office. Such contact helps to explain why the authorities readily accepted the plan proposal. The main contacts were between the planning office and the real estate and street offices, AB Stockholm Spårvägar, and the water and electric agencies, but during master plan preparation there were other contacts, such as those between the planning office and the health and welfare agencies.

For a master plan intended to be legally recognized and made binding, the 1947 building statute requires a one-month public exhibition by the building board; for a site development plan, a fourteen-day exhibition was specified. [28] Preparation of proposed plan documents was to be a coordinated effort among the various functional agencies of local government—for example, the boards of finance, building, public health, schools, and so on. This was not, however, explicitly required. Neither does the law specifically require circulation for, and reporting on, consideration and comment. However, the routine inclusion of this step is standard practice in Stockholm. It offers an opportunity to coordinate the preparation of planning documents between the various agencies of the city. And, for some agencies, particularly hospitals and education, the consideration and comment procedure was their first chance to say anything about the proposed plan; it might even be the first time they have seen the plan. To these outsiders especially, comments were important. The plan may have overlooked their needs or made them difficult to fulfill.

Södra Spånga   The first time a master plan for Södra Spånga was sent for consideration and comment was in March 1948. Among the considering bodies were the social welfare authorities. The work with this proposal was not strictly formal. The real estate office acted in parallel with the planning office and had contact with representatives of the welfare board, especially the director. Discussion included the location of an intensive-care center. No agreement was reached, and during early stages of the work, the considering bodies held diverging views on the location of public buildings.

The planning office chose to present these differing opinions in a new official report of February 1949, without completing the work of the considering bodies already done. The document files contained no detailed information about these informal contacts. However, there were letters from the authorities on health, welfare, and education questions. A letter from the welfare director showed clearly that he would not change his position.

The new report mentioned plan G 5:18. There appears to have been no consideration and comment step in the development of this plan. Before it was discussed at a meeting with the planning board, it was discussed between the heads of the important administrative bodies—real estate, streets, planning, transit, and the finance department. Discussion included the use of Grimsta Wood, the location of a cemetery, sewage lines, and the need for cost estimates on each of the master plan proposals. This meeting can be considered an informal consideration and comment procedure. The results of these discussions within the administration and the planning board were presented as plans G 5:25 and G 5:26 in March 1949. The document files contain no written consideration-and-comment work for plan G 5:18 with the alternatives G 5:25 and G 5:26.

In April 1949, in an official report, the planning office presented plan maps G 5:31 and G 5:32. While there are changes in plan map G 5:18, there is no statement of what individual authorities proposed or the reactions from the planning office and planning board. These two maps were sent for consideration and comment to the real estate board, the street office, the transit company, the board of sports and outdoor recreation, the director of elementary schools, the welfare board, the youth board, the electric and water agencies, the hospital board, the board of cemeteries, the Stockholm Retail Trade Federation, and the Spånga board. This plan, together with a map, G 2:49, for a special geographical area, was discussed by the planning office and the heads of the welfare and hospital administrations. The planning office followed the requests of these authorities and relocated certain social units from Beckomberga.

In plan G 5:50 some authorities (the electric and water agencies, the welfare board, the board of cemeteries, and the elementary school board) approved the proposal and made no requests for changes. Other authorities requested technical changes. The Stockholm Retail Trade Federation had major objections. The real estate office approved the proposal but added that the question of whether to develop the Grimsta area ought to be decided later. The board of sports and outdoor recreation did not want any residential construction in Grimsta, but the planning office did not change its opinion in the plan proposal G 5:50. However, it accepted objections from the street office, the youth board, the transit company, and the Spånga board. The Stockholm Retail Trade Federation's criticism emphasized the need for more intensive development of commercial facilities at Vällingby Center and for more dwelling units nearby.

In March 1952, plan G 5:222 was sent for consideration and comment. Again, a large number of authorities replied. Acceptance of the proposal came from the water and gas agencies, the director of elementary schools, the accounting office, the superintendent of antiquities, the director of the board of cemeteries, and the transit company.

The planning office seems to have accepted most of the objections from the considering bodies, including those of the board of sports and outdoor recreation. The real estate office had some remarks concerning the location of an athletic field. This proposal was modified through mutual agreement between the office of planning and the office of real estate.

Vällingby Center   The plan proposal that built upon plan S 6:399 was plan Pl 3885. When the latter was presented in an official report from the planning office in April 1951, the commenting bodies had taken up the following subjects for discussion; the water agency —location of a pump station; the fire chief— construction strength of the roof of the subway station; the electricity agency—location for a transformer station; Stockholm Retail Trade Federation—increase in the number of residents within walking distance, definite rather than flexible planning, and a single entrance to the rapid transit station; the gas agency—inclusion of a gas pipe system; the transit company—the transit station building and its function; and the accounting office— increasing the number of customers.

The proposals from the planning office were accepted by the real estate office and the street office. It was primarily the proposals from the Stockholm Retail Trade Federation that were not accepted by the planning office. In the other cases, the planning office usually said that changes had been made; it did not take up minor proposed changes on the comments in its official report.

For plan Pl 3994, changed from Pl 3885, the document files indicated only verbal contact between the planning office and a few municipal authorities—the real estate office, the street office, the transit company, and development companies.

For plan Pl 4140 the document files show the same commenting authorities as Pl 3885. Here, the changes were minor and technical, and there were proposals for changes in land use. The planning office accepted the proposed changes.

Farsta Development Area

Master Plan Proposals for Farsta (and Södertörns Villastad)[29]

Plan Proposal G 5:254, March 4, 1954 The 1952 master plan for Stockholm added two stations to the southern rapid transit line: one at Farsta Center, the other at the Stockholm-Nynäshamn railroad station. The Farsta station would serve 13,500 people, the other, 12,600. AB Stockholms Spårvägar wanted a maintenance yard between these two stations. South of this location an area was reserved for industrial development.

Also included in the plan were a large commercial center at Farsta, a high school in Södertörns Villastad, and a hospital at the northwestern part of Lake Drevviken. Areas were reserved for recreational use between Nynäsvägen and Lake Drevviken, and around Farsta Gård. The plan aligned the rapid transit line to allow for possible extension to Huddinge.

Certain changes were made to plan G 5:254, however. The maintenance yard was moved from Farsta to Högdalen. The planners also moved Farsta station slightly, in the hope of uncovering an area with a radius of 500 meters to develop residentially. They kept in mind, however, the possible extension of the rapid transit to Ågesta, although this question remained a minor one during the development of Farsta. Nynäsvägen and Ågestavägen were planned as major roads for through traffic; Magelungsvägen would be used as a feeder.

An area was reserved for a hospital in the same location as in the 1952 master plan for Stockholm. The high school was moved to the center at Farsta, but no change was made in the areas reserved for recreational activities. Because of the planning for the center, the industrial area was relocated to the southeastern part of the master plan area between Nynäsvägen, the railroad, and Ågestavägen.

Housing was separated into six neighborhood units of 5,000 to 7,000 people each. Apartment houses were concentrated around the center, allowing an increase in the number of row houses and detached houses. Including the dwelling at Södertörns Villastad, there would be 35,000 room units, 77 percent of them in apartment houses, housing 35,000 people. The planners thought that 15,000 to 20,000 people would find employment within the plan area.

The center was planned to serve 65,000 people. There would be a local center between the railroad station and the tentative Ågesta transit station. Five other small centers were planned.

Plan Proposal G 5:272, September 7, 1954 Proposed changes were minor.

Plan proposal G 5:272, April 22, 1955 Certain comments as a result of public exhibition are noted, but no changes were requested by the planning board.

Chronology of the Master Plan for Farsta[30] (see Fig. A1.3)

May 31, 1947. Göran Sidenbladh of the planning office stated in a letter to the real estate office that the master planning committee had drawn up a layout plan for Farsta and that he planned to begin site development plans for this area in the autumn of 1947.

January 1, 1948. In a letter to the planning office,[31] the street office said that the commission from the real estate office for making a topographical and geological report for the purpose of preparing site development plans for Farsta had been completed. Handwritten on the letter was a remark by Sidenbladh stating "we will do nothing until later."

May 12, 1953. A report from the real estate office director, Jarl Berg (a discussion of sites available for housing construction from January 1, 1955, to July 1, 1957), concluded that Farsta ought to be developed. The office wanted the area from Hökarängen to Södertörns Villastad to be planned for development and construction to begin in early 1957 near the railroad station at Södertörn. Later development could come from the north and join with the development in the south.

May 20, 1953. Jarl Berg, in a letter to the planning office, stated that the need for ground reserves required that site development plans

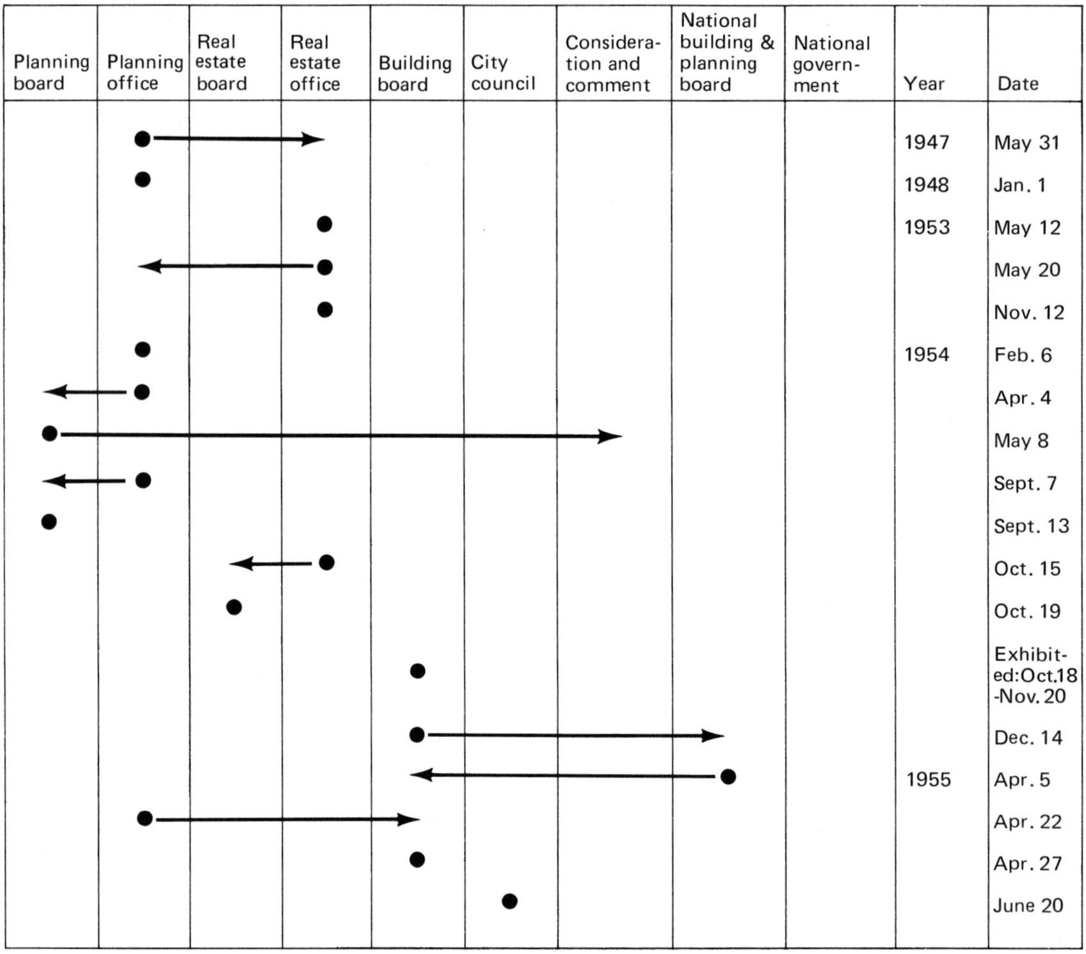

Planning board	Planning office	Real estate board	Real estate office	Building board	City council	Consideration and comment	National building & planning board	National government	Year	Date
	● →								1947	May 31
	●								1948	Jan. 1
			●						1953	May 12
	←		●							May 20
			●							Nov. 12
	●								1954	Feb. 6
←	●									Apr. 4
●						→				May 8
←	●									Sept. 7
●										Sept. 13
		←	●							Oct. 15
		●								Oct. 19
				●						Exhibit-ed:Oct.18 -Nov. 20
				●			→			Dec. 14
				←			●		1955	Apr. 5
	● →									Apr. 22
				●						Apr. 27
					●					June 20

Figure A1.3
A chronology of the master plan for Farsta.

for Farsta be finished by the middle of 1954.

November 12, 1953. In notes from a meeting concerning a layout plan for Farsta, Jarl Berg and Torsten Ljungberger, representing the real estate office, wanted a stronger concentration of dwellings around Farsta Center than at Vällingby. The influence area was smaller, and the real estate office wanted to increase construction of single-family housing. However, the real estate office did not believe it possible to create a large number of employment opportunities at Farsta. They would make an attempt but were pessimistic after the failure at Vällingby. The office also wanted a more intense development of the area between the Farsta rapid transit station and the railroad station; the railroad made a similar request.

February 6, 1954. The planning office prepared a preliminary description of the master plan for Farsta and Södertörns Villastad: map Sf 5:166.[32]

March 4, 1954. A description of a master plan for Farsta, map G 5:254 from Markelius of the planning office, proposed a significant increase in the number of people living near the suburban transit line. This was founded upon experience with Vällingby. Dwellings would be in multistory apartment houses. Of 35,000 units, 77 percent would be in multistory dwellings. In this plan the center was intended to serve areas like Hökarängen and Huddinge. The customer base would be 65,000 persons.

March 8, 1954. The planning board discussed the plan proposal and sent it for consideration and comment.[33]

September 7, 1954. Markelius talked about a new master plan after the consideration and comment procedure, map G 5:272. There were no important changes between G 5:254 and G 5:272.

September 13, 1954. The planning board approved G 5:272.[34]

October 15, 1954. The real estate office approved G 5:272.

October 19, 1954. The real estate board approved G 5:272.

October 18–November 20, 1954. The plan was exhibited by the building board.

December 14, 1954. The building board discussed G 5:272 and sent it without decision to the national planning and building board.

April 5, 1955. The national planning and building board reviewed G 5:272 and requested the city to take more account of the need for industrial areas and improvements in the traffic system. Acceptance of the plan proposal would require some changes, though these could be accomplished informally with the national board.

April 22, 1955. Sidenbladh stated that the changes needed were such that the planning office would take care of them in the site development planning phase of the work.

April 27, 1955. The planning board, which since the first of the year had been merged with the building board, approved G 5:272.

June 20, 1955. The city council approved G 5:272.

Site Development Plans for Farsta[35]

Plan Sf 6:621, March 14, 1956   Approved by the planning board, this plan did not differ materially from the master plan G 5:272 approved by the city council June 20, 1955.

The buildings at the center were bordered at the south by the road, Farstavägen. Farstavägen ran parallel to the Nynäsbanan railroad, 250 meters from it. The center buildings were aligned north-south over the valley, which also runs north-south. The area was between the plan areas Farsta VII on the west and Farsta V on the east.

After the approval of Sf 6:621 in April 1956, the real estate board appointed a five-man development committee for Farsta Center. The committee commissioned architects Backström & Reinius to plan the center. The architects worked with the city administration from the autumn of 1956 to May 1957, when it was proposed that Farstavägen be moved south to within 120 meters of the Nynäsbanan. Buildings that had been south of Farstavägen were now moved to the north side of Farstavägen adjacent to the center.

The "O" Plan, May 13, 1957 This plan was prepared by Backström & Reinius. In addition to realigning Farstavägen, this plan differed in essential features from the planning office's map Sf 6:621. It called for two groups of apartment houses, with three buildings each, one in the north of the planning area and one in the south.

Most of the commercial buildings were now grouped around a rectangular square to the southwest of the entrance to the rapid transit station. A large building, planned for offices, was now placed northwest to southeast near and parallel to the rapid transit line. A community hall, theater, and cinema were located in a building on the southwest edge of the center. A church and a youth center were placed along the pedestrian path leading down to Farstavägen from the south edge of the center. The "O" Plan allocated 17,000 square meters for shops and 36,000 square meters for offices.

Plan S 1:5106/2, November 20, 1957 This plan from the city planning office was a development of the "O" plan, and no essential changes were made.

Plan Pl 5106, April 24, 1958 After receiving comment and opinion on S 1:5106/2, Pl 5106 became the definite proposal. No significant changes were made.

Chronology of the Site Development Plan for Farsta Center[36] (Fig. A1.4)

March 14, 1956. The planning board approved the site development plan of Farsta Center, Sf 6:621. This proposal used map G 5:272, the master plan for Farsta, as a principal source. It was circulated for consideration and comment.

March 24, 1956. The real estate board approved the proposal. At this time five development delegates were chosen for the overall management of the development of Farsta Center.

In autumn 1956, there were contacts among representatives from the real estate, planning, and street offices to expedite street design and engineering without delaying the development of the surrounding areas.

March 22, 1957. In a letter to the planning board from the planning office, Göran Sidenbladh discussed the development of the area around Farsta Center in connection with the Farsta X plan. The surrounding housing areas had to be developed, but it was important that the plans remain flexible.

May 14, 1957. At the direction of the real estate board, the real estate office transmitted to the development delegates a proposal for a site development plan for Farsta Center, the "O" plan. This plan deviated from Sf 6:621, approved by the building board on March 14, 1956. The new plan added two housing clusters around the center, one to the north and one to the south. The groups each consisted of three high-rise apartment buildings. The market plaza had been relocated, and there was more parking area.

August 30, 1957. Backström & Reinius sent a changed location plan for Farsta Center. Parking area was increased.

November 20, 1957. Sidenbladh sent to the planning board a proposal for a new site development plan, S 1:5106/1. It was based upon the proposal from Backström & Reinius, with some minor changes.

December 2, 1957. The planning board approved S 1:5106/1 with minor changes.

December 20, 1957. The development delegates for Farsta approved the plan.

April 22, 1958. The planning board sent the plan to the real estate board.

April 24, 1958. The planning board decided to exhibit the plan.

April 25, 1958. The planning board approved the plan.

May 10, 1958. The real estate board approved the plan.

June 16, 1958. The city council approved the site development plan, Pl 5106 for Farsta Center.

October 7, 1958. The national planning and building board approved the plan.

Differences between Successive Plan Proposals for Vällingby and Farsta

Development of the traffic system in the Vällingby Development Area was based on an initial tramline to be followed by a rapid transit line that would, in time, extend to new stations at Johannelund, Hässelby Gård, and Hässelby Strand. Until the early 1940s planners used as a frame of reference a rapid transit line from Odenplan to Sundbyberg, continuing southwest to the north and northwest portions of Vällingby.

The successive master plan proposals indicate no essential changes to the proposed locations of the various social welfare institutions: a regional hospital at Råcksta and a retirement home and intensive-care home at Råcksta-Vällingby. However, plan proposals that followed repeatedly increased the number of people who would live in the planning area. Along with these increases were proposed changes in land use, particularly in residential density and increases in multi-story apartment dwellings at the expense of single-family homes. After the 1946 master plan proposal, the proportion of apartment units rose with each proposal, until in the mid-1950s some 80 percent of the planned population of the Vällingby Development Area was to be housed in apartments.

From 1946 onward the only large industrial area planned for the Vällingby Development Area was Johannelund. Most of the Grimsta area was reserved for recreational use. Master plan proposal G 5:31, which proposed increased residential development of the southwestern portion of Grimsta, was rejected.

Central features of each new site development plan proposal for Vällingby Center were an increase in the area allocated for shops and offices and a regrouping of public buildings. The buildings were finally clustered together at the northwestern portion of the square, west of the large commercial building.

Successive master plan proposals for Farsta and Södertörns Villastad exhibited few changes. They offer no changes either in the proposed resident population or in the types and proportions of different dwelling units. The proposal for a second rapid transit station for those areas was unfruitful, and only one station was built at Farsta. Within the planning area, intended industrial land use was relocated from the southwestern to the southeastern portion of the area. Except for a hospital, no large social welfare institutions were planned. There was no change in the location of the hospital.

However, successive site development plan proposals for Farsta Center did produce major changes, some of them prepared by Backström & Reinius. The major axis of the center was altered, as was the grouping of the buildings. Later plans grouped commercial buildings and offices around a plaza on a southwest-northeast line. Also, the area allocated for commercial and office use was increased from the first plan.

Acceptance Dates of Site Development Plan Proposals (Table A1.8)

The tabulation of the dates for the acceptance of site development plan proposals by the various local and national organizations reflects the formal structure of the city planning process in Stockholm. For each site development plan proposal, two dates concerning the planning board are usually presented. The first date indicates the initial consideration of the plan proposal at a formal board meeting. However, it does not indicate how long a time was spent developing the plan, nor does it indicate how the proposal was discussed within the administration. The second date indicates the last time a plan was dealt with in the planning board before the usual exhibition by the building board. Dates for exhibition by the building board are recorded in the appropriate column of the table. The dates for consideration of the plan by the building board, the city council, the national planning and building board, and the national government (or the office of the governor of Stockholm) are also presented. Consideration may have meant a decision to accept, recommend, pass, or approve. All dates, except those under "City planning board," indicate either a decision or a receipt of notice of decision at the planning board. All dates are from registers of either the erstwhile planning board or the building board.

Figure A1.4
A chronology of the site development plan for Farsta Center.

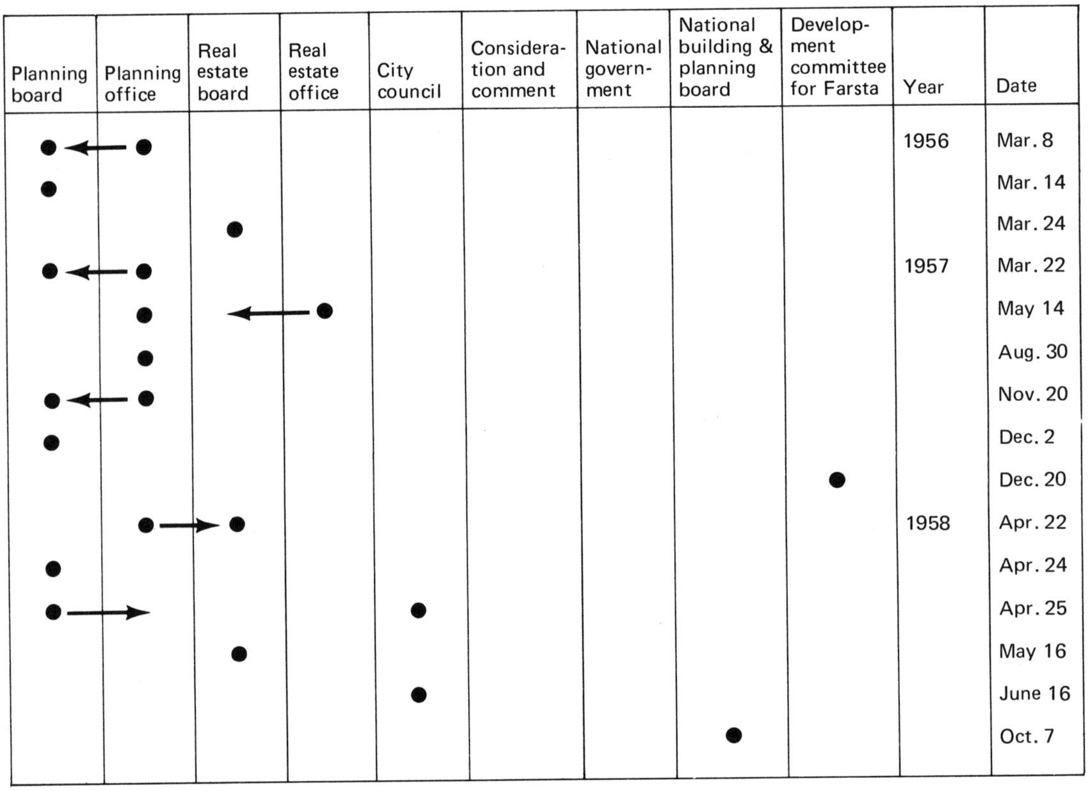

Planning board	Planning office	Real estate board	Real estate office	City council	Considera-tion and comment	National govern-ment	National building & planning board	Develop-ment committee for Farsta	Year	Date
● ←	●								1956	Mar. 8
●										Mar. 14
		●								Mar. 24
● ←	●								1957	Mar. 22
		● ←	●							May 14
	●									Aug. 30
● ←	●									Nov. 20
●										Dec. 2
								●		Dec. 20
	● →	●							1958	Apr. 22
●										Apr. 24
● →										Apr. 25
		●								May 16
				●						June 16
				●						Oct. 7

Table A1.8
Dates for the Acceptance of Site Development Plan Proposals

Plan number	Dates in City planning board	City building board	City council	National building board	National government
Hökarängen					
3121	1944 Sept. 27 1945 Feb. 14	Exhibited: 1945 Mar. 26– Apr. 14	1945 May 23	1945 June 12,	1945 Nov. 23
3145	1944 Dec. 13		1945 Sept. 17	1945 Nov. 6	1945 Nov. 23
3080 D	1944 Oct. 25 1946 Mar. 11		1946 May 20	1946 July 25	1946 July 26
3214	1944 Dec. 13		1946 Jan. 28	1946 Mar. 28	
3650 district center	1949 Mar. 14	Document file lost	1949 June 20		1949 Aug. 19
Gubbängen					
3007 portion I & II	1944 May 10 1944 May 24	Exhibited: 1944 June 10–26	1944 June 19	1944 Sept. 11	1944 Sept. 14
Blackeberg					
3600	1947 Feb. 26 1949 Apr. 13	1948 June 10– 26	1949 June 20	1949 Aug. 9	1949 Aug. 19
3762	1949 Nov. 23 1950 Mar. 22	Exhibited: 1950 Apr. 5–21	1950 Apr. 17	1950 May 23	1950 June 9
Vällingby					
I 3763	1950 Feb. 22 1950 Apr. 12	Exhibited: 1950 Apr. 25– May 8	1950 May 15	1950 Aug. 22	1950 Sept. 1
II = area center					
III 3779	1950 May 10	Exhibited: 1950 June 6–19	1950 June 19	1950 Aug. 22	1950 Sept. 1
IV 3800	1950 June 14 1950 Sept. 19	Exhibited: 1950 Dec. 15–30	1951 Feb. 19	1951 May 2	1951 May 18
V 3874	1951 Mar. 7 1951 Mar. 21	Exhibited: 1951 May 4–17	1951 June 18	1951 Oct. 31	1951 Nov. 10
VI 3868	1950 Nov. 29 1951 Mar. 7	Exhibited: 1951 May 4–17	1951 May 28	1951 July 4	1951 July 20
VII 3932	1951 June 13 1951 Aug. 22	Exhibited: 1951 Oct. 4–17	1951 Oct. 15	1951 Dec. 11	1951 Dec. 28
VIII 3875	1951 Mar. 7 1951 Mar. 21	Exhibited: 1951 May 4–17	1951 June 18	1951 Oct. 31	1951 Nov. 16
Råcksta					
I 3728	1949 Oct. 26 1950 Jan. 11	Exhibited: 1950 Mar. 15–28	1950 Apr. 17	1950 May 23	1950 June 9
II 3771 A	1949 Sept. 14	Exhibited: 1950 Mar. 22– Apr. 4	1950 Apr. 17	1950 June 8	1950 June 9
III 3764	1950 Feb. 22 1950 Apr. 12	Exhibited: 1950 Apr. 25 May 8	1950 May 15	1950 Aug. 22	1950 Sept. 1
IV 3769 I & II	1950 Mar. 2 1950 Apr. 12	Exhibited: 1950 Apr. 22– May 5	1950 May 15	1950 Aug. 22	1950 Sept. 1
V 3773	1950 Apr. 26	Exhibited: 1950 May 16–30	1950 June 19	1950 Aug. 22	1950 Sept. 1

Table A1.8 (continued)

Dates for the Acceptance of Site Development Plan Proposals

Plan number		Dates in City planning board	City building board	City council	National building board	National government
VI	4581		1956 July 18 1956 Nov. 14 Exhibited: 1956 Oct. 19– Nov. 5			
1	3987 B			1957 Jan. 28	1957 Mar. 26	1957 Apr. 5
Johannelund industrial area						
		1951 July 3 1952 Aug. 25	Exhibited: 1952 Sept. 25– Oct. 13	1952 Nov. 17	1953 Feb. 24	1953 Mar. 13
Hässelby Gård						
I & II	4008 A	1952 Mar. 31 1952 May 12		1952 June 19	1952 Sept. 30	1952 Oct. 17
III	4007	1952 Mar. 10 1952 Mar. 31	Exhibited: 1952 May 23– June 5	1952 June 19	1952 Sept. 30	1952 Oct. 17
IV	4063	1952 June 9 1952 Oct. 20	Exhibited: 1953 Jan. 22– Feb. 4	1953 Jan. 26	1953 Apr. 8	1953 Apr. 24
V	4070	1952 Oct. 20	Exhibited: 1952 Dec. 12–29	1953 Jan. 26	1953 Apr. 8	1953 Apr. 24
VI	4090	1952 Oct. 20 1952 Dec. 22	Exhibited: 1953 Feb. 18– Mar. 3	1953 Apr. 20	1953 May 12	1953 May 29
VII	4114	1953 Jan. 12 1953 Feb. 23	Exhibited: 1953 Apr. 1–14	1953 May 26	1953 July 14	1953 July 31
VIII	4255	1954 Mar. 29	Exhibited: 1954 May 29– June 14	1954 June 8	1954 Aug. 31	1954 Sept. 10
IX	4256	1954 Mar. 29	Exhibited 1954 May 24– June 10	1954 June 22	1954 Aug. 31	1954 Sept. 17
Hässelby Strand						
I	4127	1953 Mar. 31	Exhibited: 1953 Apr. 24– May 11	1953 May 26	1953 Nov. 5	1953 Nov. 6
II	4128	1953 Mar. 31	1953 May 11	1953 May 26	1953 Nov. 5	1953 Nov. 6
III	4129	1953 Mar. 31	1953 May 11	1953 May 26	1953 Nov. 5	1953 Nov. 6
IV	4160	1953 June 18	Exhibited: 1953 Aug. 28– Sept. 10	1953 Nov. 16	1954 Jan. 19	1954 Feb. 5
V	4425 B		1955 Sept. 28 1956 Jan. 23 Exhibited: 1956 Jan. 3–16	1956 Mar. 19	1956 May 23	1956 June 1
VI	4360	1954 Nov. 25 1955 Mar. 9	Exhibited: 1955 Feb. 7–21	1955 May 16	1955 Aug. 6	1955 July 15

Grimsta

I						
3948 A/3949 A		1951 June 27 1952 Mar. 31	Exhibited: 1952 May 10–23	1952 June 19	1952 Oct. 7	1952 Oct. 23
II	4563		1956 July 18 1956 Aug. 22 Exhibited: 1956 Sept. 3–20	1956 Sept. 17	1957 Jan. 12	1957 Jan. 18

Farsta

I	4264	1954 Mar. 8	Exhibited: 1954 June 12–22	1954 Oct. 11	1955 Dec. 17	1955 Dec. 28
II area center						
III	4339	1954 Sept. 13 1955 Feb. 19	Exhibited: 1955 Jan. 26– Feb. 12	1955 June 20	1955 Nov. 22	1955 Dec. 9
IV	4311	1954 Sept. 13 1955 Feb. 19	Exhibited: 1955 Jan. 26– Feb. 12	1955 June 20	1955 Dec. 17	1955 Dec. 9
V	4389	1954 Oct. 25 1955 May 26	Exhibited: 1955 May 24– June 10	1955 June 20	1955 Dec. 17	1955 Dec. 9
VI	4346 A	1954 Oct. 25 1955 Nov. 23	Exhibited: 1955 Oct. 15– Nov. 15	1956 Jan. 30	1956 June 20	1956 June 29
VII	4403		1955 Feb. 9 1955 May 26 Exhibited: 1955 May 12–25	1955 Sept. 19	1955 Dec. 17	1955 Dec. 28
VIIIa	5160a		1957 May 24 1957 Nov. 11 Exhibited: 1957 Oct. 23– Nov. 9	1958 Jan. 27	1958 May 29	1958 June 6
IX	4530		1955 Oct. 26 1956 May 23 Exhibited: 1956 May 22– June 4	1956 June 19	1956 Sept. 19	1956 Sept. 21
X	4529		1956 Feb. 22 1956 May 23 Exhibited: 1956 May 22– June 22	1956 June 29	1956 Sept. 19	1956 Sept. 21
XI	5015		1957 May 4 Exhibited: 1957 May 29– June 15	1957 June 3	1957 Oct. 21	1957 Oct. 25
XII	5625		1959 June 26 1960 May 27 Exhibited: 1960 Apr. 19– May 3	1960 June 20	1961 Jan. 30	1961 Mar. 23
XIII	5138		1957 Sept. 13 Exhibited: 1957 Oct. 4– Nov. 4	1957 Oct. 28	1958 Jan. 28	1958 Feb. 7

Table A1.8 (continued)

Dates for the Acceptance of Site Development Plan Proposals

| Plan number | | Dates in | | | | |
		City planning board	City building board	City council	National building board	National government
Farsta Gård						
I	5127		1957 Dec. 13 1958 June 6 Exhibited: 1958 May 12–29	1958 June 17	1958 Dec. 8	1958 Dec. 19
II	5510		1959 Feb. 3 1962 Sept. 21 Exhibited: 1962 Aug. 24– Sept. 14	1962 Oct. 15		Governor's Office 1963 Jan. 3
IV	5401		1958 Sept. 26 1959 Aug. 28 Exhibited: 1959 July 3–17	1959 Oct. 15	1960 Mar. 8	1960 Apr. 8
V	5419		1958 Oct. 31 1959 Aug. 28 Exhibited: 1959 July 24– Aug. 14	1959 Oct. 15	1960 Mar. 10	1960 Apr. 8
Farsta Strand						
III	5365 A		1958 Sept. 26 1965 May 20	1965 June 14	Governor's Office 1965 Aug. 5	1966 Mar. 4

Appendix 2

Measurement Conversions

Money

In recent years, the krona, or Swedish crown, has been officially converted at between 5.14 and 5.21 to the U.S. dollar. For convenience, all figures in the text have been converted at 5 kronor to the dollar.

100 öre = 1 krona

Length and Area

1 foot = 0.30 meters

1 yard = 0.91 meters

1 mile = 1.61 kilometers

1 square foot = 0.09 square meters

1 square yard = 0.84 square meters

1 acre = 43,560 square feet

= 4,840 square yards

= 4,046.9 square meters

= 0.40 hectares

1 square mile = 640 acres

= 2.59 square kilometers

1 meter = 3.28 feet

1 meter = 1.09 yards

1 kilometer = 0.62 miles

1 square meter = 10.76 square feet

1 square meter = 1.20 square yards

1 hectare = 10,000 square meters

= 2.47 acres

1 square kilometer = 0.39 square miles

Notes

Chapter 1

1. Bertil Lennart Hanson, in his monograph *Stockholm Municipal Politics* (Cambridge, Mass.: Joint Center for Urban Studies of the Massachusetts Institute of Technology and Harvard University, 1960), p. 202, writes: "The chief participants [were] all governmental figures and the decisive discussion [took] place within governmental circles. The initiative [did] not fall to lay civic leaders or to spokesmen of commercial or other private interests. The major policy objectives [were] those that [were] seen by the governmental officials." Before, on p. 164, Hanson says: "Let it be quickly admitted that all organizations are not completely powerless all of the time. Some groups do find favorable opportunities to achieve certain limited aims."

2. The following new community objectives, from a study by the Advisory Commission on Intergovernmental Relations on balanced urbanization and new community development, reported in U.S., Congress, *Congressional Record*, 90th Cong., 1st sess., 1967, 113, were realized at Vällingby and Farsta:

a. Dispersal away from overconcentrated urban centers.

b. Regulation of development, allowing planned, staged development of urban growth encouraging desirable cities and towns, based on sound principles of physical planning, using flexible approaches, viewing the total projected city as a whole, and providing for various needs on a rational basis.

c. Assurance of the most economic use of public and private resources for new urban development.

d. Provision for a wide range of single- and multifamily housing in a broad price range.

e. Presentation of the unhampered opportunity for innovation and experimentation.

f. Provision for relatively self-contained social and economic opportunities, within or easily accessible to the community, for a wide range of professional and occupational needs.

g. Provision for housing choices to all groups as a step in overcoming established patterns of segregation.

h. Relieving of pressure on central cities and built-up areas for relocation of opportunities in urban renewal, highway projects, code enforcement, and other displacements.

i. Provision for amenities and desirable residential, work, and recreational opportunities; forestalling of blight and deterioration.

j. Contribution to the sound economic development of the region.

k. Provision of direct economic benefits to the governments involved, such as a diversified tax base and economic provision of public services and facilities.

l. Provision of alternative residential and work opportunities for migration into metropolitan areas.

m. Provision for geographically dispersed alternatives to migration into the largest urban concentrations.

Also, the following organizational procedures came into play in developing Vällingby and Farsta:

a. Public development with an opportunity for participation by a wide range of public and private interests.

b. Responsibility for planning and designing, land development, and regulating of public services.

c. A mix of public and private groups (or private but provided with public funds for research and development) to take responsibility for development. Existing governments would retain more regulatory authority under these arrangements.

3. Carl-Fredrik Ahlberg presents a series of events and concepts culminating in the Vällingby and Farsta type of large-scale development in "Stadsplaneringens nya giv," *Samhällsplanering, Social årsbok 1947*, Centralförbundet för socialt arbete (Stockholm: Kooperativa Förbundets Bokförlag, 1948), pp. 16–24.

4. The *Statistical Yearbook* lists seventeen different types. *Statistical Yearbook of Stockholm 1967* (Stockholm: Stockholm Office of Statistics, 1967), Table 5, p. 5.

5. A city district has the appearance of a planning or development district. Stockholm planners described this as a unit of such size that it could be populated sufficiently to justify serving it with public transportation, a high school, and a district center.

6. For a discussion of the older areas north, west, and east of Vällingby, see Lars Persson, "Kunderna i Vällingby" ("A Shopping Center and Its Customers"), *Stadskollegiets utlåtanden och memorial—bihang* (Stockholm: Stockholms kommunalforvaltning, 1960), 1959, no. 86, pp. 34–38.

7. Information regarding the number of shops in 1957 for city districts in the Vällingby Development Area is from *ibid.*, pp. 27–38.

8. Early planning called for first a hospital, then the administrative offices of the National Post Office Savings Bank on this site.

9. In the Johannelund industrial area, leasehold land is still available for light industrial use, and development continues.

10. This religious institution cares for the sick and aged, and it operates a school that trains missionaries for service within Sweden. It is one of the few private landowners left in the area.

11. The matter of Farsta's terrain should not, however, be taken lightly. As Jan Herbert Martin of the real estate office puts it, "Farsta is such difficult country. We have an industrial estate which resembles Switzerland, with steep hills and narrow valleys. . . . It must be the largest stone quarry in Europe because we've had to pull down hundreds of thousands of cubic meters of mountains to make it possible to build. . . . The good ground went to the government. . . . They are moving the telecommunications administrative offices there, which will employ 4,000 people. What is left . . . has differences in elevation of up to forty meters. I mean it's impossible, it's absolutely impossible." From an interview March 10, 1966, with Jan Herbert Martin.

Chapter 2

1. Folke Lundin, "The Land Policy of the City of Stockholm," mimeographed (Stockholm: Stockholms stadskansli, June 1965), p. 1; and *Statistical Yearbook of Stockholm 1967* (Stockholm: Stockholm Office of Statistics, 1967), p. 229.

2. *Ibid.*, pp. 1–2.

3. *Ibid.*

4. Joakim Garpe, "Stockholm at the Opening of the 1960's," *Stockholm Regional and City Planning* (Stockholm: City Planning Commission, 1964), pp. 31–32.

5. Certain data on leaseholds in this section are from Lundin, "Land Policy," pp. 3–7.

6. *Ibid.* In new areas leasehold fees often are necessarily used to pay some of the costs for areas developed earlier.

7. *Ibid.*, p. 7.

8. Municipal land purchases in Stockholm were begun by conservatives at the beginning of the century. A former city planning administrator tied their motives to emigration and helping the poor:

It all started with emigration. A third of the Swedish people went to live in America. It was a shock seeing tens of thousands going over every year. There was a growing movement to better the conditions for these people. One plan was to give these people small farms, especially in the north, but they couldn't stand the climate and the living conditions, and it was a failure. . . . At that time, there were very few Social Democrats in this country. They had no right to vote, so they couldn't elect anybody to the city council, anyhow. But we had a more or less liberal government here in Stockholm, and they decided to provide cheap dwellings for people with small incomes. . . . And when they started all these garden suburbs, there was very little thought about whether it was socialist or liberal or whatever.

From an interview on March 10, 1966, with Jan Herbert Martin, former secretary of the planning office and later in charge of the industrial section of the real estate office.

9. Ebenezer Howard presented his ideas in *To-morrow: A Peaceful Path to Real Social Reform* (London: Swan Sonnenschein & Co., 1898), which was distributed in a second edition four years later under the new and now better-known title, *Garden Cities of To-morrow* (London: Swan Sonnenschein & Co., 1902), reissued (London: Faber & Faber, 1946), and reissued again in a paperback edition (Cambridge, Mass.: M.I.T. Press, 1965).

10. Examples of areas that later borrowed from the English pattern are Äppelviken, Smedslätten, Ålsten, and Enskede. They are garden cities, however, only superficially, since they lack their own governments, industries, and social and cultural facilities. A more accurate term for them is garden suburbs.

11. Axel Dahlberg, *Cottage Building at Stockholm* (Stockholm: Stockholm stad, 1939), p. 16.

12. *Ibid.*, p. 35.

13. Gunnar Åsvärn and Bertil Mathsson, "Fritid i Förort: Sociologisk undersökning i Årsta 1954–56," *Stadskollegiets utlåtanden och memorial–bihang*, 1958, no. 94 (Stockholm: Stockholms kommunalförvaltning, 1958), p. 13.

14. Åsvärn and Mathsson cite the most influential sources as being Flora and Gordon Stephenson, *Community Centers* (London: Ministry of Education, 1946), and Otto Dannneskiøld-

Samsøe, *Nutida engelsk samhällsplanering* (Stockholm: 1945).

15. Åsvärn and Mathsson cite the most influential sources as being Clarence Perry, *The Neighborhood Unit: A Scheme for Family Living* (New York: 1929); Clarence Perry, *Housing for the Machine Age* (New York: 1939); and Lewis Mumford's *Culture of Cities*, translated into Swedish in the 1940s.

16. Translated from Åsvärn and Mathsson, "Fritid i Förort," p. 25.

17. *Ibid.*

18. For example, the authors suggested that Årsta was perhaps too large (about 30,000 inhabitants) for its inhabitants to consider it a single unit, in the sense implied in neighborhood planning. They also pointed out that there was a much greater need for small meeting rooms for small groups than had been provided at Årsta; also, that future centers would require the services of a full-time professional organizer to organize and publicize the centers' activities. None had been provided at Årsta.

19. Edmund Dahlström, *Trivsel i Söderort, Sociologisk undersökning i Hägerstensåsen och Hökmossen 1949–1950* (Stockholm: Stockholms kommunalförvaltning, 1951), p. 279.

20. These studies include the work of Karsten (1949, 1950, 1952), Pfannenstill (1950), and Lennart Holm (1952, 1955, 1957).

21. Göran Sidenbladh, "Planning Problems in Stockholm," *Stockholm Regional and City Planning* (Stockholm: City Planning Commission, 1964), p. 56; *County of London Plan*, prepared for the LCC by J. H. Forshaw and Patrick Abercrombie (Macmillan, 1943); "Det framtida Stockholm—Riktlinjer för Stockholms generalplan," *Stadskollegiets utlåtanden och memorial—bihang*, 1945, no. 9, pp. 10–14. Hereafter to be cited as *Bihang*.

22. *Bihang*, 1945, no. 9, p. 36. See also Chapter 4 of this text.

Chapter 3

1. Sources include: *Stockholms kommunalkalender*, 1956, 1965, 1966 (Stockholm: Stockholms kommunalförvaltning, 1956, 1965, 1966); Hans Calmfors, *Local Self-Government in Stockholm* (Stockholm; Stadshuset, 1963); T. Grünthal. *Modern kommunalförvaltning*, 2nd ed. rev. (Stockholm: Bonniers, 1965); Per Edvin Sköld, Lars Sköld, and Tage de la Motte, *Kommunalkunskap*, 17th ed. rev. (Stockholm: Tidens Förlag, 1967); *Sveriges kommunallagar 1966* (Stockholm: 1966); Stockholms stads statistika kontor, *Statistisk månadsskrift för Stockholms Stads*, 1966, nos. 9–12; *Stockholms kommunallag*, SFS 1957, no. 50; and Per Langenfelt, *Local Government in Sweden* (Stockholm: The Swedish Institute, 1964). Clarence S. Stein in "Stockholm Builds a New Town," *Planning 1952*, Proceedings of the Annual National Planning Conference, American Society of Planning Officials (Chicago: American Society of Planning Officials, 1952), pp. 56–64, also discusses the organization of Stockholm government. For a discussion of politics in Stockholm, see Bertil Lennart Hanson, *Stockholm Municipal Politics* (Cambridge, Mass.: Joint Center for Urban Studies of the Massachusetts Institute of Technology and Harvard University, 1960).

2. A recent newspaper article (*Dagens Nyheter*, February 22, 1969, p. 7) stresses the power of the board of commissioners. According to a city hall spokesman, the article is based upon two confidential memoranda (PM 10:1968 and PM 1:1969) of a city hall investigation under chief administrative secretary Hans Calmfors and investigation leader Fredrik Sterzel. According to the article, the investigation memoranda conclude that "during the three years examined, 1947, 1957, and 1965, the central board of administration only once voted against a proposal by the board of commissioners." (My translation.) The article concludes that "this demonstrates the commissioners' strong position. It is they who really decide things." (My translation.)

3. While the majority party of the council may nominate all the commissioners, these posts are, in practice, distributed on a proportional basis among the various parties represented.

4. A board is a committee of laymen who meet together at regular intervals to direct the formulation and execution of policy in a given field of government activity. The five to fifteen members of each board are chosen by the city council from among the citizens of Stockholm.

5. Basic sources are Simon Jensfelt, "Lagstiftningen rörande byggnadsväsendet," a reprint from *Bygg* (Stockholm: AB Byggmästarens Förlag, 1962), pp. 3–18; *Svensk författningssamling* (SFS) (Stockholm: P. A. Norstedt & Söners Förlag); A. Bexelius, A. Nordenstam, and N. Aurén, *Byggnadslagstiftningen*, 3rd ed. (Stockholm: P. A. Norstedt & Söners Förlag, 1960); and A. Bexelius, A. Nordenstam, and V. Körlof, *Byggnadslagstiftningen*, 4th ed. rev. (Stockholm: P. A. Norstedt & Söners Förlag, 1964).

6. J. Sigurd Westholm was pensioned in 1940 and replaced by Gunnar Wetterling, who remained until 1955. Josef M. Stäck, a former member of the city planning office, recalls in some detail at least one effect Wetterling had on planning: "There were representatives of different political opinions. . . . I remember that the principle of separated segregated traffic was an idea that the right wing didn't like. They said it was too expensive, . . . used a lot of ground, and it cost a lot of money

to build underpasses and bridges, and, after all, they said, children must learn how to cross the street sooner or later. It's better for them to learn it early in life, or they will be killed later on when they come downtown. . . . The city planning commission was a little more toward the left wing. . . . Wetterling, the city architect, a man of the old school, . . . thought all those ideas like traffic separation were silly." From an interview, May 23, 1966, with Josef M. Stäck, then chief architect, development division, Stockholm City Planning Office.

7. Of the differences in outlook between the planners and the members of the old building board, city planning director Göran Sidenbladh has commented: "In those days . . . the building board didn't actually play a great part. The planning board, the real estate board, and the street board had city commissioners for chairmen, but the law prohibited a city commissioner from automatically being chairman of the building board, which was supposed to have some of the functions of a court. . . . Both [Sven] Markelius and I went there to follow the plans we made, and I remember when the secretary of the building board, who was explaining something, had to raise his voice to make himself heard. . . . So we didn't think very much of the building board in those days." From an interview, May 27, 1966.

8. From an interview, February 20, 1967, with Joakim Garpe.

9. *Stockholm Kommunalkalender*, 1956, p. 178.

10. See Kell Åström, *City Planning in Sweden* (Stockholm: The Swedish Institute, 1967), pp. 60–62; and *Kompendium i stadsbyggnad* (Stockholm: Kungl. Tekniska Hogskolan, Institutionen for arkitektur S, avdelning stadsbyggnad, 1968), pp. h1–h9.

11. Åström, *City Planning*, p. 60.

12. Sidenbladh interview.

13. Stäck interview.

14. Sidenbladh interview.

15. Stäck interview.

16. *Ibid.*

17. *Ibid.*

18. During the development of Vällingby and Farsta and until the 1960s, the National Labor Market Board was under the jurisdiction of the Ministry of Health and Social Affairs. Today, it is under the Ministry of the Interior. The board is represented regionally by county labor boards and locally by labor exchanges, all of which are national government administrators.

19. From an interview in Swedish, May 27, 1966, with labor board director F. Gunnar Karlsson, assistant to the director, Stockholm branch of the National Labor Market Board (1949–1953). (My translation.) Karlsson visited Vällingby together with his chief and the board's civil servants concerned with location questions. They agreed it made sense to tie housing to employment opportunities other than those of a purely service nature for the housing area, places of employment—industrial and handicraft—which would primarily be businesses which relocated from the central business district.

20. From an interview in Swedish, June 7, 1966, with Bengt Svensson, assistant to the director, Stockholm branch of the National Labor Market Board (1946–1953). (My translation.)

21. *Ibid.*

22. *Ibid.*

23. The national authorities determined the investment volume for the entire country, then allocated it to different sectors. One portion went to housing construction, another to industry, and a third to retail trade, and so on. Decisions regarding the local distribution of investments in industry and retail trade during the time of the Vällingby development were made in consultation with industrial and retail trade representative organizations. While new housing construction was allocated on a regional quota basis, other building activities were limited only at the national level.

24. From an interview, March 10, 1966, with Jan Herbert Martin, Stockholm Real Estate Office.

25. From an interview, April 27, 1966, with Professor Carl-Fredrik Ahlberg, director, Greater Stockholm Regional Planning Office, with the Stockholm City Planning Office, 1945–1952. Ahlberg later wrote, "It is correct [to say] that I often deliberated directly with [Helge] Berglund [the commissioner], but it is wrong [to say] that I thereby bypassed or went around [Sven] Markelius." (My translation.) From a letter in Swedish of July 22, 1969, written by Ahlberg.

26. From an interview in Swedish, April 22, 1966, with S. Albert Aronson, chief executive, AB Svenska Bostäder. (My translation.)

27. Of this dual nature of government, Herbert J. Gans observes that "in any heterogeneous community, conflicting demands from the voters force the decision-makers to set up a performing government which observes democratic norms, freeing them to reconcile these conflicts in a backstage actual government. Their decisions . . . are unresponsive to powerless minorities. . . . Local government generally neglects minority demands and rights, and the public interest as well." *The Levittowners* (New York: Pantheon Books, 1967), p. 410.

28. Of this process in Stockholm, B. L. Hanson, in *Stockholm Municipal Politics*, p. 203, says: "The public welfare is, to be sure, invariably discussed in terms of economy and efficiency and contentment. . . . Yet the basic choice is frequently made between Mr. A's plan and Mr. B's plan, and that hanging most clearly and immediately in the balance is not the public welfare but the professional reputations and the chances for promotions of the participating officials. When this happens, it is clear that the considerations made by the officials need not in fact be the same as those that would be made by the affected residents of the city."

29. Basic sources are "Tjänsteutlåtande angående den s.k. Vällingbyprincipens fortsatta tillampning m.m.," Fastighetskontoret, May 9, 1958; letter to Fastighetsnämnden from Fastighetsnämndens delegerade and Bostadsförmedlingsstyrelsens delegerade, April 29, 1958; "PM angående den s.k. Vällingbyprincipens fortsatta tillämpning," Stockholms stads fastighetskontor and Stockholms stads bostadsförmedlingskontor, April 8, 1958; Utdrag av protokoll, *Stockholms stads fastighetsnämnds sammanträde*, "Anmälan av skrivelse från FsN:s och FfS:s gemensamma delegation för prövning av frågan om den s.k. Vällingbyprincipens fortsatta tillämpning," par. 4, April 29, 1958; Utdrag av protokoll, *Stockholms stads fastighetsnämnds sammanträde*, "Fråga om den s.k. Vällingbyprincipens fortsatta användning m.m.," par. 24, May 13, 1958; and an interview, May 24, 1966, with municipal housing exchange director A. Gustav Jonasson.

30. Referred to specifically in a brief for a meeting dated March 20, 1952, to the real estate board's development committee from the real estate office.

31. It has been pointed out by the National Housing Board and others (see, for example, Owe Lundevall, *Swedish Housing Market* [Stockholm: Hyresgästernas Förlags AB, 1957), p. 52) that waiting lists do not accurately reflect the true magnitude of the housing shortage. On the one hand, the lists may be inflated by persons registering with two municipalities, by those who have found accommodation on their own but have not informed the municipal housing exchange, and by those who register many years before they will actually require accommodation. On the other hand, it is certain that many do not bother to register, knowing that a long waiting list is involved, and they either put up with their present overcrowded conditions, or if they are wealthy enough, resort to the generally acknowledged black market in apartments, especially in Stockholm.

32. Many industries did not apply for housing priority quite simply because all housing had already been occupied or otherwise optioned. The suburb does not seem to have achieved such a nondormitory character by that time, however, to justify encouraging commuting. The reasons prepared for discontinuing the Vällingby principle reflect both changing housing conditions and new planning ideas.

33. Martin interview.

34. *Ibid.*

35. *Ibid.*

Chapter 4

1. When the population of Sweden began to increase in the nineteenth century, serious housing and employment problems developed for the new citizens. The easiest outlet for them was emigration; from 1850 to the end of the nineteenth century, almost one million Swedes emigrated, chiefly to the United States. Realization of how many of these were the country's ambitious young people aroused national concern. To stem this outflow, Sweden initiated the "Own Home Movement." It aimed at providing young families with small homesteads, but by the time it was inaugurated, emigration had begun to dwindle for other reasons. See Alva Myrdal, "Developments of Population and Social Reform in Sweden," in *Ten Lectures on Swedish Architecture* (Stockholm: Svenska Arkitekters Riksförbund, 1949), p. 29.

According to Yngve Larsson, "The national 'Own Home' policy—credit policy and the like—aimed at impeding *internal* migration, keeping people in the rural areas. This policy concerned agriculture and was not applicable to Stockholm." Of Stockholm's "Own Home" policy—cheap lots for one's own home—aimed at impeding emigration to America, Larsson says: "This does not correspond to what has been said elsewhere. The city wanted to fight overcrowding with the new garden cities; the emigration had nothing to do with it. The superfluous labor force in the rural areas moved *partly* to the U.S.A., *partly* to the growing cities, especially Stockholm." From a letter in Swedish, October 25, 1969, written by Yngve Larsson. (My translation.)

2. *Stockholm in the Future—Principles of the Outline Plan for Stockholm* (Stockholm: Stockholms stads stadsplanekontor, 1946), pp. 11, 113. Also printed as *Det framtida Stockholm—Riktlinjer för Stockholms generalplan. Stadskollegiets utlåtanden och memorial—bihang*, 1945, no. 9.

3. *Stockholm in the Future*, pp. 14, 113.

4. For a discussion of planning and building the transit system in Stockholm, see Chapter 7. For a short history of early Stockholm traffic studies and proposals for a rapid transit system, see *Tunnelbanan i Stockholm* (Stockholm: Stockholms stads gatunämnd and Aktiebolaget Stockholms Spårvägar, 1957), pp. 7–17.

5. The work of a well-known professor of architecture, Paul Hedqvist. See Yngve Larsson, "Nedre Norrmalm; Historiskt och Ohistoriskt," a reprint from *Samfundet Sankt Eriks· Årsbok för 1960*, pp. 13–14.

6. Bertil Lennart Hanson, *Stockholm Municipal Politics* (Cambridge, Mass.: Joint Center for Urban Studies of the Massachusetts Institute of Technology and Harvard University, 1960), pp. 194–198.

7. *Stockholms stadsfullmäktiges tryckta handlingar, Stadskollegiets utlåtanden och memorial* (Stockholm: Stockholms kommunalförvaltning, 1944), 1944, no. 233. Hereafter to be cited as *Utlåtanden.*

8. *Stockholms stadsfullmäktiges tryckta handlingar, Protokoll jämte yttrande* (Stockholm: Stockholms kommunalförvaltning, 1944), 1944, p. 114. Hereafter to be cited as *Protokoll.*

9. *Stockholms stadsfullmäktiges tryckta handlingar, Stadskollegiets utlåtanden och memorial—bihang* (Stockholm: Stockholms kommunalförvaltning, 1945), 1945, no. 9. Here-

after to be cited as *Bihang*. The report was reprinted in 1946 with English captions and summary.

10. *Stockholm in the Future*, pp. 55–60. In a footnote, attention is called to Erland von Hofsten, *Utredning angående stadsplanen for Gubbängen* (Stockholm: Stockholms stads statistiska kontor, 1944), also published as *Stadskollegiets utlåtanden och memorial—bihang*, 1943, no. 88, where some of the points of view are discussed in greater detail.

11. Incorporation of Södra Spånga, part of the larger area of Spånga, required ratification by the national government and did not come about without a fight, in spite of the fact that Stockholm owned the property. Several years of discussions preceded the event. The county would lose revenue from Södra Spånga if Stockholm incorporated it. Other municipalities that produced county revenue adjoined Spånga. If they could annex it, the county could retain Spånga's revenue potential. The solution in effect balkanized the area. Södra Spånga went to Stockholm; the rest of Spånga was divided and incorporated by the adjoining municipalities.

12. Map G 5:50.

13. *Utlåtanden*, 1950, no. 382.

14. Interview, April 17, 1966, with Carl-Fredrik Ahlberg.

15. *Stockholms stadsfullmäktiges tryckta handlingar, Stockholms stadsfullmäktige—motioner* (Stockholm: Stockholms kommunalförvaltning, 1950), 1950, no. 1. Hereafter to be cited as *Motioner*.

16. Agrenius had to wait until 1952 for a reply to his proposal, though the delay does not appear to be exceptional. A newspaper article (*Dagens Nyheter*, March 26, 1969, p. 10), reporting that city councilman Gunnar Hjerne had to wait eighteen years for a reply to one of his proposals, quoted Hjerne as saying, "Personally, I don't think the divisions ought to sit on proposals indefinitely. A time limit of, say, two years would be desirable." (My translation.)

17. *Utlåtanden*, 1950, no. 382.

18. *Motioner*, 1951, no. 81.

19. In a statement to the city planning board on August 22, 1951, Gunnar Danielson suggests that the municipality had been lax in coordinating the development of housing and employment at Vällingby. "The question is urgent. The current construction goals at Vällingby are in sharp contrast to the intent of earlier planning. Vällingby is supposed to be the first self-sufficient community in the Stockholm area. As I see it, attainment of that goal must not be bungled by wasting more time." (My translation.) Danielson's statement was appended to the city planning board's minutes of August 22, 1951. The board decided that the central board of administration ought to contact the appropriate national government authorities, which together would take the necessary measures to ensure the coordinated construction of housing and employment at Vällingby.

20. *Protokoll*, 1952, pp. 553–555.

21. *Utlåtanden*, 1952, no. 362.

22. *Ibid.*

23. *Ibid.*, no. 179.

24. *Vällingby. Företagens framtidsstad. Skaffa firman luft* (Vällingby. Enterprise's future city. Secure breathing room for your company [My translation.]) (Stockholm: Stockholms stads fastighetsnämnd, 1952); and *Råcksta-Vällingby. Ett arbeta-bo-centrum* (Stockholm: Stockholms stads fastighetsnämnd, 1952).

25. "Fagersjö is one of the most dreadful things I had to survive," says Göran Sidenbladh, Stockholm's planning director. The 200 persons originally living there had been fighting for water and sewage facilities, and long, expensive lines were required to reach the area. From the late 1940s to the early 1960s, the planning office drew up proposals, but none satisfied the finance or real estate departments. Finally, the planning director addressed a meeting of the Fagersjö residents: "'Isn't it better to live in the paradise you have here? Suppose you don't have running water; you still live much better now than you will after this plan goes into effect.' But they insisted. 'We want water and sewers.' And in the end I don't know how many thousands of new people they got on land where before they had picked wild flowers and looked at the birds." From an interview, May 27, 1966, with Göran Sidenbladh, city planning director.

26. In a 1957 interoffice memorandum to the building board, the city planning director emphasized the urgency of continuing residential development around the Farsta Center site, but in such a way as not to restrict possible changes in the plans for the center. See *Tjänstememorial angående förslag till ändring och utvidgning av stadsplanen för kv. Luro m.m. (Farsta X) i Farsta. Pl. 5044*, March 22, 1957.

Chapter 5

1. *Swedish Shopping Centres*, 2nd ed. (Stockholm: Stockholm Chamber of Commerce, 1965), p. 18.

2. *Ibid.*, p. 12; Göran Sidenbladh, "Planning Problems in Stockholm," *Stockholm Regional and City Planning* (Stockholm: City Planning Commission, 1964), p. 59; and Per Holmgren, "Integration of Public Transport with Urban Development," paper presented to the Town and Country Planning Summer School, Sept. 16, 1965, St. Andrews, Scotland, p. 5.

3. For example, Hässelby Gård, constructed in 1955 to serve some 15,000 people, was provided with 120 parking spaces, whereas Hagsätra, constructed in 1960 and serving about the same number of people, was provided with 225. See A. Scarlat, *The Development of Shopping Centers in the Stockholm Area* (Stockholm: The Swedish Institute, 1963), p. 7.

4. Lars Persson, "Kunderna i Vällingby" ["A Shopping Center and Its Customers"], *Stadskollegiets utlåtanden och memorial —bihang* (Stockholm: Stockholms kommunalförvaltning, 1960), 1959, no. 86, pp. 368–369.

5. Respondents agreed that political preference guided housing construction. Bertil Lennart Hanson, *Stockholm Municipal Politics* (Cambridge, Mass.: Joint Center for Urban Studies of the Massachusetts Institute of Technology and Harvard University, 1960), p. 142, for example, says that "bourgeois leaders have always preferred to let the major share of public housing contracts fall to private builders, while the social democrats have preferred to let the major share fall to public and co-operative construction companies; the actual division of contracts has, for three decades, been made according to a quota system based upon the division of seats between the socialist and bourgeois parties in the city council."

6. The Bourgeois Majority had been in power since 1950 (see Table 3.1), and would probably have preferred Vällingby too, to have been developed privately. Vällingby, however, was already well under way as a public project when the Liberal-Conservative coalition gained power. To be sure, there were instances of private organizations' expressing a desire to participate in the Vällingby project. Gösta Bohman, representing the city planning committee of the Stockholm Retail Trade Federation, strongly suggested to the city planning office that the construction of Vällingby Center be shared by private as well as public building organizations. From a letter of April 29, 1950, from Gösta Bohman to the city planning office, mimeographed, p. 9.

Municipal records offer no indication that the city ever invited proposals from the private sector, but it was well known at the time that private organizations were quite unwilling to underwrite a financial experiment of the Vällingby magnitude. Nor did the city advertise for bids for Farsta. The scope of both projects was unusual and not covered by regulations concerning the solicitation of bids. It is likely that the three expressions of interest which were received April 6, 17, and 19, 1956, by the real estate director were solicited, if at all, very informally.

Public advertisements soliciting bids for Vällingby Center and Farsta Center would probably have required at least some initiative by the real estate director and the real estate commissioner. Political affiliations make it unlikely that either the commissioner during the early Vällingby years, Set Persson (1946–1950), a Communist, or the Farsta years, Gösta Wennström (1950–1958), a Social Democrat, would have assisted in furthering the interests of private enterprise.

7. From an interview March 21, 1966, with Sten Källenius, director of the Associated General Contractors and House Builders of Sweden.

8. From an interview June 1, 1966, with Bertil Odelfelt, deputy chief general manager of Svenska Handelsbanken.

9. *Ibid.*

10. Källenius interview.

11. Odelfelt interview.

12. Källenius interview.

13. This permission was formalized in an agreement between the city and the company dated October 1956.

14. From an interview March 21, 1966, with Arne T. Bergqvist, manager of AB Farsta Centrum.

15. Källenius interview.

16. Bergqvist interview.

17. Källenius interview.

Chapter 6

1. From an interview June 6, 1966, with Yngve Larsson.

2. Erland von Hofsten, *Utredning angående stadsplan för Gubbangen*, Specialundersökninaar, no. 23 (Stockholm: Stockholms stads statistiska kontor, 1943); also published as *Stadskollegiets utlåtanden och memorial—bihang*, 1943, no. 88.

3. Larsson interview. The consideration of the sociological aspects of city planning during the 1940s is described in Kell Åström's book *City Planning in Sweden* (Stockholm: The Swedish Institute, 1967), pp. 43–46:

Where "sun, light, and air" were the overriding considerations of the thirties, the sociological aspects of planning came to dominate in the forties. These were most notably expounded by Lewis Mumford, whose *The Culture of Cities* came out in a Swedish edition in 1942. His description of life in medieval towns generated renewed interest in urban intimacy, but his chief importance for Sweden was as spokesman for neighborhood planning. The city and its districts were to be divided into well-defined residential areas, each of them sufficiently large to sustain its own small center with room therein for a school, places of assembly, and stores. A small delimited community would enhance the sense of responsibility of its inhabitants and encourage each individual to become a more independent and more active citizen.
However, the original faith lost in conviction during the postwar years. The course of events soon proved the impossibility of leading contemporary mankind back to the village community. It was thought that the housing of people in small, individually comprehensible units would instill group feeling but reality belied the hopes. It was quite plain that economic, social, and technical developments were moving in another direction. In terms of function and environment, however, neighborhood planning acquired great importance.

4. Larsson interview.

5. *Ibid.*

6. *Ibid.*

7. *Ibid.*

8. From an interview April 27, 1966, with the Greater Stockholm Regional Planning Office director, Carl-Fredrik Ahlberg, member of the Stockholm city planning office from 1945 until 1952.

9. From an interview May 5, 1967, with former commissioner Joakim Garpe.

10. Bertil Lennart Hanson, *Stockholm Municipal Politics* (Cambridge, Mass.: Joint Center for Urban Studies of the Massachusetts Institute of Technology and Harvard University, 1960), pp. 198–199, presents this colorful description:

Mr. Dahlberg [had] fought for a certain subway plan in spite of the opposition of his political superior, Commissioner Sandberg. In the years that followed, an extraordinary bitterness grew between these two men. An "interpreter" used to have to sit between them when they rode in the same automobile, and memoranda they exchanged were written in an inflated bureaucratic style that was intentionally offensive. This bad feeling hampered Dahlberg's chances to advance his own ideas. In 1943, the commissioner contrived to have the Real Estate Board renew Mr. Dahlberg's appointment but for a single year in order to impress on him the need to "co-operate more fully" with the board. Mr. Dahlberg took this as a personal affront, which it was. He changed not a bit, and the next year [1944] he lost his appointment.

11. *Ibid.*, p. 199.

12. From an interview, April 29, 1966, with Göran Sidenbladh.

13. Hanson, *Stockholm Municipal Politics*, pp. 200–201.

14. The Dahlberg proposal, catalog indexed, was not available for inspection in the archives either of the city or of the real estate office. In the city archives there is a notation that the report is to be found in a particular document file, but the Dahlberg map is not there and there is no signout card. In the document files of the city archives a signout card is required for "every speck of dust."

15. "P.M. ang. förslag till stadsplan för delar av Råcksta och Vällingby i Spånga." Signed Axel Dahlberg, January 17, 1950. Recorded by Stockholm stads stadsplanenämnd: Ink 17/1 1950, Dnr 1949/330:22.

16. Larsson interview.

17. Ahlberg interview.

18. From an interview in Swedish, May 23, 1966, with Åke Grauers, chief executive, Hyreshus i Stockholm AB (a municipal housing company), formerly real estate office industrial development chief and chief executive, AB Korphoppet (a municipal industrial buildings development-management company).

19. Letter from Sven Markelius, June 24, 1969.

20. From an interview in Swedish, March 29, 1966, with former city planning director, Sven Markelius. Markelius develops this opinion in his article "The Structure of the Town of Stockholm," *Byggmästaren*, 1956, A3, p. 74:

Town Sections, Not "Satellite Towns".—Reference has been made to these new districts as independent communities and they have been inaccurately represented as a kind of satellite town. Publicity in connection with the vast and risky undertaking of the development of Vällingby has, with the essential and desireable aim of stimulating interest, been more popular than precise. We who have had charge of the planning work have, right from the beginning, been quite clear on the subject and have often pointed out that these town sections or suburb groups cannot be expected to function as satellite towns in the proper sense. The distance to the town's main working districts and to the great magnet Stockholm City is far too small.
Many of the things to be found here, the central main thoroughfares with their elements of art exhibitions, theaters, super cinemas, restaurants, and other places of public entertainment will, as in the case of the central cultural institutions, universities, scientific institutions, the big libraries, museums, etc., still be felt to belong to the town as a whole as well as to the region and, to a certain extent, to the whole country. By this very fact we realize that the town in important respects functions as one unit even if it is composed of independent parts.
The independence, the self-support, is a question of contentment, comfort, and rational organization, but it does not mean isolation. The Stockholmer at Vällingby, Hogdalen, or Farsta still remains a Stockholmer as much as the inhabitants of Ostermalm, Södermalm, or Kungsholmen and the quick and comfortable communications make it just as easy for the one as for the other to move about within the big town.

The position that the new suburban communities were not intended to be self-supporting is repeated by Göran Sidenbladh, quoted in Giorgio Gentili, "The Satellite Towns of Stockholm," reprint from *Urbanistica*, no. 24–25, dated Stockholm, February 1960, p. 2: "It has never been the intention [of the department of planning and building control] to make Vällingby and the other suburban groups into actual self-supporting satellite towns." Such statements on the part of the planning department by Markelius and Sidenbladh—indicating that the self-sufficiency of the new suburban communities, particularly with regard to employment opportunities, was unintentional—are somewhat at variance with both the spirit and letter of those remarks made in the city council when the master plan for Södra Spånga was under consideration. The staff statements just quoted serve to reinforce two points concerning the suburban development process: (1) It is extremely difficult for local politicians to come to grips with, guide, and understand the implications of an increasing number of large municipal projects; and (2) guidelines, implementation, and outcome of these municipal projects are often determined and controlled by the city's technical "experts." In spite of what was said in the city council concerning the self-supporting nature of the new suburban communities, Markelius maintains that the original ideas, as expressed in *Det framtida Stockholm*, were never changed.

21. By then Axel Dahlberg had been succeeded as real estate director by Jarl G. Berg, with whom Markelius enjoyed excellent relations. Markelius also states that his relations with Dahlberg were quite satisfactory. Markelius adds that although Dahlberg often tended to have differing points of view on many questions—and was sometimes immovable on them—in many respects Dahlberg was extremely sensible. Opposed to a repetitive development of high-rise apartment houses, he fought for apartments in three-story buildings, sufficiently narrow to provide each dwelling with a double exposure and cross ventilation. (Markelius interview.)

22. As specific examples, Markelius now feels that Vällingby's pedestrian ways, important elements in his traffic system, could have been more attractive and better tied to essential areas. "A pedestrian way should not be just a path, it should be a street." The green spaces containing schools, playgrounds, and recreation areas are too spread out to give the pedestrian way the feeling of activity. Markelius suggests a partial reorientation of the surrounding housing to give the residential façades better contact with the pedestrian ways, green areas, and the clusters of neighborhood shops. Markelius was also not satisfied with the coordination between the architecture and the detailed site planning, but this he attributed to the organizational factor of having each facet of planning in different hands. (Markelius interview.)

23. From an interview in Swedish, April 22, 1966, with S. Albert Aronson, chief executive, AB Svenska Bostäder.

24. Martin interview.

25. Aronson interview.

26. *Ibid*.

27. *Ibid*.

28. *Ibid*.

29. Gösta Brännström is currently chief executive of ICA Restaurant AB and former planning director for the NK-Farsta department store.

30. From an interview, June 4, 1966, with Rudolf Kalderén.

31. From an interview, May 25, 1966, with Gösta Bränström.

32. *Ibid*.

33. *Ibid*.

34. Kalderén interview.

35. *Ibid*.

36. *Ibid*. Kalderén later expanded NK even further. He had the downtown store remodeled and expanded and added a new branch store in the city of Malmö.

37. From an interview May 13, 1966, with Axel Wennerholm, former managing director of the Stockholm Retail Trade Federation. (Although Gösta Bohman made available a number of pertinent documents, the pressure of his duties prevented him from being interviewed. To speak for the activities of the Stockholm Retail Trade Federation during the period under examination, Mr. Wennerholm graciously consented to be interviewed.)

38. See letter of June 1949 from the Stockholm Retail Trade Federation to the city planning office, mimeographed, 6 pp.; and letter of April 29, 1950, from Gösta Bohman to the city planning office, mimeographed, 9 pp. Shortly after the celebration of the second inauguration of Vällingby Center in 1966, Gösta Bohman, in a *Svenska Dagbladet* article, May 5, 1966, p. 5, reviewed the planning for retail trade in Stockholm's new suburban communities, particularly Vällingby:

It may be useful to reexamine the 1948–1950 debate on the planning problems of Stockholm's retail trade—not primarily to verify the foresight of the trade associations but to gain a better understanding of such problems in this field today and in the future.

At that time, the city was in the process of drafting a master plan for the [newly] incorporated [area of Södra] Spånga. Regarding the question of distribution of goods in the city, the trade associations, as it was pointed out in a June 24, 1949, *Dagens Nyheter* editorial, had not yet achieved "the interplay between suburban centers of different sizes and the large downtown business and entertainment centers." In other words, our experience in Stockholm was insufficient to prove which was best: "the solution of the suburban center problem as seen by Stockholm's city planners or the alternative proposed by the Retail Trade Federation at midsummer."

The editorial was a result of a statement in the Stockholm Retail Trade Federation master plan proposal. In this the federation criticized the previous city planning principles, according to which the purchasing needs of the various city districts were to have been satisfied by retailing centers in relatively small residential areas. The federation asserted that up to that time the city had not "in one single area" succeeded in realizing the proposed goals. Even if the then practiced building control had contributed to the poor result—a condition of immediate interest today with a corresponding necessity for retail trade to obtain a license for its building activities—planning techniques then in practice were inadequate to solve the distribution problems of the suburban areas.

The federation stated that the center premises had to be attractive and comprehensive from both the consumer's and the retailer's point of view. Among other things this implied extensive centers with a greater range of shops than had been theretofore realized, larger city districts with more concentrated building development around the center, a variety of industries and employment opportunities, social and cultural institutions, and generally a more purposeful building and traffic planning.

The opinions of the federation did not meet with immediate approval from the city authorities. A city planning office memorandum on Vällingby Center estimated—as late as March 1950—that the retail area, including banks, a liquor shop, and a pharmacy would require only 3,300 square meters.

The Stockholm Retail Trade Federation, to support its demands for a large center, countered this with an investigation of its own dealings with the retail trade supply in Norra Spånga [Sundbyberg]. The federation said that the retail area in Vällingby should be no less than that of [the municipality of] Sundbyberg, or roughly 12,000 square meters. In a letter of April 29, 1950, it was reemphasized how urgent it was to make Vällingby a natural center for "the present and future residential and industrial areas in Spånga and neighboring parts of the country." The site development plan should therefore be framed so that the built-up areas could be accommodated to the demands of progress; for this, suitable land areas should be kept in reserve for future development. The federation made a further suggestion—which later became the case—that a special coordinating body should be formed.

The municipal planning authority, followed by the city council, eventually accepted the essential elements of the federation's position, and it can now be seen that the outcome of the "Vällingby experiment" has proved the correctness of that position to an even greater degree than had been foreseen by the retailers. Further, the experience gained concerning the feasibility of relocating specialized downtown retailers has been used in the planning of Farsta . . . among others. [My translation.]

39. See *Generalplan för Stockholm 1952* (Stockholm: Stockholms stads stadsplanekontor, 1952), pp. 199–207.

40. Wennerholm interview. Like Vällingby Center, Farsta Center drained customers from nearby neighborhood shops and neighborhood centers. This conclusion is documented in a report by the Swedish Retail Trade Federation's city planning office, prepared during the summer of 1964. The results show that neighborhood shops and neighborhood centers, depending upon their distance from the center, have lost up to half their total turnover. Some shops as close as four or five hundred meters from the center have closed. See *Undersökning av butikskoncentrationers inverkan på befintliga närhetsbutiker* (Stockholm: Sveriges Köpmannaförbunds stadsplanebyrån, September 5, 1964).

41. Wennerholm interview.

42. From an interview, May 16, 1966, with Bertil Hedin, director of finance and administration at Svenska IBM AB.

43. *Ibid.*

44. Grauers interview.

45. *Ibid.*

46. In 1966, AB Korphoppet was again active as a building company in the southern part of central Stockholm, Södermalm, where it was constructing a building to provide quarters for small businesses in areas of the central city undergoing redevelopment. While Korphoppet's participation was not vital—the businesses could have found other quarters themselves—it made possible a more controlled and more orderly evacuation of buildings slated for demolition.

47. Grauers interview.

48. From an interview May 24, 1966, with Håkan Birke, SIAB director.

49. *Ibid.*

50. *Ibid.*

51. *Ibid.*

Chapter 7

1. For a short history of transit commissions and transit planning, see *Tunnelbanan i Stockholm* (Stockholm: Stockholms stads gatunämnd and Aktiebolaget Stockholms Spårvägar, 1957), pp. 11–17; and *T-banan i ord och bild* (Stockholm: Stockholms stads gatunämnd and Aktiebolaget Stockholms Spårvägar, 1964), pp. 7–10. For a detailed presentation of transit commissions and transit planning up to and including the 1930 Års Trafikkommitté, see Stockholms stadsfullmäktige, *Stadskollegiets utlåtanden och memorial—bihang*, 1934, nos. 10A, 10B, and 10C, *Lokaltrafikens ordnande i Stockholm: Betänkande med förslag*, report of the 1930 Års Trafikkommitté (Stockholm: Stockholms kommunalförvaltning, 1934), Del I, Huvudbetänkande, pp. v–x, 3–89. For a description of the politics and personalities of the 1930s and early 1940s behind the development of the transit system, see Bertil Lennart Hanson, *Stockholm Municipal Politics* (Cambridge, Mass.: The Joint Center for Urban Studies of the Massachusetts Institute of Technology and Harvard University, 1960), pp. 189–194.

2. See Hanson, *Stockholm Municipal Politics*, pp. 189–194; and *Tunnelbanan i Stockholm*, pp. 14–16.

3. Except for a very few privately held shares, Spårvägar was entirely owned by the city of Stockholm. The company operated in the black until about 1946, and since that time its deficit has been covered by the general operating budget of the city. At the beginning of 1967, Spårvägar's relation to the city changed when the company was incorporated into a new body, the Greater Stockholm Traffic Board.

4. From an interview of May 4, 1966, with Bror K. G. Hillbom, then technical director of Spårvägar. Hillbom was head of research and development during the planning of the transit system that connects Farsta and Vällingby with downtown Stockholm.

5. *Ibid.*

6. As quoted in *Tunnelbanan i Stockholm*, p. 15. (My translation.)

7. There were no major technical difficulties involved by the lengthening of the stations, but providing for four subway tracks across and under Söderström and Norrström, as Spårvägar proposed, entailed considerable problems. It appeared impossible to solve this problem within the framework of the railroad station agreement of 1940, which left the main railroad line in its old tunnel. However, by moving the new main line approach to the west of Södergatan, the city planning office, through its chief engineer, Gösta Lundborg, succeeded in achieving a satisfactory solution both from the technical and the economic points of view during the spring of 1945. An agreement to realize the project was reached between the parties during the autumn of 1947. From *The Söderström Bridges* (Stockholm: The Harbor Authority and the Public Works Office of the City of Stockholm, 1960), pp. 12, 14.

8. Hillbom interview.

9. From an interview June 6, 1966, with Stig Samuelson. While at Spårvägar, Samuelson was chief of the development department, which prepared proposals for the development of the rail rapid transit system. He worked closely with Hillbom, who succeeded him when Samuelson left in 1949.

10. Hillbom interview.

11. Samuelson interview.

12. *Ibid.*

13. *Ibid.*

14. *Ibid.* In a recent letter, Yngve Larsson clarified the development of Stockholm's rail rapid transit system. His remarks are lengthy but worth noting in detail:

Since the beginning of the century, the rail rapid transit system was projected, not as a trolley line, but as a local railroad line. The Södertunneln [south tunnel] is part of this system and was, from the beginning, intended for future railroad use. During the 1940s, new estimates of the city's future population and its economic resources required a radical raising of standards of earlier projects: for example, longer platforms and a third rail instead of an overhead wire, making necessary the elimination of level crossings. The true projector of the rail rapid transit system was the chief engineer, Gösta Lundborg, of the city planning office, who is now dead.

Larsson provides greater detail concerning the earlier rapid transit projects:

The Södertunneln of 1931 and the north-south and east-west rapid transit system proposal made by the 1934 traffic committee were for railroad service, not tunnels for trolley cars.

These proposals were, in fact, continuations of earlier projects to relocate the National Railways local traffic from its connecting line to a special north-south local line; there were even earlier projects on an east-west local line (in Kungsgatan) that were supposed to serve the traffic from Djursholm, Sundbyberg, and other communities. These projects were presented as results of governmental investigations and were undoubtedly serious. . . .

The local line question was carried on in a series of governmental and municipal traffic investigations during the 1910s and 1920s. Our proposal for a south tunnel was self-evidently connected to all these earlier investigations. The tunnel was built as the first part of a north-south local line with railroad traffic, though it was clear that it would have to serve as an approach for the trolley lines via Skanstull for a long time. That it was a real railroad tunnel is proved by its section, broader than necessary for trolley cars. It was also meant to be able to incorporate the Saltsjöbanan—undoubtedly an important railroad!—sometime in the future when that line would be relocated from Stadsgården to Skanstull, an idea that was abandoned later.

If I—who was responsible to the city council of 1931 for the "Slussen regulation" as well as the Sodertunneln—had not been able to show that it was technically possible to continue the tunnel northward as a local line, I would have risked not getting a majority for the project.

In the further planning of the rapid transit system during the 1930s, railroad traffic was obviously implied, not trolley cars. It is correct that the standard was lower than what Stockholms Spårvägar—for excellent reasons—demanded later, but it was, nevertheless, up to railroad standard, and the platforms were constructed for a train with six cars, while a trolley has no more than three cars. . . .

One has to remember that in the 1930s we were predicting a considerably smaller future population than what proved to be the case. In 1928, the Stockholm Office of Statistics stated Stockholm's future population to be a maximum of 600,000; in 1939, von Hofsten estimated Greater Stockholm at a maximum of 900,000, give or take 50,000. It wasn't until around 1944 that we got the figure of 1,300,000 estimated by the director of the Swedish National Bank, [Per] Åsbrink, at that time an official of the city accounting office.

We also underestimated the financial resources of the city and its capacity for investments that large. We did not dare define the time for the development and use of the rapid

transit lines—they lay in an indefinite future. Even the basic decision of 1941, which was passed in spite of strong resistance from the politically powerful finance commissioner, was only an approval of the plan in principle—the time of effecting the plan was left open. I would have risked not getting a majority if I had fixed the groundbreaking date at what it really became—1944, when we started work from the west with the enlargement of Drottningholmsvägen from Tranebergsbron to Fridhemsplan.

How fast times were changing appears from the fact that when the public works director and I applied for permission to start this work in 1944 and presented the whole rapid transit project, I met with the well-motivated question: 'Why didn't you begin earlier?''

My honored friend Stig Samuelson, who deserves all the credit for raising the subway standards—longer platforms for eight-car trains, four tracks instead of two over Strömmen, a third rail instead of an overhead powerline—had come to Stockholms Spårvägar only in 1938; from that time Spårvägar showed a new interest in the rapid transit projects. The former chief of Spårvägar, Gösta Hellgren, who left his post in 1940, had, of course, been a member of the earlier delegations, but without really getting involved in the project—I think he considered it a wise tactic to seem uninterested, so that Spårvägar would escape as cheaply as possible when it came to the subway capital account. With a new chief and the 1941 resolution, the costs of the subway fell entirely to the city, and with Samuelson's skillful contributions, the project was considerably improved. We also got a new population forecast and had to take a substantially larger traffic figure into account.

But Stig Samuelson, an excellent engineer, entirely underrates the earlier qualifications of the rail rapid transit system when he calls it a mere trolley-car tunnel. In the interview that has been printed in this study, he mentions that he encountered opposition from my part, that I was even supposed to have suggested that Stockholms Spårvägar should not meddle in population estimates, and so on. I do not recall any problem of that kind, and it would have been stupid if I had said anything to that effect. What appalled me was the demand for four tracks over Söderström, which required both doubling the size of the subway bridge and, even worse, moving the [National Railways] connecting line bridge westward, from Slussen to the extension of Södergatan. So we got a heavy railroad bridge there that we had not foreseen. Söderström and Riddarfjärden have been blighted to a great extent by these operations. Had we known in 1931 what we learned in the 1940s, we would probably have put the subway under Söderström instead of over it. Once the Södertunneln was operating, it was too late to change this; it was essential to the great expansion going on south of Skanstull.

It was probably these consequences of the rail rapid transit system expansion, unfortunate for Stockholm's appearance, that caused my ill humor.

From a letter to me in Swedish, October 25, 1969, from Yngve Larsson. (My translation.)

15. *Ibid.*

Appendix 1

1. Document file 1948, no. 166, Stockholms stads stadsarkiv.

2. *Ibid.*

3. Stockholms stads statistiska kontor, *Statistisk undersökning rörande Stockholmsfamiljer X. Specialundersökningar, 1947, no. 24*; also printed as *Stadskollegiets utlåtanden och memorial—bihang*, 1947, no. 88.

4. Document file 1948, no. 166.

5. Record of the city planning board.

6. Document file 1948, no. 166.

7. *Ibid.*

8. Record of the city planning board.

9. From a description of the master plan for Södra Spånga, text accompanying map G 5:50.

10. Document file 1948, no. 166.

11. *Ibid.*

12. Record of the city planning board.

13. Thus, Blackeberg and most of Vällingby-Råcksta were excluded.

14. Document file 1948, no. 166.

15. Document files 1950, no. 190; 1952, no. 129; and 1953, no. 125, Stockholms stads stadsarkiv.

16. Document file 1950, no. 190.

17. Record of the city planning board.

18. Document file 1950, no. 190.

19. *Ibid.*

20. Record of the city planning board.

21. Document file 1950, no. 190.

22. *Ibid.*

23. *Ibid.*

24. *Ibid.*

25. Data from February 13, 1952, through July 26, 1952, from document file 1952, no. 129.

26. Data from February 20, 1952, through October 12, 1954, from document file 1953, no. 125.

27. From official reports of the plan proposals and the statements of the bodies considering the proposals. Document files 1948, no. 166; 1950, no. 190; 1952, no. 129; and 1953, no. 125.

28. The Building Statute of 1959 [Kungl. Maj:ts Byggnadsstadga den 30 December 1959 (Nr. 612)], chap. 2, par. 17, subsection 1, changed the public exhibition time required to three weeks in both cases.

29. Document file 1947, no. 247, Stockholms stads stadsarkiv.

30. *Ibid.*

31. Letter of January 1, 1948, from the street office to the planning office.

32. Record of the city planning board.

33. *Ibid.*

34. *Ibid.*

35. Document file 1959, no. 5106, Stockholms stads stadsbyggnadskontor.

36. *Ibid.*

Glossary

This glossary, which lists a number of frequently used planning and administrative terms in Swedish and English, is intended as a convenient aid to those using other texts about Swedish planning or investigating the sources cited in the Notes and Selected Bibliography.

The use of words within square brackets depends upon context. Words within parentheses are an alternative translation.

akt	document file
ålderdomshem	retirement home; home for the aged
antaga	adopt
arbetarklassen	working class
Arbetsförmedlingen	Labor Exchange
Arbetslöshetskommittén	Unemployment Committee
Arbetslöshetsnämnden	Unemployment Board
Arbetsmarknadsstyrelsen, Kungl.	National [Swedish] Labor Market Board
arbetsnämnden	labor board
arbetstillstånd	work permit
Arbetsvårdsnämnden	Board for Vocational Training and Rehabilitation
Arkivnämnden	Board of the City's Archives
Barnavårdsnämnden	Children's Welfare Board
Besvärsnämnden	Board of Appeals
betänkande	report, opinion
Biblioteksnämnden	Board of the City's Libraries
bifall	approval, sanction
bihang	appendix
borgarråd	commissioner
borgarrådsberedningen	commissioners' council, board of commissioners
borgerlig	bourgeois; nonsocialist, non-working-class
bostadsområde	residential area
Bostadsstyrelsen, Kungl.	National [Swedish] Housing Board
brandchefen	fire chief
bygga	to build
byggnadsinspektör	building inspector
Byggnadsnämnden	city planning and building control board; building control board
byggnadsplan	(rural) site development plan; literally, building plan
Byggnadsstyrelsen, Kungl.	National [Swedish] Board of Building and Planning
byråingenjör	staff engineer
byteshandel	bartering
centerpartiet	Center Party
Centralstyrelsen för undervisning och vård av psyk. efterblivna	Board for the Mentally Deficient

centrum — commercial, social, and cultural center

city — downtown; CBD

Civilförsvarsnämnden — Civil Defense Board

Delegation för Stor-Stockholmsfrågor — Delegation for Greater Stockholm (Regional) Questions

detaljplanering — detailed planning

direktion — board

Direktion för rätts- och polisväsendet — Legal and Police Board

Direktionen för uppbörds-sverket — City Tax Board

Direktionen över Eastman-institutet — Eastman Institute Board

direktör — director

direktörskonferens — directors' conference

dispositionsplan — layout plan; literally, disposition plan

drabantstad — satellite town

Drätselnämnden — Finance Board

Drätselroteln — Finance Division

Elektricitets- och Vattenverket — (municipal) electricity and water supply agency

exploatering — development

exploateringsdelegerade för Farsta — development committee for Farsta

Familjebidragsnämnden — Board for Family Allowances

Fastighetskontoret — (municipal) real estate office

Fastighetsnämnden — (municipal) real estate board

Fastighetsroteln — Real Estate Division

fastställa — approve, affirm

fattigvård — poor relief

fattigvårdsdirektören — municipal welfare director; director of poor relief

Fattigvårdsnämnden, Fattigvårdsstyrelsen — Board for Poor Relief

finansavdelning — finance section

Flyghamnsstyrelsen — Airport Board

folkpartiet — Liberal Party

Folkskoledirektionen — Elementary School Board

Folktandvårdsstyrelsen — Public Dental Care Board

förort — suburb, suburban community

förortsbana — suburban rail line

förortsutbyggnad — suburban development; suburban expansion

församling — parish

förslag — proposal

förstad — suburban municipality

förtroendeman — fiduciary, delegate, representative

gångstråk, gångväg — footpath; walkway

Gasverket — (municipal) gas supply agency

Gatu- och trafikroteln — Division for Streets and Traffic Services

Gatukontoret — (municipal) street office

Gatunämnden — Board for Streets

generalplan — master plan, general plan

generalplanearbete — general plan work

generalplaneberedningen — master planning committee

grannskapsenhet — neighborhood unit

Hälsovårdsnämnden — Public Health Board

Hamnstyrelsen — Harbor Board

Handels- och Sjöfartsnämn-den — Trade and Shipping Board

handlingar — proceedings, transactions; documents

Hemhjälpsnämnden — Domestic Aid Board

Hemvärnsnämnden — Home Guard Board

högerpartiet — Conservative Party

höghus — high-rise building

huvudväg — major road

hyreshus — (multistory) rental apartments

Hyresnämnderna — Rental Boards

icke antaga — not adopt

Idrotts- och friluftsstyrelsen — Board of Sports and Open-Air Life

Idrottsstyrelsen — Sports Board

Industriroteln — Industrial Division

Industriverksstyrelsen — Water, Gas, and Electricity Board

ingenjör — engineer

Kammarkontoret — Stockholm Accounting Office

kommunallag — municipal law

kommunalt bolag — municipal company

kommunikation — communication, transportation

Kommunikationsdeparte-mentet, Kungl. — [Royal Swedish] Ministry of Communications

kommunistiska partiet — Communist Party

konsortium — consortium, syndicate, association, combine, combination, pool, group, joint venture

Konsum — Co-op

kontor — office

Kristidsnämnden — Crisis Board

krona — crown (money); (cap.) the Swedish state

Kulturroteln — Cultural Division

Kungl. Maj:t — [Swedish] government (administration), the King [in Council], the Crown

kyrkogårdsdirektören	director of the Board of Cemeteries	Rådhusrätten	City (Town; Magistrates') Court
Kyrkogårdsnämnden	Board of Cemeteries	Rätts- och polisdirektionen	Legal and Police Board
län	county	regionplan	regional plan
Landstinget	County Council	remiss	circulation for consideration and comment
Länsskolenämnden	County School Board		
Länsstyrelsen	County Administration	remissinstans	body to which a matter is referred for consideration and comment; considering body
Lärlings- och yrkesskolestyrelsen	Apprentice and Trade School Board		
Löneavtalsnämnden	Municipal Employees Salary Agreement Board	remissvar, remissutlåtande, remissyttrande	a statement (report) of the opinion of a body in a matter submitted to them for consideration
Lönenämnden	Municipal Employees Salary Board	remittera	send for comment
Luftskyddsnämnden	Air-Raid Board	Revisionsutskottet	Revision committee
Magistraten	Stockholm Civic Court	Rikets Allmänna Kartverk	Geographical Survey Office [of Sweden]
Mantalsnämnden	Census-Registration Board	Riksdagen	Riksdag (Swedish Parliament)
matargata	feeder street		
motion	motion, proposal, measure	rotel	division
motionera, göra motioner	make a motion	rumsenhet	room unit
Museinämnden	Board of the City's Museum	sanering	redevelopment
nämnd	board	självförsörjande	self-supporting
Nämnd för medling i hyrestvister	Rental Mediation Board	självständig	independent
		sjukhem	nursing home
Nykterhetsnämnden	Temperance Board	Sjukhusdirektion, Stockholms Stads	Stockholm City Hospitals Directorate
område	area		
ordförande	chairman	sjukvård	medical care
organisationsdirektör	director of organization, responsible for organizational improvement in the Stockholm municipal administration	Sjukvårdsdirektionen	Stockholm (municipal) Hospital System
		Sjukvårdsroteln	Public Health Division
Överförmyndarnämnden	Committee of Chief Guardians	Sjukvårdsstyrelsen	Hospital Board
överingenjör	chief engineer	Skoldirektionen	School Board
översiktsplan	layout plan, disposition plan	Skolöverstyrelsen, Kungl.	National [Swedish] Board of Education
översiktsplanering	comprehensive planning		
Överståthållarämbetet	Office of the Governor of Stockholm	"Skönhetsrådet"	Council for Beautification of the City
överståthållaren	royal governor of Stockholm	Slakthus- och saluhallsstyrelsen	Board of Slaughterhouses and Markets
parkväg	path, park path		
Pensionsnämndens delegerade	Pensions Delegation	småhus	detached single-family dwelling
Personalutbildningsnämnden	Personnel Education Board	smalhus	narrow block (walk-up garden apartments)
Polisnämnden	Police Board		
politiker	politician	småstuga	cottage; detached single-family dwelling
praxis	practice	socialdemokratiska partiet	Social Democratic Party
promemoria	memorandum	Socialdepartementet, Kungl.	[Royal Swedish] Ministry of Health and Social Affairs
protokoll	minutes, protocol, report of the proceedings		
		Socialnämnden	Public Assistance Board
punkthus	point block (tower apartments)	Socialroteln	Social Welfare Division
		sovstad	dormitory suburb
radhus	attached single-family dwelling, row house	Spångarådet	Spånga Board
		Spårvägen	see Stockholms Spårvägar, AB

stadsantikvarien	municipal antiquarian; chief of antiquities
stadsarkitekt	city architect
stadsbyggnad	civic design, urban building, urban design, city planning; literally, town building
stadsbyggnadsdirektör	director of city planning and building control
stadsbyggnadskontor	city planning office, office of planning and building control
Stadsbyggnadsroteln	City Planning (Building) Division
stadscentrum	city center
stadsdel	city district
stadsförnyelse	urban renewal
stadsfullmäktige	city council
stadshuset	city hall
stadsingenjör	city engineer
Stadskansli	City Chancery
stadskärna	urban core
stadskollegiet	Central Board of Administration
stadsmätningsavdelningen	city surveying office
stadsplan	(urban) site development plan, detailed plan; literally, town, city plan
stadsplaneförslag	site plan proposal
stadsplanedirektör	city planning director
stadsplanekontoret	city planning office
stadsplanenämnden	city planning board
stadsplanering	city planning
stadstyp	city type
Statens Järnvägar	National [Swedish] Railways
Statistiska Centralbyrån, Kungl.	[Swedish] Central Bureau of Statistics
Statistiska Kontoret	Office of Statistics
Stockholms Köpmannaförbund	Stockholm Retail Trade Federation
Stockholms Spårvägar, AB	Stockholm Tramways, Inc.
Stor-Stockholmsroteln	Greater Stockholm Division
styrelse	board
Styrelsen för bostadsförmedlingen	Housing Exchange Board
Styrelsen för hyresnämndernas centralkansli	Rent Control Administration
Styrelsen för rättshjälpsanstalt	Legal Aid Board
Sveriges Köpmannaförbund	Swedish Retail Federation
tätort	densely built-up area
Telestyrelsen, Kungl.	[Swedish] Board of Telecommunications
tjänsteman	official, employee
Tjänstenämnden	Board of Municipal Officials
tjänsteutlåtande	official message, official report
tomträttsavgäld	leasehold fee
trafik	traffic
trafikfrågor	traffic questions
Trafik- och Stadsbyggnadsroteln	Traffic and City Planning (Building) Division
träsk	marsh
trivsel	comfort; contentment; well-being
tunnelbana	rail rapid transit line; subway
Tunnelbanedelegerade	Central Board of Administration transit delegation, appointed February 23, 1939, reported September 6, 1940
utlåtande	report, pronouncement
utredning	investigation
utredningsavdelning	research section
Utskänkningskommittén	Liquor License Board
Väg- och Vattenbyggnadsstyrelsen, Kungl.	National [Swedish] Road Board
Valkommittén	Election Committee
valkrets	voting district
Valnämnden	Board of Elections
våningsyta	dwelling unit surface area
vårdanstalt	treatment center; nursing home
vårdhem	nursing home
Vattenfallsstyrelsen, Kungl.	National Power Board [of Sweden]
Vattenverket	(municipal) Water Supply Agency
verkställande direktör	managing director; president; chief executive
villa	detached single-family dwelling
Yrkesskolstyrelsen	Trade School Board
yttrande	remark, statement, opinion, expression, comment, report

Selected Bibliography

The bibliography includes official publications of the city council and the Central Board of Administration. Their published debates and decisions were available at the municipal administration (*Tekniska nämndhuset*) library. In addition, detailed information was found in the records of the real estate office and the city planning office.

The archives of the real estate office provided information from 1935 until the present. Most of this material consisted of reports and letters between municipal offices. Material available included the incorporation of Spånga and the development of Vällingby and Farsta.

To follow the development of a plan proposal, information was available from maps and files in the city planning office and in the city archives. The city archives are the repository for most of the municipality's records, documents, and files. Data from the records of the old city planning board (*stadsplanenämnden*) and city planning office were available from the document files at the city archives.

The city planning board and the building board (*byggnadsnämnden*) were amalgamated in 1955 as a new building board (*byggnadsnämnd*, or board of city planning and building control), and therefore the records of the old city planning board cease after 1954. The records of the building board are available in the archives of the city planning office. All plan maps and accompanying written descriptions from 1955 to the present are on file at the city planning office.

Personal interviews are those referred to in the text. They were in English, except as noted.

Ahlberg, Carl-Fredrik. "Stadsplaneringens nya giv," *Samhällsplanering, Social Årsbok 1947*. Stockholm: Kooperativa Förbundets Bokförlag, 1948.

Ahlberg, Carl-Fredrik. "Småhus i Stor-Stockholmsregionen," *Småhus i grupp*, 1960, pp. 19–26.

Ahlberg, Carl-Fredrik, "Miljömässiga synpunkter på stadsplaneläggningen," *Småhus 1963*, pp. 59–75.

Ahlberg, Carl-Fredrik. *Shopping Centers and Satellite Towns in the Stockholm Region*, Meddelande 4–1965, Kungliga Tekniska Högskolan, Institutionen för stadsbyggnad R. (Lecture at a study conference on Regional Planning and Retailing at the Gottlieb Duttweiler Institute for Economic and Social Studies, Zürich, February 25, 1965.)

Ahlberg, Carl-Fredrik. Director, Greater Stockholm Regional Planning Office; staff member, Stockholm city planning office, 1945–1952. Personal interview, April 27, 1966.

Ahlberg, Carl-Fredrik. "The Regional Plån for the Stockholm Area," UN Department of Economic and Social Affairs, *Planning of Metropolitan Areas and New Towns*, Document No. ST/SOA/65, 1967.

Ahlberg, Carl-Fredrik. Letter in Swedish, July 22, 1969.

Ahlberg, Gösta. *Stockholms befolkningsutveckling efter 1850*. Stockholm: Stockholms kommunalförvaltning, 1958.

Ahlgren, Magnus. "Tunnelbanestationen Vällingby centrum," *Byggmästaren*, 1956, No. A4, pp. 86–88.

Ahlgren, Magnus. "Tunnelbanestationen Vällingby centrum," *Byggmästaren*, 1956, No. A 4, pp. 86–88.

Allen, Muriel I. (ed.). "New Communities: Challenge for Today," an American Institute of Planners Background Paper—No. 2, October 1968.

Allmännyttiga Bostadsföretagen i Stockholm, De. *Kommunalt Bostadsbyggnade i Stockholm*. Stockholm: De Allmännyttiga Bostadsföretagen i Stockholm, 1966.

Altshuler, Alan. *The City Planning Process*. Ithaca, N.Y.: Cornell University Press, 1965.

Aronson, S. Albert. "Vällingby Centrum—från idé till verklighet," *Byggmästaren* 1956, No. A4, pp. 77–79.

Aronson, S. Albert. "Centrum," *Byggform*, 1963, No. 7. pp. 9–15.

Aronson, S. Albert. Chief executive, AB Svenska Bostäder. Personal interview in Swedish, April 22, 1966.

Artle, Roland. *Studies in the Structure of the Stockholm Economy Towards a Framework for Projecting Metropolitan Community Development*. Stockholm: The Business Research Institute at the Stockholm School of Economics, 1959.

Åström, Kell. *City Planning in Sweden*. Stockholm: The Swedish Institute, 1967.

Åsvärn, Gunnar, and Mathsson, Bertil. "Fritid i Förort: Sociologisk undersökning i Årsta 1954–56," *Stadskollegiets utlåtanden och memorial—bihang*, 1958. No. 94. Stockholm: Stockholms kommunalförvaltning, 1958.

Backström, Sven, and Reinius, Leif. "Centrumbyggnaden i Vällingby," *Byggmästaren*, 1956, No. A4, pp. 80–85.

Backström, Sven, and Reinius, Leif. "Torget och byggnaderna i Farsta centrum," *Arkitektur*, 1961, No. 3, pp. 44–47 and 53–59.

Banfield, Edward C. *Political Influence*. New York: Free Press, 1961.

Banfield, Edward C., and Wilson, James Q. *City Politics*. Cambridge, Mass.: Harvard University Press, 1965.

Bergqvist, Arne T. Formerly, manager, Farsta Center, Inc. Personal interview, June 16, 1965, and March 21, 1966.

Bexelius, A., Nordenstam, A., and Aurén, N. *Byggnadslagstiftningen*. 3rd ed. Stockholm: P. A. Nordstedt & Söners Förlag, 1960.

Bexelius, A., Nordenstam, A., and Körlof, V. *Byggnadslagstiftningen*. 4th ed. revised. Stockholm: P. A. Nordstedt & Söners Förlag, 1964.

Birke, Håkan. Director, Svenska Industribyggen Aktiebolag. Personal interview, May 24, 1966.

Bock, Edwin A. (ed.), Felser, James W., Stein, Harold, and Waldo, Dwight. *Essays in the Case Method in Public Administration*. The Inter-University Case Program, 1962.

Bohman, Gösta. "Morgondagens detaljhandel," *Svenska Dagbladet*, May 5, 1966, p. 5.

Brännström, Gösta. Chief executive, ICA Restaurant AB; formerly, planning director for the NK-Farsta department store. Personal interview, May 25, 1966.

Calmfors, S. Hans. *Local Self-Government in Stockholm*. Stockholm: Stadshuset, 1963.

Calmfors, S. Hans. Chief administrative secretary, city of Stockholm. Personal interview, March 31, 1966.

Cassen, Robert. "Welfare State's Role," *New Society*, No. 141 (June 10, 1965), pp. 12–14.

Central Bureau of Statistics, *Statistical Abstract of Sweden*. Stockholm: Central Bureau of Statistics, 1963, 1964, 1965, 1966, 1967, 1968.

Dagens Nyheter, February 22, 1969, p. 7.

Dagens Nyheter, March 26, 1969, p. 10.

Dahl, Robert A. *Who Governs?* New Haven, Conn.: Yale University Press, 1961.

Dahl, Robert A., and Lindblom, Charles E. *Politics, Economics, and Welfare*. New York: Harper and Brothers, 1953.

Dahl, Torsten, Wieselgren, Oscar, and Hildebrand, Bengt (eds.). *Svenska män och kvinnor*. Stockholm: Bonniers Förlag, 1948.

Dahlberg, Axel. *Cottage Building at Stockholm*. Stockholm: Stockholms stad, 1939.

Dahlberg, Axel. "P.M. ang. förslag till stadsplan för delar av Råcksta och Vällingby i Spånga." Signed Axel Dahlberg, January 17, 1950.

Dahlström, Edmund. *Trivsel i Söderort: Sociologisk undersökning i Hägerstensåsen och Hökmossen 1949–1950* [Comfort and contentment in the suburbs: A sociological investigation in Hägerstensåsen and Hökmossen 1949–1950] Stockholm: Stockholms kommunalförvaltning, 1951.

Danielson, Gunnar. Letter to the city planning board, August 22, 1951, 4 pp.

Davidoff, Paul, and Reiner, Thomas A. "A Choice Theory of Planning," *Journal of the American Institute of Planners*, Vol. XXVIII (May 1962), pp. 103–115.

Eichler, Edward P., and Kaplan, Marshall. *The Community Builders*. Berkeley and Los Angeles: University of California Press, 1967.

Elvander, Nils. *Intresseorganisationerna i dagens Sverige*. Lund: CWK Gleerup Bokförlag, 1966.

Engkvist, Olle. "Farsta Centrum," *Arkitektur*, 1961, No. 3, pp. 41–43.

Farsta Centrum, AB. *Farsta*. Stockholm: AB Farsta Centrum, 1959.

Feuk, Sverker. Production chief, AB Svenska Bostäder. Personal interview, April 22, 1966.

Fog. Hans, and Dahlberg, Gun-Britt. *Den fysiska samhällsplaneringens administrativa strukter; Synpunkter på samspelet mellan stat och kommun* (An Outline of Regional Town and Country Planning in Sweden). Rapport 32:1965, Statens Institut för byggnadsforskning, Stockholm.

Foley, Donald L. *Controlling London's Growth*. Berkeley: University of California Press, 1963.

Foley, Donald L. "The London Metropolitan Region." Institute of Governmental Studies, University of California, Berkeley, December 1967, preliminary draft.

Folmer, Alf. "Farsta Centrum," *Plan*, Vol. 13, No. 2 (1959), pp. 47–56.

Fredriksson, Hans Einar. Administrative secretary to hospital director Carl Gösta Pehrson full time until 1953, one-half time until 1960. Personal interview, April 5, 1966.

Gans, Herbert J. *The Levittowners*. New York: Pantheon Books, 1967.

Garpe, Joakim. "Stockholm at the Opening of the 1960's," in *Stockholm Regional and City Planning*. Stockholm: City Planning Commission, 1964.

Garpe, Joakim, Former commissioner. Personal interviews, February 20, 1967, and May 5, 1967.

Gentili, Giorgio. "The Satellite Towns of Stockholm," reprint from *Urbanistica*, No. 24–25 (September 1958), Stockholm, February 1960.

Godschalk, David R. "Creating New Communities: A Symposium on Process and Product," *Journal of the American Institute of Planners*, Vol. XXXIII, No. 6 (November 1967).

Grauers, Åke. Chief executive, Hyreshus i Stockholm AB (a municipal housing company); formerly, chief, real estate office, industrial development section and chief executive, AB Korphoppet (a municipal industrial buildings development-management company). Personal interview in Swedish, May 23, 1966.

Grebler, Leo. "Urban Renewal in European Countries," in the special issue on "City Planning in Europe," *Journal of the American Institute of Planners*, Vol. XXVIII, No. 4 (November 1962), pp. 229–238.

Greer, Scott. *Governing the Metropolis*. New York: John Wiley & Sons, 1962.

Grünthal, T. *Modern kommunalförvaltning*. 2nd ed. revised, Stockholm: Bonniers, 1965.

Gutheim, Frederick. "Continental Europe Offers New Town Builders Experience" in H. Wentworth Eldredge (ed.), *Taming Megalopolis*, Vol. II, pp. 828–838. New York: Doubleday & Co., 1967.

Hamrin, Eva, and Wirén, Erik. *Town and Country Planning in Sweden Today*. Stockholm: The Swedish Institute, 1964.

Hanson, Bertil Lennart. *Stockholm Municipal Politics*. Cambridge, Mass.: Joint Center for Urban Studies of the Massachusetts Institute of Technology and Harvard University, 1960, ditto.

Harbor Authority, the, and the Public Works Office of the City of Stockholm. *The Söderström Bridges: An Account of the New Railway, Road and Underground Railway Bridges between Södermalm and the Old Town*, Stockholm: The Harbor Authority and the Public Works Office of the City of Stockholm, 1960.

Heckscher, Gunnar. *Svensk statsförvaltning i arbete*. 2d ed. revised. Stockholm: Studieförbundet Näringsliv och Samhälle, 1958.

Hedin, Bertil. Director of finance and administration, Svenska IBM Aktiebolag. Personal interview, May 16, 1966.

Hedqvist, Paul. "Hyreshus i Vällingby," *Byggmästaren*, 1965, No. A12, pp. 299–301.

Hillbom, Bror K. G. Employed by AB Stockholms Spårvägar since 1945; head of research and development. Personal interview, May 4, 1966.

Hofsten, Erland von. *Utredning angående stadsplanen för Gubbängen*. Stockholms stads statistiska kontor. *Specialundersökningar*, 1943, No. 23. Also printed as *Stadskollegiets utlåtanden och memorial—bihang*, 1943, No. 88.

Holm, Lennart. "Bostad, arbete och fritid i Gustavsberg," 1952, mimeographed.

Holm, Lennart (ed.). "The Master Plan for Stockholm and Master Plans for Some Other Swedish Towns," *Att Bo*, Special Issue (1953).

Holm, Lennart. *Familj och bostad*. Stockholm: Hemmens forskningsinstitut, 1955.

Holm, Lennart. *Hem, arbete och grannar—Bostadsvaneundersökning i Örebro*. Stockholm: Statens nämnd för byggnadsforskning, 1957, mimeographed.

Holm, Per. "Community planning and the future development of trade (Samhällsplanering och handelns framtida utveckling)," *Plan*, Vol. 10, Nos. 4–5 (1956), pp. 153–160.

Holm, Per. *Swedish Housing*. 2d ed. Stockholm: The Swedish Institute, 1959.

Holm, Per. "Physical Planning and Local Economic Development: Reflections on a Case Study," *Regional Science Association, Papers*, Vol. XII (1964), pp. 29–46.

Holmgren, Per. "Integration of public transport with urban development." Paper presented to the Town and Country Planning Summer School, St. Andrews, Scotland, September 16, 1965.

Howard, Ebenezer. *To-morrow: A Peaceful Path to Real (Social) Reform*. London: Swan Sonnenschein & Co., 1898.

Howard, Ebenezer. *Garden Cities of To-morrow*. London: Swan Sonnenschein & Co., 1902. Reissued London: Faber & Faber, 1946.

Hoyt, Homer. "The Structure and Growth of American Cities Contrasted with the Structure of European and Asiatic Cities," *Urban Land*, Vol. 18, No. 8 (September 1959), pp. 3–8.

Hunter, Floyd A. *Community Power Structure*. Chapel Hill, N.C.: University of North Carolina Press, 1953,

"Hyreshus i Vällingby," *Byggmästaren*, 1955, No. A11, pp. 280–283.

Jensfelt, Simon, "Lagstiftningen rörande byggnadsväsendet," in a reprint for Stockholms stads stadsbyggnadskontor from the handbook *Bygg*. Stockholm: AB Byggmästarens Förlag, 1952.

Johansson, Gotthard. "Experimentet Vällingby: en ny stadstyp," *Svenska Dagbladet*, November 12, 1954.

Jonasson, A. Gustav. Director, municipal housing exchange. Personal interview, May 24, 1966.

Kalderén, Rudolf. Former president, Nordiska Kompaniet. Personal interview, June 4, 1966.

Källenius, Sten. Director, The Associated General Contractors and House Builders of Sweden. Personal interview, March 21, 1966.

Karlsson, F. Gunnar. Assistant to the Director, Stockholm Labor Board, 1949–1953. Personal interview in Swedish, May 27, 1966.

Karsten, Eva. *Sociologisk undersökning i Haga, våren 1949*. Gothenburg: Gothenburg Office of Statistics, [1949], mimeographed.

Karsten, Eva. *Sociologisk undersökning i Lundby, våren 1950*. Gothenburg: Gothenburg Office of Statistics, [1950], mimeographed.

Karsten, Eva. *Sociologisk undersökning i Johanneberg och Guldheden, 1952*. Gothenburg: Gothenburg Office of Statistics, [1952], mimeographed.

Kidder Smith, G. E. *Sweden Builds*. New York: Albert Bonnier, 1950.

Klemming, Hjalmar. "Två hyreshusområden i Vällingby," *Byggmästaren*, 1955, No. A11, pp. 275–279.

Kungl. Tekniska Högskolan, Institutionen för arkitektur S, avdelning stadsbyggnad. *Kompendium i stadsbyggnad*. Stockholm: Kungl. Tekniska Högskolan, Institutionen för arkitektur S, avdelning stadsbyggnad, 1968.

Langenfelt, Per. *Local Government in Sweden*. Stockholm: The Swedish Institute, 1964.

Lalli, Frank. "New Towns: Are They Just Big Subdivisions with Big Problems?" *House & Home*, Vol. XXIX, No. 6 (June 1966), pp. 92–103.

Larsson, Yngve. "Nedre Norrmalm; Historiskt och Ohistoriskt," a reprint from *Samfundet Sankt Eriks Årsbok för 1960*.

Larsson, Yngve. "Stadsbyggarens villkor (betraktade från Stockholms horisont)," *Att Bo*, 1962, pp. 177–182.

Larsson, Yngve. Former city planning commissioner. Personal interview, June 6, 1966.

Larsson, Yngve. "Municipal, Regional, and National Planning in Sweden," pp. 1–24, in Larsson, Yngve, deWolff, Pieter, and Currie, Lauchlin, *Government Planning and Political Economy*. Berkeley: Institute of Governmental Studies, University of California, 1967.

Larsson, Yngve. Letter June 18, 1969.

Larsson, Yngve. Letter, October 25, 1969.

Lilienberg, Albert. "Tunnelbanans Ödesstunder," *Svenska Dagbladet*, May 16, 1965, p. 4.

Lindberg, Gunnar. *Saltsjöbadens historia*. Prepared for Saltsjöbadens kommunalfullmäktige. Uppsala: Almqvist & Wiksell, 1959.

Lindström, Pär. "Coordination of land-use planning and urban transport planning in Sweden—a background and some examples." Stockholm: Ministry of Communications, 1966, mimeographed.

Lindström, Pär. "Measures for Insuring the Integration of Land-Use Planning and Transport Planning," European Conference of Ministers of Transport, Committee of Deputies, Urban Transport Group, CS/AUC (66)5, Paris, February 24, 1966.

London County Council. *The Planning of a New Town: Data and Design Based on a Study for a New Town of 100,000 at Hook, Hampshire*. London: A. Tiranti, 1961.

Luce, R. Duncan, and Raiffa, Howard. *Games and Decisions*. New York: John Wiley & Sons, 1957.

Lundborg, Gösta. "Järnvägar och broarna över Riddarholmen," *Samfundet Sankt Eriks Årsbok för 1957*.

Lundevall, Owe. *Swedish Housing Market*. Stockholm: Hyresgästernas Förlags AB, 1957.

Lundin, Folke. "The Land Policy of the City of Stockholm." Stockholm: Stockholms stadskansli, June 1965, mimeographed.

McKean, Roland N. *Efficiency in Government through Systems Analysis*. A Rand Corporation Research Study. New York: John Wiley & Sons, 1958.

Makielski, Stanislaw J., Jr. *The Politics of Zoning*. New York: Columbia University Press, 1966.

March, James G., and Simon, Herbert A. *Organizations*. New York: John Wiley & Sons, 1958.

Markelius, Sven. "Synpunkter på moderna bostadsplaner," in *Stadsbyggnad: Svenska Kommunal-Tekniska Föreningens Stadsbyggnadsvecka IV*, 1948.

Markelius, Sven. "Stockholms struktur—The structure of the town of Stockholm," *Byggmästaren*, 1956, A3.

Markelius, Sven. "Structure of Stockholm," *Town and Country Planning*, Vol. 24 (November 1956), pp. 575–580; Vol. 24 (December 1956), pp. 636–642; and Vol. 25 (February 1957), pp. 87–91.

Markelius, Sven, and Sidenbladh, Göran. "Town Planning in Stockholm," in *Ten Lectures on Swedish Architecture*. Stockholm: Svenska Arkitekters Riksförbund, 1949.

Markelius, Sven, et al. "Stockholms City," *Arkitektur* 1962, No. 11.

Markelius, Sven. Former city planning director. Personal interview in Swedish, March 29, 1966.

Martin, Jan Herbert. Stockholm real estate office, industrial section; formerly, secretary to commissioner Yngve Larsson and later administrator for city planning director Sven Markelius. Personal interview, March 10, 1966.

Meijer, Hans. Chapter entitled "Från uppslag till betänkande," *Kommittépolitik och kommittéarbete: Det statliga kommitéväsendets utvecklingslinjer 1905–1954, samt nuvarande funktioner och arbetsformer*. Samhällsvetenskapliga studier, No. 13, Statsvetenskapliga institutionen, Lunds universitet. Lund: Gleerup, 1956.

Meyerson, Martin, and Banfield, Edward C. *Politics, Planning, and the Public Interest*. New York: Free Press of Glencoe, 1955.

Monson, Donald, and Monson, Astrid. "Report on Sweden," *Journal of the American Institute of Planners*, Vol. 15 (Spring 1949), pp. 16–21, and Vol. 15 (Summer 1949), pp. 33–39.

Myrdal, Alva. "Developments of Population and Social Reform in Sweden," in *Ten Lectures on Swedish Architecture*. Stockholm: Svenska Arkitekters Riksförbund, 1949.

"Nybyggd stad," *Aftonbladet*, November 14, 1954.

Odelfelt, Bertil. Deputy chief general manager, Svenska Handelsbanken. Personal interview, June 1, 1966.

Olsson, Per-Olof. "Acceptera Farsta?" *Arkitektur*, 1961, No. 3, pp. 67–68.

Osborn, Sir Frederic J., and Whittick, Arnold. *The New Towns: The Answer to Megalopolis*. New York: McGraw-Hill Book Co., 1964.

Osborn, Sir Frederic J. "Britain's Place in Town Planning," in H. Wentworth Eldredge (ed.), *Taming Megalopolis*, Vol. II, pp. 819–822. New York: Doubleday & Co., 1967.

Paulsson, Thomas, and Ahlberg, Carl-Fredrik. "Täby och Vällingby—två stadsbildningar—två strukturer," *Byggmästaren*, 1956, No. A1, p. 10.

Persson, Lars. "Butikshandeln i Vällingby centrum," *Plan*, Vol. 11, No. 6 (1957), pp. 184–190.

Persson, Lars. *Kunderna i Vällingby (A Shopping Center and Its Customers)*. Stockholm: Stockholms kommunalförvaltning and Företagsekonomiska Forskningsinstitutet, The Stockholm School of Economics, 1960. Also printed as *Stadskollegiets utlåtanden och memorial—bihang*, 1959, No. 86.

Pfannenstill, H. *Sociologisk undersökning i Augustenborg*. Malmö, 1950.

"Radhus i Vällingby," *Byggmästaren*, 1956, No. A 12, pp. 239–242.

Rodwin, Lloyd. *The British New Towns Policy*. Cambridge, Mass.: Harvard University Press, 1956.

Rose, Arnold M. *The Power Structure*. New York: Oxford University Press, 1967.

Rouse, James W. "The City of Columbia, Maryland," in H. Wentworth Eldredge (ed.), *Taming Megalopolis*, Vol. II, pp. 838–848. New York: Doubleday & Co., 1967.

Ryman, Nils E. (ed.). *Studies of the Building and Community Planning Process*. Report No. 27, 1965, National Swedish Institute for Building Research.

Samuelson, Stig. Chief engineer, employed by AB Stockholms Spårvägar from April 1938 until 1949 as chief of the development department. Personal interview, June 6, 1966.

Sayre, Wallace S., and Kaufman, Herbert. *Governing New York City: Politics in the Metropolis*. New York: Russell Sage Foundation, 1960.

Scarlat, A. *The Development of Shopping Centers in the Stockholm Area*. Stockholm: The Swedish Institute, 1963.

Sidenbladh, Göran. "Planning Problems in Stockholm," in *Stockholm Regional and City Planning*. Stockholm: City Planning Commission, 1964.

Sidenbladh, Göran. "Stockholm: A Planned City," in *Scientific American*, Vol. 213, No. 3 (September 1965), pp. 107–118.

Sidenbladh, Göran. City planning director. Personal interviews, April 29, 1966, and May 27, 1966.

Simon, Herbert A. *Models of Man*. New York: John Wiley & Sons, 1956.

Simon, Herbert A. *Administrative Behavior*. 2d ed. New York: The Free Press, 1966.

Sköld, Per Edvin, Sköld, Lars, and de la Motte, Tage. *Kommunalkunskap*. 17th ed. rev. Stockholm: Tidens Förlag, 1967.

"Stadshusets toppolitiker vill koncentrera makten," *Dagens Nyheter*, February 22, 1969, p. 7.

Stein, Clarence S. "Stockholm Builds a New Town," *Planning 1952*. Proceedings of the Annual National Planning Conference, American Society of Planning Officials, pp. 56–64. Chicago: American Society of Planning Officials, 1952.

Stein, Clarence S. *Toward New Towns for America*. Cambridge: The M.I.T. Press, 1966.

Stein, Harold (ed.). "The Kings River Project" and "The Cambridge City Manager," *Public Administration and Policy Development: A Case Book*, pp. 533–572 and pp. 573–620. New York: Harcourt, Brace & World, 1952.

Stockholm Chamber of Commerce. *Swedish Shopping Centres*. Stockholm: Stockholm Chamber of Commerce, 1961; 2d ed. 1965.

"Stockholm och Vällingby," *Svenska Dagbladet*, November 12, 1954.

Stockholm Office of Statistics. *Monthly Statistical Review*, 1966, Nos. 9–12.

Stockholm Office of Statistics. *Statistical Yearbook of Stockholm*. Stockholm: Stockholm Office of Statistics, 1965, 1967, 1968.

"Stockholm, Tapiola, and Cumbernauld," *AIA Journal*, July 1967.

Stockholms stads borgarrådsberedning. Board of commissioners report 188, June 9, 1955. Presentation by city planning office of master plan for Farsta including map G 5:272 prepared 1954.

Stockholms stads drätselrotel. Tjänsteutlåtande re: Farsta. Drätselroteln, April 5, 1954.

Stockholms stads fastighetskontor. Tjänsteutlåtande med anledning av motion nr 81/195 angående riktlinjer för exploateringen av nya stadsdelar samt framställning i samma ärende från Stockholms Köpmannaförbund.

Stockholms stads fastighetskontor. Official report No. 152, April 7, 1956, from the real estate office to the real estate board.

Stockholms stads fastighetskontor. Official report No. 446, October 12, 1956, of the real estate office.

Stockholms stads fastighetskontor. "P.M. angående den s.k. Vällingbyprincipens fortsatta tillämpning," Stockholms stads fastighetskontor and Stockholms stads bostadsförmedlingskontor, April 8. 1958.

Stockholms stads fastighetskontor, "Tjänsteutlåtande angående den s.k. Vällingbyprincipens fortsatta tillämpning m.m.," Fastighetskontoret, May 9, 1958.

Stockholms stads fastighetsnämnd, *Råcksta-Vällingby, Ett Arbeta-Bo-Centrum*. Stockholm: Stockholms stads fastighetsnämnd, 1952.

Stockholms stads fastighetsnämnd. *Vällingby: Företagens Framtidsstad. Skaffa firman luft* [Vällingby: Enterprises' Future City. Secure breathing room for your company]. Stockholm: Stockholms stads fastighetsnämnd, 1952.

Stockholms stads fastighetsnämnd. *Utdrag av protokoll, Stockholms stads fastighetsnämnds sammanträde*, April 24, 1956.

Stockholms stads fastighetsnämnd. *Utdrag av protokoll, Stockholms stads fastighetsnämnds sammanträde*, "Anmälan av skrivelse från FsN:s och Ffs:s gemensamma delegation för prövning av frågon om den s.k. Vällingbyprincipens fortsatta tillämpning," par. 4, April 29, 1958.

Stockholms stads fastighetsnämnd. *Utdrag av protokoll, Stockholms stads fastighetsnämnd sammanträde*, "Fråga om den s.k. Vällingbyprincipens fortsatta användning m.m." par. 24. May 13, 1958.

Stockholms stads fastighetsnämnds delegerade. Letter to Fastighetsnämnden from Fastighetsnämndens delegerade and Bostadsförmedlingsstyrelsens delegerade, April 29, 1958.

Stockholms stads fastighetsnämnds exploateringsdelegerade. *Protokoll*, December 17, 1951, through March 9, 1952, and May 12, 1956, through April 20, 1959.

Stockholms stads gatunämnd and Aktiebolaget Stockholms Spårvägar. *Tunnelbanan i Stockholm*. Stockholm: Stockholms stads gatunämnd and Aktiebolaget Stockholms Spårvägar, 1957.

Stockholms stads gatunämnd and Aktiebolaget Stockholms Spårvägar. *T-banan i ord och bild*. Stockholm: Stockholms stads gatunämnd and Aktiebolaget Stockholms Spårvägar, 1964.

Stockholms Köpmannaförbund. Letter of June 1949 from Stockholms Köpmannaförbund to Stockholms stads stadsplanekontor (6 pp., mimeographed).

Stockholms Köpmannaförbund. Letter of April 29, 1950, from Gösta Bohman, Stadsplanekommittén, Stockholms Köpmannaförbund to Stockholms stads stadsplanekontor (9 pp., mimeographed).

Stockholms Köpmannaförbund. Letter of April 28, 1954, from Sven G. Holmberg, Stockholms Köpmannaförbund to Stockholms stads stadsplanekontor (2 pp., mimeographed).

Stockholms Köpmannaförbund. Letter of June 16, 1956, from Sven G. Holmberg, Stockholms Köpmannaförbund to Stockholms stads stadsplanekontor (3 pp., mimeographed).

Stockholms stads stadsarkiv. Document files, 1947, No. 247; 1948, No. 166; 1950, No. 190; 1952, No. 129; 1953, No. 125.

Stockholms stads stadsbyggnadskontor. Document file, 1956, No. 5106.

Stockholms stads stadskollegiets reklamkommité, *Stockholm stads markområden 1965*. Stockholm: Stockholms stads stadskollegiets reklamkommité, 1966.

Stockholms stads stadsplanekontor. *Det framtida Stockholm— Riktlinjer för Stockholms generalplan. Stadskollegiets utlåtanden och memorial—bihang*, 1945, No. 9. The report was reprinted in 1946 as *Stockholm in the Future—Principles of the Outline Plan of Stockholm* with English captions and summary.

Stockholms stads stadsplanekontor. *Utlåtande över det framtida Stockholm från offentliga organ och enskilda.* Stockholm: Stockholms stads stadsplanekontor, 1946.

Stockholms stads stadsplanekontor. Promemoria till ärende vid stadsplanekommitténs sammanträde den 20 maj, "P.M. angående generalplan för Södra Spånga," May 14, 1949 (2 pp., mimeographed).

Stockholms stads stadsplanekontor. Official report (*tjänsteutlåtande*) from Sven Markelius, director, city planning office, to the city planning board, December 9, 1949, presenting a proposal for a site development plan for an area north of the Råcksta transit station (Råcksta II).

Stockholms stads stadsplanekontor. "P.M. nr. 2 angående utbyggnad av Vällingby Centrum," signed Göran Sidenbladh, Stockholms stad, March 10, 1950 (3 pp., mimeographed).

Stockholms stads stadsplanekontor. "Tjänsteutlåtande angående förslag till stadsplan för del av Spånga (Vällingby Centrum, Vällingby II), S 6:399 och S 6:402," to Stadsplanenämnden from Sven Markelius, November 14, 1950 (8 pp., mimeographed).

Stockholms stads stadsplanekontor. *Generalplan för Stockholm 1952.* Stockholm: Stockholms stads stadsplanekontor, 1952.

Stockholms stads stadsplanekontor. "P.M. angående principförslag till stadsplan för Farsta Centrum, Sf 6:621," from Bertil Karlén, March 8, 1956 (4 pp., mimeographed).

Stockholms stads stadsplanekontor. To the building board from the city planning director: *Tjänstememorial angåenda forstag till ädring och utvidgning av stadsplanen för Kv Lurö m.m. (Farsta X) i Farsta. Pl 5044, March 22, 1957.*

Stockholms stads stadsplanenämnd. Minutes of August 22, 1951, paragraph 8.

Stockholms stads statistiska kontor. *Statistisk undersökning rörande Stockholmsfamiljer. X. Specialundersökningar,* 1947, No. 24. Also printed as *Stadskollegiets utlåtande och memorial — bihang,* 1947, No. 88.

Stockholms stads statistiska kontor. *Statistisk månadsskrift för Stockholms Stad.* 1966, Nos. 9–12.

Stockholms stads statistiska kontor. *Statistisk årsbok för Stockholms stad.* Stockholm: Statistiska kontoret, 1965, 1967, 1968.

Stockholms stads statistiska kontor. *Folk- och bostadsräkningen den 1 november 1965.* "Sartryck ur del 1, områdesindelningen i stor-stockholm": "Del IV, bostäder i stor-stockholm": "Del VI, pendlingen i stor-stockholm." Stockholm: Statistiska kontoret, 1968.

Stockholms stadsfullmäktige. *Stockholms stadsfullmäktiges tryckta handlingar: I. Motioner, II. Stadskollegiets utlåtanden och memorial, III. Stadskollegiets utlåtanden och memorial— bihang, IV. Protokoll jämte yttrande.* Stockholm: Stockholms kommunalförvaltning, 1935–1960.

Stockholms stadsfullmäktige. *Stadskollegiets utlåtanden och memorial—bihang,* 1934, Nos. 10A, 10B, and 10C. Report of the 1930 Års Trafikkommitté, "Lokaltrafikens ordnande i Stockholm: Betänkande med förslag." Stockholm: Stockholms kommunalförvaltning, 1934.

Stockholms stadsfullmäktige. *Stadskollegiets utlåtanden och memorial—bihang,* 1940, Nos. 10A and 10B. Report of (1939) tunnelbanedelegerade, "Tunnelbanedelegerades betänkande." Stockholm: Stockholms kommunalförvaltning, 1940.

Stockholms stadsfullmäktige. "Tunnelbaneplan för Stor-Stockholm," *Stadskollegiets utlåtanden och memorial—bihang* 1965, No. 85. Stockholm: Stockholms kommunalförvaltning, June 1965.

Stockholms stadskansli. *Kommunal författningssaming för Stockholm,* 1957, No. 66. Stockholm: Stockholms kommunalförvaltning, 1959.

Stockholms stadskansli. *Stockholms kommunalkalender.* Stockholm: Stockholms kommunalförvaltning, 1936, 1937, 1941, 1946, 1947, 1950, 1952, 1953, 1956, 1959, 1960, 1961, 1965, 1966.

Stockholmstraktens Regionplanenämnd. *Förslag till regionplan för Stockholmstrakten.* Stockholm: Stockholmstraktens Regionplanenämnd, January 18, 1958.

Stockholmstraktens regionplanekontor. *Skiss 1966 till regionplan för stockholmstrakten.* Stockholm: Stockholmistraktens regionplanekontor, 1967.

Stäck, Josef M. Then chief architect, development division, Stockholm city planning office. Personal interview, May 23, 1966.

Svenska Bostäder, AB. Appendix to 1964 Annual Report "Statistics from AB Svenska Bostäder 1/10 1963–30/9 1964." Stockholm: AB Svenska Bostäder, 1965.

Svenska Bostäder, AB. *Vällingby.* Stockholm: AB Svenska Bostäder, 1966.

Svenska Dagbladet, May 5, 1966.

Svenska Dataregister AB. "The Five Biggest Stockholm Shopping Centers," *Sweda News,* No. 52ab. Stockholm: Svenska Dataregister AB, 1964.

Sveriges Köpmannaförbunds stadsplanebyrån. *Undersökning av butikskoncentrationers inverkan på befintliga närhetsbutiker.* Stockholm: Sveriges Köpmannaförbund stadsplanebyrån, September 5, 1964.

Svensson, Bengt. Assistant to the director, Stockholm Labor Market Board, 1946–1953. Personal interview in Swedish, June 7, 1966.

Sweden. *Svenska Författningssamling* (SFS). Stockholm: P. A. Nordstedt & Söners Förlag.

Sweden. *Bostadssociala utredningen. Statens Offentliga Utredningar* (SOU), 1945, No. 63.

Söder, Tore. "Vällingby, Sweden," in *The Application of the New Towns Concept.* The Hague: International Union of Local Authorities, 1964.

Tannenbaum, Robert. "Planning Determinants for Columbia, a New Town in Maryland," *Urban Land,* Vol. 24, No. 4 (April 1965). Washington, D.C.: Urban Land Institute, 1965.

Thompson, Wilbur R. *A Preface to Urban Economics.* Baltimore: Johns Hopkins Press, 1965.

United Nations. Department of Economic and Social Affairs. *Planning of Metropolitan Areas and New Towns,* "Part five. New Towns planning and development." Document No. ST/SOA/65, 1967, pp. 149–252.

U.S. *Congressional Record,* Vol. 113, No. 166.

"Välkommen Vällingby," *Morgon-Tidningen,* November 14, 1954.

"Vällingby Centrum—huvud utan kropp," *Expressen,* August 3, 1954.

"Vällingby—ett experiment," *Dagens Nyheter,* November 15, 1954.

"Vällingbys framgång," *Svenska Dagbladet,* April 9, 1966.

Weissbourd, Bernard, and Channick, Herbert. "An Urban Strategy," *The Center Magazine* (Center for the Study of Democratic Institutions), Vol. I, No. 6 (September 1968).

Wendt, Paul F. "Lessons from the Old World for America's City Buildings." Reprinted from *The Appraisal Journal,* July 1961. Reprint Number 22, Real Estate Research Program, Institute of Business and Economic Research, University of California, Berkeley.

Wendt, Paul F. *Housing Policy: The Search for Solutions.* Berkeley: University of California Press, 1962.

Wennerholm, Axel. Past managing director, Stockholm Retail Trade Federation. Personal interview, May 13, 1966.

William-Olsson, W. *Stockholm Structure and Development.* Uppsala: Almqvist and Wiksells Boktryckeri AB, 1961.

Index*

*Page numbers for figures are
in italics.